I0131084

"The conduct of governance at the local level is increasingly challenging. This is so for those preparing for careers in management, planning, and law, and particularly for current practitioners – most especially elected officials. Demands on their time are extreme – thus of most importance, Professor Fisher approaches the topic of local government in practical terms. I would hope that each city, village, and township hall would have a copy of this book for reference, especially for newly elected and appointed officials."

William C. Mathewson, *Legal Consultant, and former General Counsel, Michigan Municipal League. Honorary Life Member, Michigan Municipal League*

"Local government affects people daily in ways that both enhance and limit their freedoms and wealth. But many Americans, including local officials, don't understand what 'local' encompasses, where local government powers come from, what power citizens have in making local law, and their rights to witness and review local government decisions. Mr. Fisher's book is an enjoyably readable and concise treatment of local government law; it should be read by all who take on the responsibilities of local elected officials and members of local boards and agencies."

Joseph DiMento, *Distinguished Professor of Law, University of California, Irvine*

"It's common to think that being elected to local office, or being a local official, doesn't require any special understanding of local government – either the laws it works with or the procedures it must follow. That's just not true. This guidebook, organized and written for local officials themselves, will be an invaluable aid to both new and experienced local officials alike, as well as to students of local government."

Richard K. Norton, *Ph.D., J.D., Professor, Urban and Regional Planning Program, Program in the Environment, Taubman College of Architecture and Urban Planning, University of Michigan*

"The law is often hard to understand, but this guidebook provides the reader with a fundamental understanding of how it works for local officials. This work not only provides an up to date look at the law, but also the history of how it came to be. Understanding where we have been, helps us know where we are and where we are going."

Christopher Johnson, *General Counsel for the Michigan Municipal League*

"The book will be of great value to persons considering running for office, or desiring to be appointed to various boards or commissions. However, it may have the greatest value to newly elected members of the governing body or persons on boards appointed by elected officials. It will also be useful for young local government professionals who have been trained in a particular discipline (like engineering, accounting, law enforcement, planning, or law), but have not yet been exposed to all aspects of local government operations."

Mark A. Wyckoff, *FAICP. Fellow, American Institute of Certified Planners. Professor Emeritus, Michigan State University. Editor,* Planning and Zoning News

"Gerald A. Fisher has been a preeminent force in Michigan for over forty years as a municipal attorney, consultant, author, educator, and advocate for local government. The number of local units of government that have benefited from his advice is incalculable.

Mr. Fisher's experience, insight, and intellect is brilliantly displayed in the most comprehensive guidebook ever written for local governmental officials. *Local Governmental Law* explains both the opportunities and pitfalls local officials face in today's complicated environment. The guidebook is clearly written, well organized, and provides excellent examples of practical problems and solutions. Whether a newly elected or long-serving veteran, every local official would be wise to have a copy of Mr. Fisher's book on their desk."

Richard K. Carlisle, *Fellow, American Institute of Certified Planners. President, Carlisle/Wortman Associates*

Local Government Law

Local Government Law provides a unique resource with concise, easy-to-understand explanations of important legal issues faced by local public officials, community boards, and city councils. From the moment officials take office, they face decisions related to basic principles found in state and federal law. The same is true for those in the private sector aiming to work successfully with local governments. This practical guidebook will empower public and private representatives with a functional grasp of legal principles, with chapters explaining what a local government is, the requirement to follow due process, local land use controls, the basics of the Freedom of Information Act, and many other important subjects that regularly arise. As a practical guidebook on local government law, this book provides a basic and empowering understanding for officials and private actors in the local government arena.

Gerald A. Fisher practiced local government law for 20 years at a mid-sized law firm in southeast Michigan, representing cities, villages, and townships, and serving as a senior partner and manager of a large municipal practice group. He then taught for 15 years as a full-time professor at WMU Cooley Law School, teaching property law, constitutional law, and state and local government law. Mr. Fisher is the contributing co-editor of a text entitled *Michigan Municipal Law*, and co-author of a text entitled *Michigan Zoning, Planning, and Land Use Law*. He has appeared in many state and local government cases in the Michigan Supreme Court, and has been a long-term member of the Council, and past chairperson, of the State Bar of Michigan Government Law Section. He continues to serve as a legal consultant for local governments, and as a mediator in local government disputes. He has been listed in *The Best Lawyers in America* in land use and zoning, and in 2001 was named a Lawyer of the Year in Michigan by *Michigan Lawyers Weekly*. He recently completed 10 years of services as chairperson of the Oakland County Parks and Recreation Commission, and is a board member for Scenic Michigan.

Local Government Law

A Practical Guidebook for Public
Officials on City Councils, Community
Boards, and Planning Commissions

Gerald A. Fisher

Routledge
Taylor & Francis Group

NEW YORK AND LONDON

First published 2021
by Routledge
605 Third Avenue, New York, NY 10158

and by Routledge
2 Park Square, Milton Park, Abingdon, Oxon, OX14 4RN

Routledge is an imprint of the Taylor & Francis Group, an informa business

© 2021 Taylor & Francis

The right of Gerald A. Fisher to be identified as author of this work
has been asserted by him in accordance with sections 77 and 78 of the
Copyright, Designs and Patents Act 1988.

All rights reserved. No part of this book may be reprinted or reproduced
or utilised in any form or by any electronic, mechanical, or other means,
now known or hereafter invented, including photocopying and recording,
or in any information storage or retrieval system, without permission in
writing from the publishers.

Trademark notice: Product or corporate names may be trademarks
or registered trademarks, and are used only for identification and
explanation without intent to infringe.

Library of Congress Cataloging-in-Publication Data
Names: Fisher, Gerald A., 1945– author.
Title: Local government law : a practical guidebook for public officials on
    city councils, community boards, and planning commissions / Gerald A.
Fisher.
Identifiers: LCCN 2020050224 (print) | LCCN 2020050225 (ebook) |
    ISBN 9780367856038 (hardback) | ISBN 9780367856014
    (paperback) | ISBN 9781003013846 (ebook)
Subjects: LCSH: Local government—Law and legislation. | State-local
    relations.
Classification: LCC K3428 .F57 2021 (print) | LCC K3428 (ebook) |
    DDC 342.73/09—dc23
LC record available at https://lccn.loc.gov/2020050224
LC ebook record available at https://lccn.loc.gov/2020050225

ISBN: 978-0-367-85603-8 (hbk)
ISBN: 978-0-367-85601-4 (pbk)
ISBN: 978-1-003-01384-6 (ebk)

Typeset in Adobe Garamond Pro
by Apex CoVantage, LLC

Contents

Acknowledgments

Special gratitude to my son, Martin Fisher, who used his legal and other skills to provide assistance in many capacities leading to the completion of this book, including his editing, patience, humor, conceptualization, and critical analysis.

I am also grateful to Professor Devin Schindler, and attorneys Steve Joppich and Patrick McGow, for their assistance in untying abstract knots and providing helpful suggestions and assurances on particular subjects.

Introduction

Local officials can do astoundingly good things for their communities. They have unique opportunities to participate in making their cities, villages, townships, and counties better places to live, work, and play. Their efforts contribute by improving people's lives through advancements in housing, transforming downtown areas, adding parks and green spaces, and enlarging cultural opportunities. Officials generally try to operate their governments in a manner which is unifying and responsive.

Local government is widely recognized as a critical component in the American system of government. There is a deep-rooted view that matters of local concern can best be addressed by those nearest to the people, and that the close relationship between the people and their representatives at the local level serves to promote an enhanced quality of life. From day one in office, local officials work to carry out their representative duties, and in the process must make decisions of lasting duration. There is no question, however, that issues confronting local officials have become increasingly complex, making local government service more challenging. One of these increasingly complex issues is local government law.

Where can officials find understandable insights on local government law? Unfortunately, the sources of plainly-written material available to directly inform an official's legal sense are very limited. Treatises on local government law fill volumes, but are written in the language of lawyers, judges, and other professionals who have been trained to understand legal terminology.

Likewise, attempting to negotiate through case opinions, statutes, and other technically written materials can be challenging for most.

When local officials are elected or appointed to office, they usually arrive with significant practical experiences and common sense. Nevertheless, they certainly cannot be expected to bring with them a well-informed sense for "the law." The goal of this book is to provide basic, user-friendly explanations on some of the most fundamental principles of law regularly met by local public officials as they carry out their responsibilities. The aim is a practical guide to bridge the gap between common sense and principles of local government law, to enhance the work of local officials on several levels. On the overarching level, the author's ultimate aspiration is to enable the understanding of officials on important components of local government law in order to enhance their contributions to *good government* at the local level.

On a more individual level, the subjects covered in the chapters of this book have been selected with the view of furnishing local officials with *practical* guidance, to assist them in being more productive and empowered within the current environment of local government law. Securing the knowledge to improve their work within the permissible bounds of the sunshine laws, and to maneuver confidently within the web of Robert's Rules of Order, will *facilitate performance on a day-to-day basis.* With other subjects, such as understanding where local government fits in the overall federal-state-local system, recognizing limitations imposed on local government by the Bill of Rights and Fourteenth Amendment, and understanding the history and contemporary issues relating to fair housing, will provide tools to *go beyond the day-to-day*, and *elevate leadership abilities* in important respects.

In addition, the materials included in the several chapters of the book are intended to provide enhancement on a dimension that does not regularly appear on the radar screen. Namely, an important goal of the author was to provide an opportunity for officials to *enrich their enjoyment* of local government work. Having a more complete picture of such things as land use regulation, local government finance, intergovernmental cooperation, the structure of local governments, and again, the ability to function knowledgeably with the maze of Robert's Rules of Order, can open the door to pursuing stimulating avenues that may have otherwise seemed too uncharted to attempt.

The necessary focus of the book is on *general principles* of law applicable throughout the country. Although this general guidebook is not able to directly provide every particular of the law applicable in each of the local governments around the country, several questions are provided at the end of each chapter to stimulate a new engagement with the reader's local government attorney, and with the local government association(s) that offer training in the reader's state. These questions are designed to connect the general principles covered in the book to the reader's own state and local law, as a means of empowering readers to develop an ongoing working understanding of basic legal principles applicable in their own communities.

A point implicit throughout this book is that there is no substitute for the community's professional legal counsel. With this in mind, the material in this volume will better prepare officials to recognize when professional legal assistance should be called upon, and to facilitate a more meaningful working relationship with the community's legal counsel.

The path to excellence as a public official is influenced by available information, including access to comprehensible explanations about the rules of local government law. The aspiration of this book is to contribute in a meaningful way to providing a practical yet fundamental understanding of important local government law principles that will assist officials in developing individual productivity and enjoyment in their work, with the goal of ultimately contributing to the achievement of good government.

Chapter 1

Just What Is a "Local Government?"

You have just been elected or appointed to serve as a local government official. Great! Your involvement allows you to make a meaningful contribution and provide a service to your community. But one nagging question may be in the back of your mind: what *precisely* is a "local government?" This question leads to others, such as: what are the limits of local government authority? Of all the actions that can be taken by local, state, and federal government, what can local officials legitimately set their sights on accomplishing? These are very basic and legitimate questions.

To begin answering these and related questions, we start by examining the allocation of authority among the local, state, and federal governments with the goal of seeing where local government fits in the overall scheme. Where the *functional* lines are drawn between these three levels of government is certainly not within the bounds of common knowledge. It can safely be assumed that local, state, and federal governments should not all perform the same functions. If they did, it would result in ongoing conflicts and confusion, with tasks and positions duplicated, all leading to maximum inefficiency. Instead, when our system is functioning at its best, each level of government stays in its own lane. For local governments, this involves doing such things as determining how residents are to be provided with public safety services, such as police, fire, and emergency response, and quality of life enhancements, such as local parks or a thriving commercial center. Stated more broadly, local government can best look out for matters which are predominantly of *local concern*. The federal government cannot account for or accommodate the nuances of such local matters, just as local governments couldn't hope to independently provide for the national defense.

A. The Federal-State Model

> The *federal* government was designed to have limited powers, with the *states and the people* having broad authority.
>
> The constitution "enumerates" specific powers delegated to the federal government.
>
> At the time the constitution was initially ratified, ten amendments, known as the "Bill of Rights," were approved. The Tenth Amendment declares that *if the constitution does not expressly enumerate a power as belonging to the federal government, it is reserved to the states or the people.*

Starting with a broad overview, here is a look across some key organizing principles.

The *federal* government was designed to have limited powers, with the states and the people having all the rest. Specifically, the federal constitution "enumerates" specific powers delegated to the federal government. At approximately the time the Constitution was initially ratified, ten amendments, known as the "Bill of Rights," were added. In precise explanatory language, the Tenth Amendment declares that if the Constitution does not expressly enumerate a power as belonging to the federal government, it is reserved to the states or the people.

Moving to the *states*, each state has its own constitution. These constitutions lay out the plan of government, including the recognition and establishment of local governments in various forms, such as cities, villages, towns, townships, and counties.

To ascertain the authority of a *local government*, the place to start looking is the state constitution, which may contain a direct delegation of authority to local government, or may direct the state legislature to establish and authorize local governments. Most likely, the constitutional plan of government will provide a general delegation and direct the legislature to fill in the details.

Local governments are actually considered to be a subdivisions of the state government, contributing an essential role specialized around unique local conditions and issues – with authority over matters of local concern to be exercised closest to the people.

B. Our Founding Documents Begin the Story

1. Viewing "local government" in the broad context

To view local government in context, we must start at the top of the power structure – the federal government. In the creation of the federal government, the sphere of state authority was defined. From there, we look to state constitutions and laws, which in turn enable and define local governments uniquely in each respective state.

2. "Splitting the Atom" of Sovereign Authority into State and Federal Spheres

In place of a king reigning over our government, the framers of the U.S. Constitution established a system of "checks and balances."

Consistent with this notion of distributed authority, the drafters established two separate levels of government: one "sovereign" federal government, and several "sovereign" state governments, with powers divided between them.

This division of federal and state power created what is known as a "federalist" system.

The Supreme Court has commented that: "Federalism was our Nation's own discovery. The Framers *split the atom of sovereignty*. It was the genius of their idea that our citizens would have two political capacities, one state and one federal, each protected from incursion by the other. The resulting Constitution created a legal system unprecedented in form and design, establishing two orders of government."

The Constitution was drawn up in an era when, throughout the world, the power of a country was typically focused on lone "sovereigns," or supreme rulers, sometimes known as "kings" and "queens." The drafters of our constitution were all too familiar with the inequities of life under the King of England, and wanted no part of this form of government. So, an attempt was made to *create a dispersed power structure* within the government to make sure that no person or body had too much authority.

In place of a supreme ruler for our government, the framers of the Constitution established a system of authority bifurcated into federal and state levels, with the view of preventing (in theory) abuses of power. Consistent with this notion of distributed authority, the drafters established two separate levels of sovereign government: one "sovereign" federal government, and several "sovereign" state governments, with powers divided between them so as to leave neither the feds nor the states as an all-powerful supreme ruler. Instead, there is a requirement for cooperation and coordination among these sovereign powers. This division of federal and state power created what is known as a "federalist" system. A justice of the US Supreme Court once offered the following insightful comments about this dual "sovereign" arrangement:

> Federalism was our Nation's own discovery. The Framers split the atom of sovereignty. It was the genius of their idea that our citizens would have two political capacities, one state and one federal, each protected from incursion by the other. The resulting Constitution created a legal system unprecedented in form and design, establishing two orders of government . . . [1]

The federal constitution draws a line of demarcation between the powers of the federal and state governments. It names ("enumerates") specific, concrete powers of the federal government, and leaves everything else to the states. The theory was that the power of the federal government would be strong but narrowly limited, and the power of the state governments would be expansive – but subordinate to the federal government on the matters specifically delegated to it.

As another part of the system of "checks and balances," the first three chapters ("articles") of the Constitution divide the federal government itself into three co-equal branches, each with independent duties: the legislative branch (Congress), the executive branch (president), and the judicial branch (court).

Here are some of the significant *enumerated powers* granted to Congress in the Constitution:

■ to establish and collect taxes;
■ to provide for the defense of the country;

- to regulate interstate and foreign commerce;
- to coin money;
- to establish post offices;
- to establish patent, copyright, and trademark laws;
- to set up the federal court system under the Supreme Court;
- to declare war, and make rules concerning captures on land and water;
- to raise and support the army and navy, and provide for calling up and organizing of the militia to execute laws of the Union, suppress insurrections, and repel invasions;
- to make all laws necessary and proper for the execution of all the powers vested by the constitution.[2]

The Constitution also contains a list of powers effectively *forbidden* to the states. In joining the federal union, the states agreed to *fully* delegate these powers to the federal government in order to prevent conflicts among individual state actions. This list applies to local governments as well because local government is an extension of state government. Powers forbidden to the states (and to local government) include:

- entering into any treaty, alliance, or confederation;
- coining money;
- making anything but gold and silver coins a tender in payment of debts;
- passing an ex post facto law (one that retroactively changes the legal consequences of actions that were committed before the enactment of the law), bill of attainder (one that singles out an individual or group for punishment without a trial), or any law impairing the obligation of contracts.[3]

And the Constitution *restricts* states from the following actions *unless* Congress gives its consent:

- charging a tax or duty on imports or exports (with limited exceptions);
- charging a duty for the weight of cargo;
- keeping troops or ships of war in time of peace;
- entering into any agreement or compact with another state or foreign power;
- engaging in war unless actually invaded or faced with imminent danger.[4]

The first ten amendments to the Constitution, the *Bill of Rights*, were adopted by the states about the same time as the Constitution, in the latter part of the 1700s. Rather than explaining the rights *of* the federal government, The Bill of Rights names important rights of the people in the form of protections *from* the federal government. Some of the most familiar protections of the people include the right to freedom of speech and religion (First Amendment), the right to bear arms (Second Amendment), and the right to due process (Fifth Amendment).

The last amendment in the Bill of Rights is the Tenth Amendment. This amendment does not identify a specific right of the people. Rather, the Tenth Amendment declares the all-important *division of authority* between federal and state governments, which indirectly *defines the powers* of state governments in the federal-state system. The Tenth Amendment says that any power not expressly delegated to the federal government or prohibited to the states is automatically reserved to the states. In other words, the Constitution specifically assigns certain key powers to the federal government, and then announces that any power it did not assign to the federal government belongs to the states. Although it has not always been interpreted with such simplicity, this basic formula created the essential power dynamic that on the one hand facilitated the uniting of individual states into one great nation and on the other hand (but at the same time) preserved the "sovereignty" (independent authority) of the individual states.

C. State Constitutions and Legislatures Complete the Story

Rather than creating local governments as full "sovereigns" of their respective realms, state constitutions and laws paint a picture showing local governments as *extensions* or *subdivisions* of the state government structure. They are essentially "creations" of the state, providing local governmental mechanisms closer to the people in order to better address matters of local concern.

While the federal government and the states are separate spheres of sovereign authority, local governments are not independent powers. Instead, the general rule is that states delegate specific powers to local governments, with the state retaining the right to adjust this delegation.

Picking up where the federal constitution leaves off, the several states have each adopted their own respective constitutions. These state constitutions cover a lot of ground. For starters, they lay out the basic plan or system of government for the state, generally identifying the same division of power into co-equal branches at the state level as were established at the federal level: the legislative branch (state legislature), the executive branch (the governor), and the judicial branch (the state courts).

State constitutions provide a general idea, but not the full story, on how authority is divided between state and local governments. Rather than creating local governments as full "sovereigns" of their respective realms, state constitutions, and laws paint a picture showing local governments as *extensions* or *subdivisions* of the state government structure. They are essentially "creations" of the state, providing local governmental mechanisms closer to the people in order to better address matters of local concern. One of the most respected treatises on the subject of municipal law characterizes local governments in the following terms of admiration:

> Since our country was conceived on the theory of local self-government, political power has, from the beginning, been exercised by citizens of the various local communities. Having been so dedicated by long practice, local self-government has come to be regarded as the most important feature in our system. The American people have always acted upon the deep-seated conviction that local matters can be better regulated by the people of the locality than by the state or central authority. One controlling idea of local self-government is to bring the officials nearer to the people whose interests are immediately affected by official conduct, in deference to the fundamental maxim in the American system of government that the nearer the officers are to the people they represent, the more easily and readily are reached the evils that result from political corruption and the more speedy and certain the cure. Local self-government is, thus, a guaranty of individual liberty.[5]

State constitutions largely do *not* emulate the federal constitutional model by delegating only limited, enumerated powers to the state government and leaving the rest of the power to local government. Quite the opposite. While the federal government and the states are separate spheres of sovereign authority, local governments are not intended to have independent powers. Instead, the general rule is that states have given local governments *enumerated* powers, and such powers are limited to those expressly and impliedly delegated, either by constitution or by law.

There was a controversy some 100 years ago over whether local governments have a degree of *inherent authority*. However, the now long and widely-held view is that local governments are completely subject to state power delegation.[6] If this description sounds to you like the state is free to move the goalposts of local authority from time-to-time, you are absolutely right. States *can* move significant goalposts, and occasionally they do so. If the power delegation is by law, the state legislature can unilaterally make a change. However, if the delegation of local authority derives from the state constitution, a change requires an amendment of the constitution.

Peering across the country, there is simply no uniform model that applies in all the states in terms of how the system of local government is structured, or exactly what powers are delegated. In all cases, however, a local government's authority derives directly from a grant by the state constitution, state legislature, or both. Getting down to the fine points, the paragraphs that follow describe the variety of local government models created by the states.

1. Local Home Rule

A local government which has been granted "home rule" authority is one that is expressly granted a greater degree of open-ended *self-rule* to address matters of local concern (such as by charter), as compared to non-home rule local governments that must operate under narrower rules provided by the state legislature.

The term "home rule" is frequently used as a general characterization of the extent of autonomy enjoyed by a local government in a state. A "strong home rule state" is one where the state's constitution and laws generally recognize local governments as performing important functions in the state and emphasize the value of granting local control over matters of local concern. At a more technical level, however, "home rule" refers to a specific type of power delegation from the state to certain forms of local government.

A local government with "home rule" authority is one which has expressly been granted a greater degree of open-ended *self-rule* to address matters of local concern, as compared to non-home rule local governments that must operate under narrower rules provided by the state legislature. The most common method used for granting home rule authority is to give cities and perhaps other forms of local governments the authority to adopt local *charters*. Charter authorization enables the people in the community to create a government structure that best matches the array of particular facts and circumstances unique to the local government. A local charter might address such issues as whether the community will be managed by an elected mayor or appointed manager, the size of the legislative body (such as the city council), the limits on local taxation, the power to enact various types of ordinances, the authority to enter into contracts, the authority to borrow money, and the ability to deal with many other issues faced by modern local governments. In each area of authority, a home rule local government can fashion its own charter, and later amend it as the people determine appropriate.

There is a large variation from state-to-state in the specific legal mechanisms used to empower local governments with home rule authority. A good number of states provide home rule authority to local entities by direct *constitutional* delegation, while in many other states the delegation of home rule is made by the state *legislature*. Some states provide an *open-ended* right to govern "matters of local concern," and others provide a detailed *itemization* of "necessary," "permitted," and "prohibited" powers that govern the contents of a local charter.

As alluded to above, not all local governments in a state will be granted broad home rule autonomy. Predominantly, this authority is granted to cities and villages, and perhaps to "towns" in some parts of the country. For "non-home rule" local governments, the state legislature must adopt "enabling acts" to specifically delegate or "enable" the local government's structure and authority to act. For these communities, power may be strictly limited to the scope of the delegation made by the state enabling law. This type of arrangement applies most frequently to counties and townships, which typically have no broad home rule authority to employ in fashioning a unique charter on matters of local concern.[7] Instead, "non-home rule" entities[8] must follow the fixed track laid out within the state statute – and this can result in very inflexible arrangements, possibly ill-suited to the unique circumstances present in the particular local communities. Some states attempt to walk the middle path, delegating non-home rule power only by enabling statute, but granting recipient communities a degree of flexibility and open-ended authority to address local issues that arise.

A local official in a non-home rule community may legitimately ask: why doesn't my local government have as much autonomy as the home rule communities? One observation on this point is that cities and villages historically differed dramatically in size and population, and they often had more complicated municipal issues to address, such as public water and sewage disposal systems, local street construction and maintenance, and local police and fire departments. As a result, there was a greater need in these communities, as compared to more historically rural townships, for broad authority to fashion their structure and authority to best suit their individual needs. There is no doubt, however, that in the modern setting there is a large variation in the size and complexity of non-home rule communities, particularly in metropolitan areas, which may suggest a need to update the enabling authority in state law or constitution to provide more fitting delegations to larger non-home rule local governments.

It is also important to recognize that, for both home rule and non-home rule local governments, there are "general laws" provided by the state legislature that create additional authority and limitations for local governments. These general laws are typically applicable to *all* local governments in the state, providing local government authority for such things as land use regulation, traffic control, fire protection, finance authority for capital improvement projects, and environmental protection. They set minimum standards and specifications, with the aim of achieving state-wide uniformity.

2. Local Government Control Is Limited to Matters of Local Concern

An important limitation of authority that an official must recognize is that a local government's power is limited to matters of *local concern*. Matters of regional and statewide concern are for state legislatures to deal with. And *one* local government has no right, in the absence of an express grant from the legislature, to directly govern private rights and property usage within any *other* local government, even a neighboring community.

Considering that some issues are regional in nature – say there is a contaminated water supply issue that spans a city, a township, and a village – local governments are generally authorized by state constitution and law to participate in decision making that extends outside of their individual borders by entering into *intergovernmental, or interlocal agreements* aimed at addressing a specific regional issue. Such agreements are common to achieve cooperative ventures, such as transportation, solid waste disposal, power generation, and the like. This subject is discussed more fully in Chapter 11.

A local law-maker must also be familiar with the concept of "preemption" by state or federal law. This refers to particular subjects on which there is an intent on the part of the state or federal legislature to sweep aside any *conflicting* regulation at the local level. Local officials should receive the advice of the local government attorney before enacting a local ordinance addressing a subject covered by the state legislature or Congress. Suffice it to say that when a local government attempts to establish a regulation that conflicts with or differs from a state or federal law, it is venturing into waters with potential legal undercurrents. This is particularly the case where the state legislature or Congress has expressly stated its intent to "preempt" local regulation on the subject, usually with the goal of ensuring uniform laws throughout the state or nation. Needless to say, where the legislature and Congress have not expressed the intent to preempt local regulation on a subject, disputes can arise in attempting to draw lines between matters of state-wide or federal concern and those of local concern, and in weighing arguments on whether there is a need for broad uniform regulation on a subject. There is no doubt that "politics" can have a hand in certain decisions of this nature.

States will often permit a local government to create a regulation which is *stricter* than a state law. However, if a state grants a specific permission to, or imposes a specific prohibition on the rights of the people, a local regulation may not contradict the state rule. A careful reading may be necessary on whether the state has created a standard which local governments may exceed, or a standard which may not be altered. The good news is that state legislatures often make their intent known with regard to the circumstances and degree that a local government is permitted to make a more stringent or more lenient regulation in relation to a state law. For example, a state law may say something to the effect that "these regulations are intended to provide minimum requirements, and local governments may establish more demanding standards." In the absence of such clarity, there are rules of interpretation that apply in helping to determine whether local regulations are out-of-bounds. Of course, these rules are not always adequate, and questions on the validity of local regulations claimed to be in conflict with state law are regularly litigated in and decided by the courts.

To round out the picture of limitations on local control, it is important to at least raise the topic of *federal protections on individual liberties* established by constitution and law (see Chapter 5). Are these protections effective only against the actions of the *federal* government, or do they also extend to the actions of state and *local* governments? For example, suppose a claim is made that a local government is violating the First Amendment constitutional guarantee of free speech (such as by zoning in a way that restricts putting up signs on certain properties), or First Amendment "freedom of religion" rights (such as by intending to target certain action because it involves religious beliefs), or Fifth Amendment "due process" rights (by an ordinance that allegedly violates a person's basic liberty), or Fourteenth Amendment "equal protection" rights (by a regulation that allegedly discriminates by race). What to expect in these scenarios will be the subject of Chapter 5, but the short answer for now is that *yes*, local governments generally *are* subject to these federal protections established for the people. Indeed, these federal issues arise on a regular basis, and local officials must seek to avoid serious conflicts with constitutional safeguards of citizens and property owners when enacting local regulations.

Another federal regulation applicable to local governments was enacted by Congress to prohibit discrimination in the regulation of housing. Known as the Federal Fair Housing Act,[9] it will be addressed in detail in Chapter 7.

D. Summary of Local Government Powers

Here are some key take-away points from the lengthy big-picture discussions above:

- Local governments are subdivisions of their respective states, and are an integral part of the overall state power structure.
- The sphere of local government authority is limited to addressing matters of local concern: local authority exercised by the officials closest to the people.
- A local government has no "inherent" power; it has only the authority delegated to it by the state constitution, laws passed by the state legislature, or a combination of the two.
- Each state has taken its own approach to empowering its local governments. Most states grant some local governments greater autonomy known as "home rule" authority, which permits the community to customize the structure of local government to best address local concerns. Home rule is normally limited to cities, villages, and towns.

- Local governments not granted "home rule" authority must follow a less flexible structure spelled out in specific enabling laws passed by the state legislature. Counties and townships tend to be "non-home rule" local governments, although there is a trend to allow greater autonomy for counties.
- All forms of local government, home rule or not, receive various additional powers and requirements from "general laws" enacted by the state legislature. The zoning power is a good example of such a general law – it grants local governments a power reserved (under the Tenth Amendment) to the states, which in turn delegate that power to local governments, to be implemented at the local level.

E. The Power Structure *within* Local Governments

Each local official has a role within the local government "power structure." That structure will include both a *legislative* body as well as bodies and officials with *administrative* authority. The precise structure will vary from state-to-state and also *within* a state, depending on the type of community. A city may have a city council, while a county may have a county commission, and a township may have a township board. Please be on guard, as the upcoming explanations of alternative power structures will be required to split a few hairs. But the pain will be of short duration, and the details will provide important insights.

There are three broad categories of local government power structures: a non-home rule (or "general law") government, a home rule government with authority granted by state statute, and a home rule government with authority delegated directly by the state constitution:

1. *"Non-Home Rule"* Government

If a public official has been elected or appointed to serve in a "non-home rule" community, the structure of power within which the official must operate is generally spelled out in laws enacted by the state legislature. There are likely to be distinct state laws for townships and counties. Broadly speaking, the state laws that apply to these non-home rule communities effectively serve as the local "charter." Of course, the state legislature does not pass a separate law for each individual community, and considering that one set of rules applies to communities of a particular type (such as townships or counties) the static rules have little flexibility to account for differences in the size and complexity of communities with significantly varying circumstances. Moreover, the community will likely lack authority to amend the rules in the state statute in order to tailor them to unique needs. Historically, local governments with this form of static power structure were rural communities where a highly structured delegation was not needed. In many cases, however, these rural communities have now matured into entities within metropolitan areas that must address sophisticated issues, such as public utility construction and maintenance, labor and employment relations, finance, and economic development. Generally speaking, townships in this situation must either continue to function under the static one-size-fits-all legal structure, or seek to become a home rule community by applying for city or village status.[10]

2. "Home Rule" Delegated by State Law

When the state provides "home rule" delegation by state statute, the state *legislature*, by passing a state law, grants local governments the authority to act. The legislature may provide a broad authorization, such as permitting cities to make provision for matters of local concern. Or the legislature may create a more elaborate statutory scheme that specifically lays out the areas of government that can be covered by a charter, such as the requirement to specify the official who will serve as the chief executive officer (such as a city manager), the authority of the city clerk and treasurer, the authority to enact ordinances for specified purposes, a ceiling on the rate of property taxation, and the like. The statutory scheme may also specify the limits on the authority that may be provided by charter. The predominant rule in the country is that, where the delegation of authority is made by statute, the legislature has substantially complete control over local government. So, if the state legislature determines that some aspect of the delegation given to local government is not functioning properly, it has the authority to simply pass a law changing the details.

3. "Home Rule" Delegated by State Constitution

The delegation of "home rule" power may be provided directly by state constitution for certain types of local governments. Such a grant can be very significant because it is granted directly by the people in approving the state constitution. So a grant of home rule authority to a local government cannot be changed by the legislature. A modification would require an amendment of the constitution.

In states where the home rule delegation is provided by constitution, a local government is generally granted the authority to adopt a local charter spelling out the authority it intends to exercise, which of course must be within the scope of the constitutional delegation, and cover only matters of local concern.

4. Structure of a Home Rule Government

A local government that receives home rule authorization is empowered to determine its own internal structure. Any number of organizational configurations are possible – and some communities have been very creative. The basic power structure will almost always call for an elected legislative body (such as city or village council), typically with five or more members. From there, the rest is flexible. The most significant variation is in how the local government's *executive* authority is established. The "executive" may be a *mayor*, who may or may not also be a member of the legislative body, or may be a professional *manager*. Here are some of the alternatives:

- A mayor may be elected by citizens, or may be elected to be a member of the legislative body and then appointed mayor by the members of the legislative body. The mayor may be a regular voting member of the legislative body, or might only be permitted to break tie votes.
- Particularly where the mayor is elected by the people, the form may be a traditionally structured "strong mayor" arrangement, in which the mayor is empowered as the head of the "executive branch" of the local government, analogous to a state governor. A "strong mayor" essentially administers the local government on a day-to-day basis, with authority to propose legislative initiatives, head-up contracting and other administrative matters, and veto actions of the local legislative body.
- A modified form of mayor in some home rule communities is assigned a somewhat lesser level of power, such as having only policy control over heads of departments, while a hired professional administrator serves as the chief *operating* officer.
- In what is likely the most prevalent modern form of executive arrangement, which addresses the sophistication of issues now facing local governments, the mayor serves primarily as the chairperson of the legislative body and ceremonial representative of the local government. For the

"heavy lifting" executive tasks, a person with a degree and experience in public administration is hired and fully authorized as a "manager" of the local government. This arrangement is sometimes referred to as the "weak mayor" form of local government. A key feature of this structure is that the manager is an appointed professional, and is not directly responsible to the electorate – which can be an important advantage when unpopular actions must be taken. Of course, to some people in the community, this may be considered a disadvantage because of the lack of direct accountability for executive decisions.

F. Recognize the Difference between *Legislative* and *Administrative* Officials and the Actions They Take

> The most fundamental distinction between administrative officials and members of the legislative body is that administrative officials are *appointed* to serve, and legislative body members are *elected* to represent voters. As a result, administrative officials are not *directly* accountable to the electors of the community.
>
> In terms of *actions performed*, legislative officials enact ordinances. Once in place, an ordinance must be administered, that is, the general terms and provisions of the ordinance must be applied to specific individuals and circumstances. This job falls to administrative officials.

It is important for local officials to recognize the distinction between governmental *actions* which are "legislative" in character, and actions which are "administrative" in character. Why is this so important? There are two very basic reasons. First, the required *process* for taking legislative action is very different from the requirements for taking administrative action. Second, the manner in which a court reviews the two types of action is quite distinct to each.

The most fundamental *distinction* between administrative officials and members of the legislative body is that administrative officials are *appointed* to serve, and legislative body members are *elected* to represent voters. As a result, administrative officials are *not directly accountable* to the electors of the community. While this absence of accountability might be considered a short-coming to some, this quality provides an important advantage. Specifically, once the *elected representatives* make policy for the local government, *administrative* officials are tasked to carry out that policy, even when it runs counter to the whims of certain members of the public in particular cases. For example, in the realm of land use control, administrative officials are able to make their decisions based purely on whether the land use proposal submitted for consideration complies with the intent and merits of the policy established by the legislative body. If administrative officials were *elected*, they might be pressured to conform their decisions directly to the whims and desires of *influential members of the electorate* on a case-by-case basis instead of even-handedly.

Moving on from the discussion of officials themselves, it is also important to understand the distinction between the legislative and administrative *actions* that these officials may take.

1.   Legislative action

Enacting and amending "legislation" is one of the most important functions performed by local government. Legislating involves the *establishment of community-wide policies* for the local government. As a technical matter, an ordinance is a local *law* that may only be created by the *elected* legislative body. If the public is unhappy with the ordinances adopted by the legislative body, the remedy is at the ballot box – that is, the electors can vote new members into office.

2.   Administrative action

Once in place, an ordinance must be *administered*. Specifically, the *general* terms and provisions of the ordinance must be applied to *specific* individuals and circumstances. This job falls to administrative officials.

Ordinance administration generally requires administrative officials to *apply the rules in an ordinance to particular people or properties*. In many cases, an *individual administrator* acts alone, such as the building official issuing a building permit. In other cases, ordinance administration calls for more formal action by a *multi-member body*, such as a planning commission.

Administrative officials are not elected, so if members of the community are unhappy with the actions of a particular administrative official, their remedy is to address their grievances with the local government's chief administrative officer, who is in charge of hiring. If that fails, electors may need to focus their attention on making changes on the legislative body that appoints administrative officials.

G. Last Words

Local governments are a critical part of the American mosaic of representative government. Learning the basic characteristics of local government, and its place in the larger picture, can be invaluable to public officials in their endeavors to make contributions and provide services to the community.

In establishing the format for the nation's governance, the Constitution's framers "split the atom of sovereignty," creating a "sovereign" federal government with limited, specifically delegated powers, and providing for "sovereign" state governments which, under the Tenth Amendment, would have all of the powers not specifically delegated to the federal government. This created what is known as a "federalist" system.

Local officials can also benefit by understanding the state-local power dynamic created by state constitutions. First of all, state constitutions do not create an arrangement that parallels the federal-state relationship. That is, a state constitution does not reserve a specific set of limited powers for the state, while leaving all of the unstated powers to local government. Indeed, it has long been held that local government has no such broad or inherent powers. Rather, the state-local power structure created under state constitutions preserves all sovereign power, or substantially all of it, at the state level. It is the local governments which are given specific and limited powers. Far from being co-equal sovereigns, local governments are extensions of the state government, dependent on state constitutions and law for their authority.

Local government officials would also benefit by understanding that state constitutions and laws create a variety of local government types, each with a unique authorization. In particular, officials can ascertain whether their particular local government has been delegated "home rule" authority, granting the ability to shape and mold their power structure and organization (typically by charter) to meet local needs and opportunities. In the alternative, they may be delegated "non-home rule" authority (typically as prescribed by state statute) which is more fixed and static in its authorization. A home rule community's executive power may reside in an elected strong mayor, an appointed professional manager, or some variation created by charter.

Officials should recognized that local government actions may be legislative or administrative in nature. Legislative actions taken by elected officials involve the creation of public policy for the community, consistent with state law. Administrative actions instead involve carrying out that policy as it relates to specific persons, properties, and situations within the community.

Understanding all of these delegations and authorizations can help reveal the capabilities and opportunities inherent in a local government office, empowering officials to better achieve *good government* within their federal-state-local system.

H.   Now on to the Local Story

If this chapter has invigorated your appetite for practical legal guidance, you can continue the story by exploring the law applicable to your own particular form of local government, and the law of your particular state. Suggested storytellers include both your local government attorney and your state's local government association, which offers training for community officials. Your local story might begin with responses to these questions:

1. Is ours a "home rule" community? If so, is home rule authority delegated by the state constitution, the state statute, or both? If both, what is the delegation by constitution, which cannot be altered without a constitutional amendment?
2. If ours is a "home rule" community, is the delegation from the state to the community accomplished by open-ended self-rule, granting power in general terms, such as "authority to address matters of local concern?" Or is the delegation from the state more specific, such as authorization to adopt a charter only with specified mandatory, permissive, and prohibited provisions?
3. If ours is not a "home rule" community, has the legislature enacted state statutes specifying the form, administration, and authority of the local government? In general terms, how is this delegation structured? For example, is the community given any flexibility in governance, or is the delegation unalterably fixed for our type of local government?

Notes

1. *U.S. Term Limits, Inc. v. Thornton*, 514 U.S. 779, 838, 115 S. Ct. 1842, 131 L.Ed.2d 881 (1994) (Justice Kennedy concurring).

2. Article I, Section 8.
3. Article I, Section 9.
4. Article I, Section 10.
5. McQuillin's Municipal Corporations, 2019, § 1:40 (3d ed.) (accessed in 2020).
6. *Hunter v. City of Pittsburgh*, 207 U.S. 161, 28 S. Ct. 40, 52 L. Ed. 151 (1907); *City of New York v. State of New York*, 86 N.Y.2d 286, 655 N.E.2d 649 (1995).
7. Counties are uniformly the basic unit of government below the state (except in Louisiana, where there are parishes). Traditionally, counties, along with townships, were not granted home rule authority, and have received their authority directly by legislative enabling acts. Modernly, however, it appears that more than half the states have decided to permit counties to adopt charters, even though relatively few have exercised this authority.
8. It is important here to distinguish the conceptual notion of "home rule" and the more technical delegation of authority. A "non-home rule" township may still enjoy the benefits of being part of a conceptually strong home rule state in which, for example, the policy for interpreting state laws may give local governments the benefit of the doubt on whether they are authorized to act on a particular subject where a delegation is ambiguous.
9. 42 U.S.C. 3601 *et seq.*
10. In some states, legislatures have recognized the urbanization of many such townships and counties, and have created authorizations that permit greater flexibility.

Chapter 2

Open Meetings Requirement

The idea that the public's business should be carried on in a "transparent" manner is now universally agreed upon throughout the United States. But this concept is of relatively recent vintage. A national movement that culminated in the widespread passage of "sunshine laws" took hold in the 1970s, mandating that members of the public must be permitted to be present for government decision-making, and that the public must be allowed access to the written records used by government.

The transparency requirements established in the sunshine laws potentially impact nearly all public officials considering that many members on the local government "team" become involved, in one way or another, in the process of preparing documents that relate in some manner to government decision-making.

To more fully appreciate the transparency requirements that apply to local governments, it is helpful to understand why these rules exist. Only a few decades ago, it was routine for important policy discussions to occur in private ("behind closed doors"), followed by a disclosure to the public of only the ultimate conclusions reached in private. In many instances, no explanations or records of the decision-making process were disclosed. President Lincoln famously described the United States as having a government "of the people, by the people, for the people." The full promise of this important phrase cannot be realized unless "the people," in the broadest sense, are permitted to participate in the decision-making process employed by their government. Another way of thinking about this point is to recognize that local government officials have unique opportunities to improve quality of life in their communities. Part of that life quality involves the ability of the public to knowledgeably participate in the important activities of their community.

The sunshine requirements are replete with technical definitions and detailed rules that attempt to make sure that public body deliberations and decision-making are open to the public, and that local government records are accessible to the public. An increasing number of people, including members of the media, pursue information about government under these laws, making them an important topic to include in this book. The fact that the rules are on the technical side means that the reader may occasionally encounter explanations which must be somewhat intricate in order to successfully communicate the meaning of the laws. Of course, an effort has been made to avoid legalese wherever possible!

It often takes a considerable amount of "on the job training" for public officials to comfortably navigate the mechanics of these sunshine laws. Indeed, local government associations routinely provide educational seminars that seek to foster an understanding of the relevant definitions and rules to promote compliance with these laws.

We will begin the discussion of the "sunshine laws" with the *open meetings* component that compels government decision-making to occur at open meetings. Chapter 4 will address the second component of the sunshine laws, known as the "freedom of information" requirements.

It is not suggested that this book is a substitute for the local government attorney with regard to the sunshine requirements. There are many rules which are unique to each state. So, the intent here is to provide a *foundation* that will make the guidance provided by the attorney more efficient and effective, and empower local officials to recognize transparency issues before they become legal problems.

The *open meetings requirement* applies to "meetings" of "public bodies." Accordingly, the first step to successfully navigating a state's open-meetings law is to develop an intuitive grasp of these two fundamental definitions, to know when the requirement applies, and also a working knowledge of when the requirement does *not* apply. First, it is critical to recognize what a "meeting of a public body" is, because when such a "meeting" occurs, the requirements of the act take effect – requiring public notice of the meeting and making it mandatory to provide the opportunity for public attendance and participation. Second, it is equally important to know *when a recognized exception applies,* which will mean that an open meeting of the public body is not required, and that a "closed session" may be held.

The exact requirements for open meetings are established by state law. Importantly, the rules among the states differ in various respects. This means that, when it comes to the fine details, a public official must become familiar with definitions and requirements in the particular state.

A.   Know When the Law Calls a Meeting a "Meeting"

Officials who are members of a public body must learn to recognize the magical moment at which a particular gathering of members of that body becomes, in the eyes of the law, a "meeting." It is worth repeating: once the gathering is a "meeting," officials must satisfy the transparency requirement by conducting the meeting in a manner fully open to the public unless an "exception" to the open meeting requirement applies. So, this section will focus on recognizing a "meeting."

The first technical ingredient for a "meeting" is that there must be a "quorum" of the members of the "public body." A "quorum" is the minimum number of members of the body required to be present in order to lawfully conduct business. State law does not require the presence of all members of a public body to be present in order to make decisions. If that were the rule, there could never be absences – which we know is unrealistic. Indeed, such a requirement would result in an undue hurdle in the progress of business. At the same time, there must be a sufficient number of members present in order to be representative of the public body. The law defines this "sufficient" number of members as a "quorum." So, to have a "meeting" at which official, binding decisions of the public body are made, there must be a quorum – often a simple majority – of members present.

An official might instinctively say, "Of course I know when I'm in a 'meeting.' It's when a quorum of members of my city council (township board, planning commission, or the like) comes together in a meeting room in response to a notice sent by the clerk." Well, this instinctive conclusion is largely correct, but . . . it does not paint the whole picture.

> ## What's the Point of Having an Open Meetings Requirement?
>
> 1. It makes public officials accountable to voters.
> 2. It gives members of the public the opportunity to show up and participate in discussions.
> 3. It allows the public to be informed about how policy decisions are being made for the public body.

Laws are best understood by recognizing their intent. So, before turning to the details, it is worth focusing on the purpose of the open meetings requirement. The underlying objective is to prevent a public body from making decisions on behalf of the public (formulating public policy) without informing members of the public what is going on. In other words, as the old saying goes, the intent is to prevent business from being conducted "behind closed doors." Requiring open meetings achieves several important purposes. It makes public officials accountable to voters, those people for whom they are making decisions. It gives members of the public the opportunity to show up and participate in discussions and it allows the public to be informed about how policy decisions are being made for the public body.

Assume a city council consists of five members, and that the city charter requires a minimum of three members to lawfully conduct business and make a decision. If three of the five members happen to get together to help out at a charity event, this certainly does not have the appearance of being a secret gathering that would violate the purpose of the sunshine law. But when officials gather, and if the opportunity arises for this quorum of council members to discuss issues scheduled on the next council meeting agenda, there is a realistic possibility that policy discussions will occur – and this may well result in a "meeting" being conducted, giving rise to the open meetings requirement.

Suppose such policy discussions do occur, but without an intent to hide anything from the public. "It wasn't a serious discussion; we just happened to talk about a policy on the next agenda." Regardless of intent, the important thing is the *fact* that potentially significant issues may have been discussed by enough voting individuals to carry a decision at the next meeting of the council. In such case, the *public could not witness the discussion*, and *the public could not participate in the discussion*. Thanks to their casual private talk, these officials could already know each other's view on the issues and very possibly have no need for further discussion at a formal "open" meeting. In that event, a quorum of the members of the public body can skip straight to a decision-making vote without ever bothering to disclose what the actual reasons were that led to the conclusion reached. Members of the public will have no clue with regard to any legitimate reasoning that underpinned the decision, or to the value judgments exercised. The other two members of the council who weren't present at the charity event may have had important contributions to the discussion that now cannot be taken into account. And any input from members of the public is skipped past and never heard. The contributions of the other two public body members, and those of the public, always have the potential of changing the opinion of one of the three members who inadvertently held a private "meeting" at the charity event. The decision at stake never gets discussed and debated at a public meeting. The simple point is that the discussion by a quorum of members at the charity event may well have been a *violation* of the open meeting requirement.

This hypothetical example of an innocent circumvention begins to illustrate the practical subtleties of sunshine law objectives. Of course, deciding just what the legislature needs to require in a law of this type is somewhat like a chess game in which the legislature attempts to anticipate the ways in which the open meeting requirement may be violated, and then proactively attempts to fill the gaps.

1. What Makes a Body a "Public Body"?

> Generally, the open meetings requirement takes effect when a "quorum" of a public body meets.
> *State law or the local charter should tell you when a quorum is present.*

The open meetings sunshine law requirement mandates a meeting open to the public only when a "public body" gathers. For the most part, if a "quorum" of a policy-making body of the local government gets together to discuss business, this will constitute a "meeting of a public body." Generally, state law or the local charter will dictate how many members of the public body are needed for a "quorum." Nonetheless, there are a few gray areas on whether a gathering amounts to a "public body."

When a member of the public believes a decision in violation of the act has occurred, and challenges whether a quorum of a public body has attended a particular gathering without proper notice, it sometimes takes a determination of a court to make the ultimate decision. The allegation in such a challenge would be that a "public body" has discussed, and perhaps decided, public policy, but has failed to hold an *open meeting* for such purpose as required under the open meetings law. In most cases, the complaint will be that there was a failure to provide sufficient advanced notice of the meeting, or there has been a failure to conduct the meeting in the "open" manner required.

So, how would a court make the ultimate decision? Certainly, a city council is a "public body" intended to be regulated. What else? State legislatures around the country create many other types of local government entities, such as township boards, village councils, and other policy-making bodies. Are they all "public bodies" in the eyes of the open meetings sunshine law? These entities all have in common that their members sit as "legislative" or "governing" bodies that are authorized to make public policy decisions – which are actions that impact the public, such as approvals to enter into contracts, land use approvals or denials, the enactment of ordinances, and so on. With all of these entities, public policy could be made any time a quorum of the members meets. This suggests that they are "public bodies."

A good place to start in more technically determining whether a specific group of local government officials is a "public body" is to examine the state law to determine whether the legislature has expressly made that decision. That is, in some cases, in discussing a particular local government body – say a local planning commission – the legislature will state something to the effect that "this body shall comply with the state's open meeting law requirements." This would provide a definitive answer on whether a "public body" is involved assuming a quorum was present.

The authority given to some local government bodies under state law or local ordinance is limited to *discussing* policy. They make recommendations, but they are *not authorized to be the final decision-makers*. If such a body's favorable recommendation is not required for an ultimate approval by the decision-making body, it might be argued that this type of group is merely *deliberating*, and perhaps expanding the information available for the decision-making body, but not actually *making* a decision. So, the question whether a quorum of such a group is a "public body" may be a gray area, and the laws of the particular state must be consulted in determining whether the particular public body is a regulated "public body." Generally speaking, the intent of the open meeting requirement aims at bodies that deliberate toward and then become the actual policy-makers. So, groups that not only discuss issues but also have the power to make public policy decisions should be considered to be "public bodies" under the open meetings law. There is agreement throughout the states that if a group has the power to make public policy decisions, it is a "public body."

On the other hand, let's take the case of a planning commission that conducts a hearing on a proposed zoning ordinance amendment, and when the hearing is over, the commission makes a *recommendation* to the community's legislative body for the actual decision to be made. Considering that the intent of the open meetings law is to allow public understanding and participation in policy-making, and that the planning commission is an integral part of the process, a court might recognize the planning commission proceedings as a substantive step in the process of making a new local law, and treat the planning commission as a "public body" that must hold open meetings. The best practice for this kind of "recommendation-only" body – particularly one basing its recommendations on discretionary determinations – would be to treat it as a "public body" unless the court determines otherwise. Again, however, officials should find out whether there is an express statement in the law that creates the planning commission (or other similar body) specifying whether it must abide by the open meetings requirement.

More clarification might follow from another example. Let's say that a *committee* is formed to review applications for an open city manager position. If this committee's authorization includes the narrowing of total applicants for consideration by the community's legislative body, this will mean that the committee has the power to actually reject some of the applicants. Say, for instance, that the committee is tasked with determining which applications fall short of minimum expectations, and thus should not be considered by the city council. The point that the committee is rejecting applicants makes the committee the final decision-maker with regard to those applicants who are eliminated from further consideration. That is enough to make the committee a policy-maker, and therefore a "public body." The choice of city manager is a decision affecting the public. The public would have no opportunity to witness the process or understand why particular applications were rejected by a committee that acted behind closed doors. Members of the public might wonder: "Was the committee concerned that the manager may be too responsive to the public, regardless of the expressed will of a majority of the city council?"

In the hypothetical above, the power to reject applications makes the committee a "public body," and policy decisions such as this must be made only at a public meeting. On the other hand, if the committee's task is merely to go through the applications to bookmark the page at which the applicant's resume appears in order to facilitate the council's later review, then it lacks decision-making power. It is not formulating, or even deliberating on, public policy, so it is very likely not a "public body." Finer details aside, a wise public official will tend to play it safe, and if there is even the appearance that a body is making a policy decision, an assumption should be made that it is a "public body" until a court or the local government attorney directs otherwise.

2. Is a Quorum Always a "Meeting"?

Suppose a quorum of the members of a public body happen to all be in the same place at the same time. If no other action is taken, do these facts alone point to the fact that a "meeting" is being held? Can a quorum of a public body attend the same social gathering? Or attend the same seminar on local government election procedures? If a quorum is present, is the gathering a "meeting"? The answer to these questions depends on the *behavior* of the public officials when they are together.

In the eyes of the law, a "meeting" occurs if the gathering happens *either for the purpose* or *with the effect* of deliberating toward a public policy decision by the quorum. Note the "either." Even if a quorum has not assembled for the *purpose* of deliberating toward a public policy decision, the assembly of a quorum may nonetheless *become* a "meeting" if the *effect* of the gathering is that the members discuss a policy decision -- such as in our charity event example a moment ago. An innocent get together by members of a public body that was not intended to be a "meeting" may suddenly be transformed into a "meeting" at the moment any member of the group – wittingly or unwittingly – opens a discussion on an issue the public body is authorized to decide, and a quorum participates in the dialogue. Avoiding accidental participation in such unintended "meetings" can be crucial, and requires a level of vigilance and diligence unfamiliar to most prior to becoming "public officials." The best practice when it appears that an unintended "meeting" is about to occur – that is, if a quorum is present and public policy topics happen to come up – would be for a sufficient number of members of the public body to leave the room – or the building – in order to avoid the presence of a quorum while a deliberation is occurring.

Another risky situation occurs when the members of a public body wish to attend a meeting of another body that represents the same community. For example, members of a township board may wish to attend a meeting of the community's planning commission simply to gain information about a proposed project. What happens when a quorum of township board members shows up at the planning commission meeting? Does this group abruptly become a public body that is conducting an unintended "meeting" solely because they are present together while business of the local government is being discussed? Generally, a decision on this question is not quite so automatic. A mere presence together should not transform a number of interested individuals into a public body having a meeting. As a practical matter, however, public officials should not be surprised if a person witnessing their presence later claims a violation of the open meetings sunshine law because they were together as a quorum while township business was being discussed.

For example, assume that an applicant has appeared with a proposed development before a planning commission meeting at which a quorum of the township board is present in the audience. Let's say that the applicant receives unfavorable treatment from the planning commission. If there is evidence that certain members of the township board are opposed to the applicant's project, and if it is the township board that approves appointments to the planning commission, the allegation may be made that the *mere presence* of a quorum of the township board was sufficient to intimidate the planning commission into denying the application. The best advice is to avoid even the *appearance* of impropriety by avoiding a quorum of the board attending the planning commission meeting. If the attempt at avoidance is to no avail, and a quorum of a public body decides to attend a meeting of another public body of the community, members of the quorum should not sit together, and should not electronically communicate with each other.

3. No Quorum, No "Meeting" . . . Right?

The general rule is that a public body may conduct lawful business for the local government only if a quorum of that body is present – that is, enough members are present to lawfully conduct business. Accordingly, the general rule is that a gathering of the members of a public body is considered to be a "meeting" *only* if a quorum of that body is present.

In spite of this general rule, a couple of cautionary points are in order. First, courts can make an exception for *deliberate attempts to circumvent the open meetings requirement.* For example, if a quorum of a public body is seven members, say that three members meet one morning and reach a consensus on a public policy, and four other members meet in the afternoon and reach a consensus, and then one member of the first group communicates on the phone to work out a consensus of both non-quorum groups together. No quorum, no "meeting." . . . right? Once again: maybe it isn't . . . but maybe it is. If the *intent* was to circumvent the sunshine law, a court may well find this scheme to be a violation of the open meeting requirement.[1]

A related situation arises when a public body seeks to avoid the open meetings requirement by delegating a particular task to a committee. If the committee is making an actual public policy *decision* outside of a duly noticed public meeting, and such decision would normally be made by a recognized public body, this would strongly suggest an open meetings violation.[2]

Keep in mind that the core principle of the open meetings requirement is to assure that the public has access to deliberations leading to public policy formation. In light of this goal, there is another situation in which a quorum of the public body may not be required to be physically present in order to have had a "meeting." Specifically, an issue may arise when a quorum of members engage in a "round-robin" of phone calls. If the communications relate to a public policy expected to be deliberated at a meeting of the public body, a court may find little basis for distinguishing these piecemeal communications from a deliberation with all of the members physical present. It is even easier for a violation to occur when the communications involve an email round robin – especially when the sender emails a quorum of members, and participants "reply to all."

With many communities using electronic devices to provide agenda materials, members of a public body must be especially careful to avoid exchanging a volley of emails, messages, or online posts relating to a substantive policy discussion, as such mass-communications have a good chance of reaching a quorum of members. This applies even *while members are all assembled at a duly noticed public meeting* with the public present. Online communications that are not accessible to members of the public (including those sitting in the audience) cannot be considered to have been *open to the public*, and may well be interpreted as having the intent – or effect – of violating the sunshine law.

B. A "Closed Session" Can Be Lawful, But a Wise Public Official Will Insist on Knowing the Authorized Reason for It

> To the extent there is an authorization for a closed session, it must be found in the carefully crafted sections of the open meetings law, in the form of a specific "exception" to the open meetings requirement. Exceptions involve circumstances in which the state legislature has recognized that there are legitimate public policy reasons why a meeting should be permitted to be conducted out of the presence of the public.
>
> Caution: make sure all *conditions* required for conducting the closed session have been met. If the village council can meet in closed session to discuss *pending* litigation, a mere *threat* of litigation may not be considered to involve pending litigation.

By now, the reader is undoubtedly numb from proddings that a public official must be on guard with a shield to avoid a gathering of a public body quorum that is not open to the public. So, it may come as a big surprise (and an additional burden) to hear that the law *does allow* a few, very specifically-defined opportunities for a quorum to close the meeting room door on the public and sit down together for a talk about a public policy. It is important for public officials to be cautious about participating in such a meeting, and to do so only when the justifiable reason is clear.

In most states that provide exceptions to the open meetings requirement, even if a closed session *deliberation* is permissible, the legislature does not allow public policy *decisions* to be made in a meeting not open to the public. Rather, a public body is permitted to meet and *discuss* a policy in a lawful "closed session" – but not make a decision until it returns to open session.

To the extent there is an authorization for a closed session, it must be found in the carefully crafted sections of the open meetings law, in the form of a specific "exception" to the open meetings requirement. *Exceptions involve circumstances in which the state legislature has recognized that there are legitimate reasons why a meeting should be permitted to be conducted out of the presence of the public.* To reiterate, the law permits a closed session only for very specific reasons – reasons that *may require technical conditions to be met.* When placed in a position of voting to meet in closed session, a wise course would be to *insist on knowing the particular authorized reason* for going into a closed session, and to confirm that all necessary conditions established by the law have been met. A public official may not need to personally know all the relevant reasons that allow a meeting to be closed, or all the conditions that must be met. But it would be a good habit to insist that the person proposing to close the meeting-room door, or the attorney for the public body, explain the specific justifying reason and conditions before a vote is taken to meet outside the presence of the public.

When a closed session is held, the discussions are considered confidential. If this were not the case, there would be no reason for a closed session in the first place. Accordingly, minutes of the session are typically not made public, and details of discussions should not be disclosed, unless ordered by a court.

After the *discussion* in closed session, the public body is permitted to make a *decision* based on the talk held in closed session, but only after returning to a session open to the public. This is very consistent with the point that public policy *decisions* may only be made in a session open to the public. In such cases, the public will at least be informed of the decision, though potentially deprived of the discussion leading to the decision.

Here are a few specifically identified "exemptions" that some state legislatures have found to justify meeting in closed session. These examples are intended to provide a "flavor" for the type of subjects that legislatures consider to have sufficient policy reasons to warrant being conducted outside the open meeting setting. Be cautious, however, because open meetings laws vary from state-to-state. You must verify that the law in your own state permits a closed session for a particular purpose, and whether there are any conditions that must be met for such purposes.

1. Evaluating Employees

Basic privacy issues arise when a public body considers such things as disciplining, firing, or even periodically evaluating an employee. Therefore, perhaps only if certain conditions are met, the legislature usually permits a closed session for these purposes. For any number of reasons, the person being reviewed may or may not prefer this type of discussion be held in a closed session. Some states require the person being evaluated to give consent before the evaluation can be held in closed session.

2. Collective Bargaining

Public employees are generally permitted to organize for collective bargaining purposes, and most local governments have employees. What flows from this is that there can be a need for local governments to enter into bargaining sessions to negotiate with employee unions. Each party to a negotiation must create its respective strategies calculated to lead to a compromise agreement. Obviously, a "strategy" would lose all of its meaning and effect if the opponent in the negotiation is permitted to discover all the details of the other side's plans. Recognizing this reality, and the contradiction of attempting to formulate strategy in a session open to the public, state legislatures generally allow the local government's decision-making body to *discuss and formulate its strategy* in a closed session for purposes of collective bargaining. But, again, actual *policy decisions* relating to the bargaining must be made in an open session.

3. Purchasing or Leasing Property

Parallel to collective bargaining, a party purchasing or leasing real property is generally engaged in a negotiation with the seller or lessor with regard to the price and terms of a purchase or lease. The local government purchaser will attempt to acquire an ownership or leasehold interest at the lowest fair price. The seller, of course, will be executing the opposite strategy by attempting to sell or lease at the highest price. Both sides must formulate a strategy designed to ultimately lead to a satisfactory meeting of the minds. If the seller or lessor knows in advance that the government is actually willing to pay a higher price, or pay more rent, or to enter into a purchase agreement or lease with other terms and conditions that are more favorable to the seller, it would not be possible for the local government to secure the property on favorable terms if all negotiating positions had to be publicly disclosed. The recognition of this reality has generally caused state legislatures to permit a closed session to establish a purchase strategy, at least until the price is fixed.

4. *Attorney–Client Discussions Concerning Litigation*

Two activities in litigation require confidentiality between a local government and its attorney – trial strategy and settlement strategy. For both trial and settlement purposes, there is no clear and objective course leading to how the trial will be conducted or what the terms of a fair settlement might be. There are numerous factors that can influence trial and settlement outcomes. To quote Winston Churchill during World War II as he pondered the likely action of an opposing party in the war: "It is a riddle, wrapped in a mystery, inside an enigma." Both trial and settlement strategies can make all the difference in the world in terms of ultimate result. There are likely to be numerous alternative actions and positions an attorney may take on behalf of a client depending on the circumstances. So, once again, disclosing this strategy to the opposing party may well assure an unsuccessful result. If disclosure would have an adverse impact on the government's position, the legislature generally allows the public body directing the litigation to meet in closed session to discuss trial and settlement strategy. To be confident that this exception applies, it will be important to check state law to determine whether the "litigation" in question must already be *pending,* or whether a closed session would be permissible for the public body to discuss *threatened* litigation. There may be other conditions that must be met before this exception applies.

5. *Hiring*

Hiring local government executives and other officers is a most interesting – and in some cases thorny – situation because of the possible need for a public body to review resumes and conduct interviews in open session. The local government will typically prefer to hire an officer with experience, which means that, at the time a candidate is being considered, such person may well be employed with another community. Naturally, a candidate with an existing position will likely be hesitant to announce to the current employer that consideration is being given to leaving if chosen for the new position. Of course, due to the hesitancy of disclosing the new job search to the existing employer, candidates may not apply for the position to be newly filled if resumes are reviewed and interviews held in open session. This would totally lift their "cover," and inform the current employing communities of the job search. The net effect of this situation is that, if reviews must be conducted in open session, the interviewing local government might never receive applications from many good candidates. In the interest of encouraging the best candidates to apply for positions if they desire to do so, some state legislatures have provided relief from the open meetings requirement for this hiring conundrum. The strong counter-argument for maintaining the open meeting requirement is that new officers, particularly the chief executive officer, may well have a significant impact on citizens, who in turn will want access to, and perhaps input on, the hiring process. Before participating in a closed session involving this type of hiring, public officials need to ascertain the applicable rules in their own state.

C. The Penalty for Violating the Open Meetings Law

It would be worthwhile for officials to learn about their particular state's penalties for violating the open meetings requirements. Generally, the penalty will be imposed on the local government unit, rather than the individuals involved. The penalty might involve the invalidation of whatever decision or decisions were made in a "meeting" that was not open to the public. A court may also enter a prohibitive order to avoid future violations of the open meeting requirement. And open meetings laws typically provide authority for the court to order the violating local government to pay penalty fines and attorney fees.

Some states take special interest when one or more officials *intentionally* violate the open meeting requirement and impose *criminal* penalties against the officials themselves, even for a first offense. This is obviously important information to know.

D. Last Words

Transparency in local government, including the obligation to conduct business in meetings open to the public, is a relatively new and certainly positive development in our society. Local residents and voters are impacted by the actions or inactions of public bodies. In the context of making public policy, open meetings are an important means of allowing citizens to become informed about local government business, and to be in a position to evaluate their representatives and hold them accountable. Does the open meetings requirement make the job of a local official more demanding? Of course. But weighing the benefits and burdens, the net effect of transparency is an informed public and a community with a broader sharing of responsibility for good government.

E. Now on to the Local Story

If this chapter has invigorated your appetite for practical legal guidance, you can continue the story by exploring the law applicable to your own particular form of local government, and the law of your particular state. Suggested storytellers include both your local government attorney and your state's local government association, which offers training for community officials. Your local story might begin with responses to these questions:

1. Of the public bodies in your community (legislative body, planning commission, zoning board of appeals, and so on) which ones must comply with the open meetings requirement?
2. What triggers our state's open meetings requirement? If the trigger is a quorum of members necessary to conduct business at the meeting, what is the quorum requirement for each public body that must comply in our community? If the trigger is some other measure, what is it?
3. Are there any exceptions under which our state law permits a quorum (or the relevant applicable measure) of a public body to gather without complying with the open meetings requirement, such as a social gathering or educational event?
4. For what purposes does our state law permit a meeting of a public body to be held in a "closed session" to deliberate matters of policy (such as discussing a legal opinion with the local government attorney), and for each purpose, what specific conditions must be met in order to make the closed session permissible (such as the requirement for the attorney's opinion to be in writing)?
5. Does our state law permit a public body to actually make decisions on policy matters (such as make and pass a motion to take action of some sort) in a closed session?
6. What are the penalties in our state for violating the open meeting requirement?

Notes

1. See *Booth Newspapers v. Wyoming City Council*, 168 Mich. App. 459, 425 NW2d 695 (1988), in which no violation was found because advisory committees of less than a quorum were not working in coordination.
2. *Booth Newspapers v. Regents of the University of Michigan*, 444 Mich. 211, 507 NW2d 422 (1993) (Action invalidated).

Chapter 3

Procedural Rules for Meetings

When the chairperson of a public meeting introduces an agenda item for discussion, what procedural rules govern the course of debate and decision-making? The answer is that, on the one hand, there are "rules of order," historically referred to as "parliamentary" procedure, which must be followed at a meeting. And it is safe to say that, in the absence of "rules of order," many meetings would descend into inefficiency and chaos, perhaps with the loudest voice doing most of the talking.

On the other hand, anyone who has attended formal public meetings over time will undoubtedly report that rules of order have the potential for allowing manipulative procedures that complicate how officials must introduce, debate, and finalize business on the meeting agenda. There are "motions" and "seconds" and "points of order," and other procedural maneuverings that almost seem to interfere with the clear progress of a meeting. While there are no quick solutions for explaining or deciphering the entire procedural "code," the objective of this chapter is to provide a refresher to some, and an introduction to others, by explaining enough of the basics to allow public officials who are less familiar with the rules of order to meaningfully participate.

The most accepted set of procedural rules, *Robert's Rules of Order*,[1] is used at public meetings throughout the country and beyond. These rules have deep historical roots, influenced by those established for parliamentary procedure practiced by an early U.S. Congress, which remain in use today.[2]

Robert's Rules are not always adopted in their entirety. Rather, they are frequently used in part, or in "principle," often supplemented from other sources, such as established local customs or bylaws, and from state laws such as the open meeting sunshine laws. Regardless of the particulars, there is no doubt that having *some* set of agreed upon rules is indispensable for providing an orderly path to policy creation – without shouting matches or fist fights.

The ability of each member of a local government body to fully participate in meetings is enabled, or certainly enhanced, by having a fundamental understanding of the rules of procedure used by the respective body. Rules of procedure exist for what is essentially a positive purpose – to provide order and avoid chaos. But when some of the members of a body are not familiar with the rules, it creates opportunities for other members who happen to have a superior knowledge of procedure to manipulate the course of discussion and unduly influence outcomes at the meeting. This is a case where, literally, knowledge is power. So, the goal here is to cover a nucleus of defensive and offensive rules of procedure – including those most likely to arise during the course of public meeting deliberations. A basic familiarity can make meetings more enjoyable and efficient, and minimizes the prospect of maneuvered consequences.

Because *Robert's Rules* so frequently form at least a part of the procedural backbone for local meeting procedures, every public official is likely to benefit from acquiring (and reading) a copy.[3] That said, *Robert's Rules* are complicated and extensive, with numerous definitions and classifications of the various actions that members of a body may take. "Motions" in particular get special attention – a "motion" being a request that the public body vote on whether to take a particular action. For example, "I move to direct the city treasurer to pay the September bill from the XYZ firm for consulting services." Some motions are debatable, which literally means there can be a debate on the subject before the vote is taken. A few are not – meaning a vote must be taken without any further discussion. Most motions require only a simple majority vote to pass. Others have stricter voting requirements. This chapter will try *not* to drag the reader down into the deeper weeds of complication, although they certainly do exist. The discussion here will be limited to only the most basic and frequently encountered rules, with a reminder that individual local governments have discretion to customize their own rules of order.

The discussion will start with a description of a few *preliminary* actions that typically occur at the beginning of a meeting, such as roll call and approving an agenda. For the rest of the chapter, the reader will be taken to Allswell,

U.S.A., where a hypothetical public body is discussing whether a property in the city should be dedicated for a park. Each time a member of the body makes a new type of motion, there will be a pause for "commentary" to explain the relevant rule of procedure. In light of its widespread use, it will be assumed for this hypothetical that *Robert's Rules of Order* has been adopted in its entirety as this public body's procedure "code."

A. Preliminary Actions at a Meeting of a Public Body

Each public body has a person who has been elected or appointed to serve as the presiding officer, or chair, at meetings. The chair will call the meeting to order (you will have to imagine the chair using a gavel to get everyone's attention), and ask for the roll to be called to identify the members of the body who are present. A key purpose of calling the roll is to determine whether there is a *quorum*, that is, whether there are a sufficient number of members present to permit the public body to conduct business and make binding decisions under state law.

Customarily, there is a proposed "agenda" for each meeting, which provides a "road map" identifying and sequencing the business anticipated to be discussed. The chair will call on the body to approve the agenda. One standard agenda item will have a name such as "public comment." During public comment, members of the public are permitted to address the public body. The precise nature of public comment will usually be influenced by the state's open meetings sunshine law, which may establish the "right" of members of the public to address the public body at some point during the open meeting. Some public bodies will allow public comment on any subject, and some will restrict the general public comment to subjects that do not appear as specific items on the agenda, and allow public participation on each respective agenda item as it is taken up during the course of the meeting.

B. Hypothetical Meeting Scenario in Allswell, U.S.A.

Once the preliminary actions on the agenda have been completed, it will be time to take up the "regular agenda" items.[4] In some communities, these items are divided into two categories: "old business," consisting of matters carrying over from past meetings, and "new business," matters being newly introduced to the body for consideration.

Instead of a thorough, but long and boring, series of rote pronouncements on every rule of order that might be invoked during the course of a meeting, this chapter will consider a single item of business on a hypothetical meeting agenda. Along the way through debate on this agenda item, the reader will meet several key "parliamentary rules" of order, which will be encountered in a logical sequence, as they might arise in the context of a customary meeting. Each rule will be explained as it arises. Headings are included to "announce" each new rule to assist the reader with returning at a later date to the discussion of respective rules, if needed as a refresher.

1. Background for the Hypothetical

We are going to visit a mythical city council meeting in Allswell, U.S.A. The meeting is already in progress, with the city's mayor serving as chair. There are six city council members, in addition to the mayor, who are all in attendance. At a recent meeting of the council, during "public comment," a group of citizens made a presentation to the council. The thrust of the presentation focused on a vacant and unused five-acre property located right next to the Allswell City Hall. The citizens advocated that this property should be dedicated as a park, with two principle purposes. First, the land would be used by members of the public as a "speaker's corner" to make announcements, advocate ideas, and campaign for candidates and propositions ahead of elections. Second, the park would include a band shell which could be reserved for musical and other cultural performances. The citizen group also displayed the form of a written petition it was circulating to show support for the new park idea. The petition includes additional details, such as the general location of improvements, landscaping, and sound equipment.

Two weeks before today's meeting in Allswell, the group filed its petition, replete with 1,000 signatures, and asked that it be placed on the council's agenda as soon as possible. The mayor and the city clerk, who in Allswell share the duty of producing the proposed agenda for each meeting, have placed the citizen petition on today's agenda as the first item of business. As we join the meeting in progress, the matter of the citizen petition is about to be called for discussion as agenda item number 1.

The mayor announces that "the Council will now consider regular agenda item number 1, the petition of a citizen group proposing the establishment of a new park next to City Hall." The mayor then asks a spokesperson of the citizen group to explain the proposal contained in the petition.

2. *Getting a* Main Motion *onto the Floor; Requirements for* Motion *and* Second

After the petition has been explained by the citizen group, a member of the council by the name of Mike Nolan is recognized by the mayor, and Nolan states: "I move to approve the proposal to establish the park next to City Hall and expend $200,000 for the improvements, all as specified in the citizen petition which is the subject of agenda item number 1."

> *Commentary:* At this point, the Nolan motion on this agenda item is not yet ready for discussion. In order to fully present a motion for consideration by the public body, it is necessary under the rules of order for a second member of the body to demonstrate support for the proposed action by offering a "second" to the motion.

The mayor then recognizes council member Lydia Lincoln, who states: "I second the motion made by Nolan."

> *Commentary:* Now a motion has been made and duly seconded, which means that a "*main motion*" has been properly placed on the floor for discussion, with a possible vote on the motion to occur at the conclusion of discussion.

3. *Deliberations on the* Main Motion; Motion to Postpone *to a Defined Date or Time;* Motion to Table

The mayor then restates the motion: "there is a motion on the floor to approve the proposal to establish a park next to City Hall and expend $200,000 for the improvements, all as specified in the citizen petition which is the subject of agenda item number 1."

> *Commentary:* The mayor is now ready to recognize members of the council prepared to speak 'for' and 'against' the main motion. The mayor would normally begin by recognizing the maker of the motion, Nolan, to explain the intent and reason for the motion.

In this hypothetical scenario, before the mayor is able to call on member Nolan to make a statement in support of the motion, member Carlito Carlisle raises a hand and seeks to be recognized by the mayor. Now we are treated to the first effort to use the rules of order to alter the customary course of debate. Upon being recognized, member Carlisle makes an unexpected motion, stating: "I do not believe we have enough information to intelligently address the main motion, so I move that we *postpone* discussion of the motion on the floor until the first meeting of the Council next month." The mayor asks whether there is a second, and member Abbie Adams seconds the Carlisle motion to postpone.

> *Commentary:* Normally, when a main motion has been placed on the floor for debate, it is 'out of order' for a member to make a new motion before consideration of the main motion has been completed in some fashion. But there are exceptions. One such exception is a motion to *postpone* consideration of the main motion on the floor to a *definite date or time*. This motion will *take priority* over further debate on the main motion.
>
> A motion to postpone to a definite date or time is known as a "subsidiary" motion because it does not involve discussion on the *merits* of the main motion. If passed, the motion to postpone will only alter the *manner* in which the main motion itself is addressed. If a motion to postpone is passed, all further discussion of the main motion must wait until the date or time specified in the motion to postpone. If it is defeated, the meeting discussion returns to the main motion. A motion to postpone to a definite date or time is always "debatable," meaning the chair can recognize members to debate the proposed postponement before a vote is taken.
>
> It is very important to distinguish a motion to postpone from a motion to "*table*" a pending motion. While the motion to postpone to a definite date or time automatically reschedules further debate on the main motion, a motion to table would take the pending motion *off the table indefinitely*, that is, it delays any action on the motion, until a motion is made at a later time to bring the tabled motion back onto the table and re-open discussion on it as a main motion. Unlike the motion to postpone to a definite date or time, a motion to table is *not debatable*, meaning that, once a

motion to table has been made, the only action to properly consider is an immediate vote on whether to table the main motion.

A meeting chair must be nimble under the rules of order, and needs to be ready to change course as the meeting progresses.

Now that a motion to postpone has been made and seconded, the mayor turns the Council's attention from the main motion to the postpone motion: "There is a motion on the floor to postpone the main motion on the floor, with the main motion being to approve the proposal to establish the park next to City Hall and expend $200,000 for the improvements." Because the motion to postpone is debatable, the mayor then opens the floor for debate on the motion to postpone. When debate on the motion to postpone has been completed, the mayor calls for a vote on the motion to postpone, restating that the vote before the body is "to postpone discussion on the main motion to establish the park next to City Hall until the first meeting to be held next month."

Let us assume that a majority of the members vote *against* postponement. This returns the discussion to the main motion, as if the motion to postpone had never been made.

4.   *Return of Discussion to the Main Motion;* Motion to Amend *the Main Motion*

The mayor then calls for a resumption of discussion on the main motion to approve establishing the park next to City Hall, giving Nolan, the maker of the motion, the first opportunity to speak. Nolan and a few other members speak to the motion. It becomes clear from the discussion that several members sense that the proposal to spend $200,000 for the improvements was not based on a detailed plan that could be used to calculate realistic costs, and consequently that the proposed expenditure of $200,000 was an arbitrary number, not a meaningful one. We are now ready to see the next "maneuverer" under the rules of order. The chair recognizes member Willamina Shakespeare, who is one of the members with a concern about the arbitrariness of the proposed $200,000 expenditure. Shakespeare makes a *motion to amend* the main motion "by *deleting* the authorization to spend $200,000 for improvements, and *adding* that an approval to establish the park will not take effect until a plan and cost estimate for improvements is prepared and presented by the City Planner and approved by the Council."

Commentary: A motion to amend a main motion is "in order" in most cases. Once the motion to amend is seconded, it is open for debate. Note that when a motion to amend is made, the debate and subsequent vote are limited to addressing the proposed *amendment*, not the main motion itself.

The motion to amend is seconded by member Martin King. So the mayor is once again compelled to be flexible and opens the floor for debate on the motion to amend. After debate is conducted on the motion to amend, the mayor calls for a vote on the motion to amend, as follows: "We are ready to vote on a motion to amend the main motion by deleting from the main motion the authorization to spend $200,000 for improvements and adding to the main motion that the approval to establish the park will not take effect until a plan and cost estimate for improvements is prepared and presented by the City Planner, and approved by the Council."

Commentary: If the motion to amend is passed, the discussion on the floor will then return to the main motion, *as amended*, to establish a park on the property. If the motion to amend fails to secure a majority vote, the discussion on the floor will return to the original main motion to establish a park on the property, with the authorization to spend $200,000 for improvements intact.

As we observe the vote being taken at this hypothetical meeting, we learn that the motion to amend passes by majority vote. This means that the mayor will now open discussion on the main motion, *as amended*, saying, "we are now ready to discuss the main motion as amended, namely, to approve the proposal to establish the park next to City Hall as specified in the citizen petition which is the subject of agenda item number 1, with the understanding that the approval to establish the park will not take effect until a plan and cost estimate for improvements is prepared and presented by the City Planner, and approved by the Council."

5. *Motion to* Limit Debate

Member King will now provide us with the next educational opportunity, having formed the opinion that any further discussion of the main motion would be a waste of time. Member King is recognized by the mayor and makes a "motion to *limit further debate* on the main motion to an additional one hour." The mayor asks whether there is a second, and member Shakespeare offers a second.

> *Commentary:* A motion to *limit debate* on a main motion is itself debatable – yes, the public body can *spend time debating* whether to *limit the time it will spend debating* the main motion. So, after a second is offered for the motion, the mayor will (patiently) ask if further discussion is desired on the question of whether to impose a time limit.
>
> A motion to limit debate may phrase the limit either as an amount of time remaining for debate (as in this hypothetical) or as a specified time of day at which the debate will be ended.
>
> Unlike the earlier subsidiary motion, a motion to limit debate *does* affect discussion of the merits of the main motion – by reducing the time available for that discussion. Accordingly, the motion to limit debate requires not just a simple majority but instead a two-thirds majority vote in order to carry.

The mayor then inquires whether any members of the Council wish to be recognized for continued discussion on the motion to limit debate. When all discussion is completed, the mayor calls for a vote, saying: "We are now ready for a vote on the motion to limit further debate to one hour on the main motion to establish the park." The motion goes to a vote and receives enough votes in favor to meet the two-thirds majority voting requirement. By passing this motion, the Council has limited debate on the main motion to establish the park to one additional hour.

6.   *Motion to* Call the Question *on the Main Motion*

At this point, the debate on the main motion, as amended, to authorize establishing the new park is limited to one hour. The mayor then inquires whether any members of the council wish to be recognized for continued discussion on the main motion, and counsel member Olive Holmes is recognized. She launches into a lengthy exposition on several points already discussed by the Council with regard to the proposed park, and makes no new points. After about twenty minutes of listening to member Holmes re-hash earlier discussions (and recognizing that there is still more than half an hour of debate remaining) member Shakespeare becomes frustrated and signals the mayor that she would like to be recognized. The mayor recognizes member Shakespeare, who states: "I respect all of the points being raised by member Holmes, and recognize that she is speaking in good faith; however, since all of these points being presented have already been fully debated, I move to *call the question* on the main motion on the floor, as amended." The mayor seeks a second to the motion, which is offered by member King.

> *Commentary:* A motion to *call the question* is a powerful tool. It can abruptly end all debate on the motion, or "question," which is then on the floor. If approved, a *call the question* motion brings about a significant departure from the customary procedure that permits debate to continue indefinitely. Consequently, passage of the motion to call the question requires a *two-thirds majority vote*, and is *not* debatable. If this motion passes, the mayor will move to an immediate vote on the main motion. If this motion fails, further debate on the main motion will be free to continue (up to the previously adopted restriction of one hour).

With a motion to call the question now made and seconded, and not being debatable, the mayor states: "A motion to call the question has been made and seconded on the main motion to establish a park, as that motion has been amended, and therefore the business before the Council is now a vote on the motion to call the question and cease further debate on the main motion." To properly inform the council, the mayor adds that "passage of the motion to call the question requires a two-thirds majority vote."

In this hypothetical, the motion to call the question passes by a vote of five in favor and one against (Holmes of course voted against) and so the mayor states that: "In light of the passage of the motion to call the question, the business of the Council on agenda item number 1 is to vote on the main motion." Accordingly, the mayor continues: "The Council shall now vote on the main motion to approve the proposal to establish a park next to City Hall as specified in the citizen petition which is the subject of agenda item number 1, with the understanding that the approval to establish the park will not take effect until a plan and cost estimate for improvements is prepared and presented by the City Planner, and approved by the Council."

The vote is taken, and the mayor announces the result of the vote on the main motion, namely that the main motion is approved by a vote of four in favor and two against, with members King and Adams voting against. The mayor, feeling a false sense of relief, proclaims: "the Council has finally made a decision on whether to establish a park next to the City Hall."

7. *Motion to* Reconsider; Point of Order; *Motion to* Rescind

After the meeting, word spreads in the community that an outdoor music venue is going in next to City Hall. The city starts receiving numerous complaints from residents whose homes adjoin the proposed park, all of them expressing great concern about the effects of a next-door concert venue on their peaceful residential lives.

> *Commentary:* And yet a motion approving the venue was already adopted by majority vote of the council. Is it already too late? Or can these newly concerned residents still get a chance to affect the outcome?
>
> The answer is that it is not too late: two alternatives under *Robert's Rules* would allow further review of a previously adopted motion. There is a *motion to reconsider*, and a *motion to rescind*.

To observe these motions in action, we now skip forward to the second council meeting after the park project was approved. Council member Adams has heard the resident complaints and raises the point: "During our earlier debates on establishing the park, the council entirely neglected to consider the impact of having an outdoor music venue in close proximity to a residential neighborhood." After elaborating on the noise and other related ramifications of establishing the park in that location, member Adams makes a *motion to reconsider* the previously adopted motion to establish the park. Member Nolan is influenced by the thoughts expressed by member Adams and seconds the motion to reconsider. But before the mayor asks member Adams whether the maker of the motion desires further discussion, member King provides us with our next learning opportunity. Gaining the floor, King invokes an often-used rule of procedure by stating: "*Point of order!* There are two problems with member Adams's motion to reconsider. First, it is not timely because a motion to reconsider may not be made two meetings after a motion was adopted. And second, member Adams voted in opposition to the motion to establish the park next to City Hall, which disqualifies her from making this motion to reconsider."

> *Commentary:* A *point of order* is an appeal to the procedural rulebook. It takes precedence over the pending question on the floor, requires no second, and needs no vote. The meeting chair has a duty to enforce the rules of the council without delay, and may do so with or without allowing a debate or vote by the full council. Any member of the council who notices the breach of a rule has the right to insist upon its enforcement by raising a point of order.
>
> A *motion to reconsider* a previously adopted motion can be used to bring about a new debate on a subject that has already been resolved by a previously adopted motion. But it comes with important limitations, both as a matter of established *procedure* and as a matter of basic *fairness*.
>
> From a procedural standpoint, as raised by member King:
>
> (1) A motion to reconsider must be made within a limited period of time, namely, at the *same meeting* at which the motion proposed to be reconsidered was adopted, or at the *very next meeting*; and
>
> (2) A motion to reconsider can only be made by a member who *voted in favor* of the motion proposed for reconsideration – although any member may second the motion.
>
> In terms of fairness, the main concern is whether there has been *reliance* on the adopted motion. "Reliance" refers to any scenario where residents (or businesses) learned of the council's vote, assumed it was binding, and took action that depended on the outcome. For example, if one of the residents sold her home (at a discount, in a hurry) to escape the upcoming noise, by selling in reliance on the previously passed motion, she would have suffered that financial loss and personal inconvenience for no reason if the council changed its decision. With that concern in mind, here are some circumstances where a motion to reconsider is generally not allowed:
>
> (1) If the adopted motion allowed or motivated a person to take certain action, and that person has already begun to take the action, a motion to reconsider is not permitted;

(2) If something happened after the vote was taken that makes it impossible or meaningless to change the vote, a motion to reconsider is not permitted; and

(3) If the vote approved a contract, and the other party to the contract has been notified of the vote, a motion to reconsider is not permitted.

Also in recognition of basic "fairness," no question can be twice reconsidered unless it was materially amended after its first reconsideration.

A motion to reconsider that passes brings the action being reconsidered (in this case the adopted motion to establish the park) back before the council for a new debate and a new vote. A motion to reconsider that fails leaves the previously approved action standing, and no further debate or vote may be taken on it.

Returning to our hypothetical, member Adams didn't make the motion to reconsider until two meetings after the council adopted the motion to establish the park next to City Hall. Since a motion to reconsider is only permitted at the *same meeting* at which the motion proposed to be reconsidered was adopted, or at the *very next meeting*, the mayor properly rules that "the *point of order* raised by member King was correct on that point." The mayor properly continues: "The second *point of order* raised by member King was also correct because member Adams did not vote in favor of the motion to establish the park next to City Hall, so member Adams was not qualified to make the motion to reconsider." For both of those reasons, the mayor declares that, "The motion to reconsider is *out of order*, and will not be recognized."

Member Adams accepts the mayor's rulings on the point of order raised by member King. However, without hesitation member Adams now makes *a motion to rescind* the motion adopted to establish a park next to City Hall. Member Nolan seconds the motion to rescind.

Commentary: The second rule of procedure that allows the undoing of a previously adopted motion is a *motion to rescind.* Rather than proposing to bring the previously adopted action back for a new vote (as in the case of a motion to reconsider), a successful motion to rescind essentially nullifies, or strikes out, the earlier action. A motion to rescind may be brought by any member of the body, and is debatable. But it has some very specific features. In particular, a motion to rescind requires a *two-thirds majority vote* to pass – *unless* it was announced in advance that the motion to rescind would be raised. If it was announced at the previous meeting, or in the publication announcing the current meeting, that there would be a motion to rescind made at the current meeting, the motion to rescind needs only a *majority* vote to pass. Also, like a motion to reconsider, a motion to rescind recognizes the basic "fairness" concern of *reliance*. So, like a motion to reconsider, a motion to rescind may not be made if the adopted motion allowed or motivated a person to take certain action, and that person has already begun the action; or if something has happened since the vote was taken that makes it impossible or meaningless to change the vote; or if the vote was to approve a contract, and the other party to the contract has been notified of the vote, a motion to rescind is not permitted.

In our hypothetical, the clerk examines the relevant records and confirms that there was no advance notice given prior to the meeting at which Adams's motion to rescind was made. Passage of the motion will therefore require a two-thirds majority vote. The mayor states: "A motion to rescind has been made and seconded to nullify the motion adopted two meetings ago to establish a park next to City Hall." The mayor then asks the maker of the motion, member Adams, if there is any further discussion to be offered. Adams declines. The mayor then turns to the rest of the council to invite debate. After a brief debate, the mayor presents the question to the council, stating: "We are ready for a vote on the motion to rescind the motion adopted two meetings ago to establish the park next to City Hall. Passage of this motion to rescind will require a two-thirds majority vote because there was no advance notice given that this motion would be presented at this meeting."

> *Commentary:* If the motion passes, it will wipe out the earlier action, as it if had never been taken. At that point, it would take a *new main motion* to consider any action on the Citizen petition. On the other hand, if the motion to rescind fails to secure the necessary two-thirds majority vote, the earlier motion to establish the park next to City Hall will stand, despite any concerns about the citizen complaints.

The fate of the motion to rescind, and of the proposed park, are left to the reader's imagination.

C. Last Words

Robert's Rules of Order is a large collection, containing many more rules than were discussed in this book. Each rule is given a classification, a priority among the other rules, and special characteristics. In short, *Robert's Rules* are lengthy and complicated. It is fair to say that very few public officials have a full grasp of all of *Robert's Rules* and their properties. But, having a set of procedural rules is important, and members of a public body would benefit by having at least a basic understanding of and comfort level using a basic set of rules. Individual local governments generally have discretion to customize their own rules of order, and it is very smart policy to periodically bring in an expert to review those rules with members of the body and consider adopting amendments to them.

D. Now on to the Local Story

If this chapter has invigorated your appetite for practical legal guidance, you can continue the story by exploring the law applicable to your own particular form of local government, and the law of your particular state. Suggested storytellers include both your local government attorney and your state's local government association, which offers training for community officials. Your local story might begin with responses to these questions:

1. Has our community adopted *Robert's Rules of Order*, in whole or in part? If adopted in part, has the community adopted the particular *Robert's Rules* used as examples in this chapter?
2. Has our community adopted other authoritative or statutory rules of procedure to govern our public body meetings? If so, what do they require?
3. Does our community have a formal resolution that spells out the rules of order applicable to our meetings?
4. As part of the normal business of organization, is a person in each our public bodies appointed or designated to determine compliance and enforce the rules of procedure adopted by the community (a parliamentarian)?
5. Would it be helpful to bring in an expert for a training program on rules of order when a new class public body members are seated?

Notes

1. *Robert's Rules* can be found online at http://www.rulesonline.com/ (accessed in 2020).
2. See https://participedia.net/method/185 (accessed in 2020).
3. http://www.rulesonline.com/ (accessed in 2020).
4. Many public bodies also have an agenda item with a name such as "Consent Agenda" or "Consent Items." This agenda item is used to avoid unnecessary formalities and debate on matters that all members are likely to approve without debate. If a consent agenda is utilized, members of the body may request that one or more items be removed from the consent agenda and placed on the regular agenda for full debate. Otherwise, the chair may call for a vote on the entire consent agenda, and in that manner approve several items that require the consent of the public body but do not require debate.

Chapter 4

Public Access to Government Records

Sunshine laws are all about providing members of the public with information about the government. It has been said that the *core purpose* of these laws is to help the public understand government operations and activities.[1] And as we are all painfully reminded while filling out tax forms each year, government operations and activities involve not just public meetings but also substantial paperwork, that is, "public records." With the same motive that inspired the "open meetings" sunshine laws discussed in Chapter 2, state legislatures have adopted *access to information* sunshine laws, often called "freedom of information acts" (FOIA).

A state's FOIA generally allows any member of the public to request *existing* public records. In response to a request, the government must provide access to the identified record within a relatively short period of time unless the government no longer has the record or the legislature has found good reason why this particular type of record should be exempted from disclosure. In general terms, the FOIA creates a benefit for members of the public and places a burden on the government – all for the worthy purpose of furthering the public's understanding of government operations and activities.

It is invaluable for all public officials to gain at least a basic knowledge of the FOIA. It is true that the day-to-day work of processing FOIA requests generally falls on the shoulders of a relatively small number of local officials, sometimes referred to as "FOIA administrators." Nevertheless, in the final analysis, when the records are released to the public, the most important aspect is their *contents*. This is what will be consumed by the public.

The content of records requested under FOIA can relate in some manner to the actions of nearly any member of the local government, regardless of role. So, all members of the local government team must recognize that, as they are *creating records*, the content of their expressions may well be consumed by any member of the community – as well as the media. Now that FOIA requirements have been in place for a few decades, most public officials are careful with the content of their communications, knowing that they are available for review.

To ensure that FOIA requirements are workable under real-world circumstances, state legislatures have built into these laws important definitions, along with processes for making and responding to public record requests. In addition, legislatures have carefully fashioned exceptions for certain types of records. And, of course, there are penalties for failing to comply.

A. FOIA Definitions

You cannot tell the baseball players without a program, and you cannot understand the FOIA without knowing the key definitions. The most important definition for FOIA purposes is the term that encompasses its main subject: "public records," or precisely what the act intends to make available to members of the public upon request. Because the goal of the FOIA is to make information widely available, the definition of "public record" is very broad; it includes nearly all existing local government records that are not specifically "exempt" from disclosure. Records maintained in electronic form are included, with the exception of software. So, simply stated, a "public record" is any existing record of the local government that does not qualify under an exemption.

Knowing the FOIA definition of "public body" is also essential, just as it was under the open meetings sunshine laws discussed in Chapter 2. This term is important because it helps to confine and identify the *only* type of records that must be made available. Namely, to qualify as a "public record" that must be produced, a record must relate directly to a "public body," and as some states say, it must be material prepared, owned, used, in the possession of, or retained by a "public body."

Take note, however: the open meetings law and FOIA use *different* definitions for "public body." The FOIA definition is much *broader*, and with good reason. The open meetings law focuses on public access to policy decisions being made. For local governments, policy decisions generally occur only when authorized decision-makers meet and discuss, and then decide policy. Therefore, the focus of the open meetings law is limited to meetings involving *bodies of policy-makers*. But from a FOIA perspective, nearly all government records are important, whether used or generated by policy-making bodies or by the many other local departments and commissions who don't vote or make policy at meetings. So, a "public body" for FOIA purposes normally includes not only a deliberative council or board, but also the *administrative* boards, commissions, and departments of a local government.

Indeed, if the goal of the FOIA is to help the public understand government operations and activities, then any recorded material, if prepared, possessed, or used by a public body, must be treated as a "public record." Of course, there are fringe cases that might escape inclusion. For example, what happens if written or electronic material was prepared for the local government by a consultant, such as an attorney, engineer, or planner, but never actually used or possessed by the public body? When the consultant prepared the document, was this consultant temporarily acting *as* a "public body" in connection with the assignment *for* a "public body"? There may be legitimate differences of opinion on whether these consulting materials which were never used or received by the public body are "public records" subject to FOIA requirements. Ultimately, this issue may be resolved based on whether the court considers the consultant an "agent" of the local government, or a part of the "public body," or how state law or the local charter defines the relationship between the local government and the particular consultant.

A more common disqualification of a record from being a "public record" comes into play where a person requests a compilation or summary of records. FOIA requirements apply only to records that *exist*, whereas a compilation or summary – if not previously prepared – would be a *record to be created* from on other materials. Suppose, for example, that a person seeks to review a series of checks written by the local treasurer. While a request is certainly permitted for copies of each of the checks, the local government does not have the obligation to create a new document summarizing the contents of the checks. The FOIA only requires release of the local government's existing records.

FOIA laws generally *do* allow requests for records to be converted to an electronic format. If the information either exists in this format already or can be converted without unreasonable effort or expense, the request for electronic format should be honored.

B. FOIA Process: Requests, Responses, and Appeals

1. Making a FOIA Request

> A person making a request must adequately *describe the record* in a way that allows the public body to find it.
>
> The description requirement is one that can easily lead to litigation.
>
> The public body must make a reasonable effort to interpret the request, as made, and find the record if feasible.
>
> Remember, the purpose of the act is to make records available, and those making requests may not be familiar with technical terms and details.

The first step for a person seeking a public record is to find out whether state law requires a request to be *in writing.* Next, the person must adequately *describe the record* in a way that allows the public body to find it. The description requirement is one that can easily lead to litigation. The public body must make a reasonable effort to interpret the request, as made, and find the record if feasible. Remember, the purpose of the act is to make records available, and those making requests may not be familiar with technical terms and details. On the one hand, the legislature or court may place a sizable burden on the government to "figure it out." On the other hand, government officials assigned to search for the records normally do not possess supernatural powers, and a description must provide sufficient clues for identifying the desired record.

The typical FOIA request is made in the form of a letter or other writing directed to the person at the local government responsible for administering the act. While the customary request seeks the production of *copies* of the record, there is an alternative. Generally, a person may instead ask the public body for an opportunity to *inspect* the public record. If an inspection is requested, an appropriate facility for examination must be provided, with the understanding that the local government can and should take steps during the inspection process to prevent alteration, loss or destruction of the records by imposing special restrictions as needed. After a person has inspected records, a request copies of relevant portions may be made. By making such an inspection, the person seeking a particular record can save a substantial amount of copying and production compared to what might otherwise have been a wholesale request. The savings will include per-page copying fees, hourly wages for copying time by the FOIA administrator, and less *time* spent by the FOIA administrator, who typically has other responsibilities in the local government, which would be derailed searching and copying.

2.   Responding to a FOIA Request

There are various responses the public body may make to a FOIA request – entirely dependent on the facts. The basic alternatives are straightforward. First, if it is feasible to do so, the required response is to *grant* the request in full, either by producing or allowing inspection of all the records requested. Second, if all the records sought are either non-existent as "public records" of the public body, or entirely exempted from disclosure, the public body will deny the request in full, with an explanation for the denial. Finally, the request may be granted in part and denied in part, which may mean that only some of the records exist as public records, or that some of the records sought are exempt. It may also be that *parts* of a record must be provided, perhaps because an exemption applies to other parts. The specific response must follow the facts.

If individual records contain both exempt and non-exempt material, it is not permissible to simply deny the request to produce the entire document. Instead, to the extent feasible, the administrator must "redact," that is, block the view of the part of the record which is exempt, and then produce the record as redacted. It may be unclear precisely what must be produced, and in some cases there will be legal issues which will blur the line between exempt and non-exempt. In such instances, the local government official responsible for administering FOIA requests will routinely need to call for assistance from other officials, including the local government attorney, to determine exactly how to respond. Getting the exemption just right, including the scope of redactions, can seriously impact the records that are ultimately disclosed, and disagreements can easily become lawsuits.

The government must respond to a FOIA request within the time limits provided in the law. This is to prevent a frustration of the purpose of the act by effectively refusing to produce records by simply delaying the response. However, it may be that the time deadline simply cannot be met in spite of a good faith effort, particularly when factoring in the total effort of searching for the record, plus sorting and separating exempt from non-exempt material. Under these circumstances, the public body is generally permitted a limited time extension, with the details depending on the individual state's FOIA language. Taking advantage of an extension will require an explanation to the person making the request that an extension is being taken, and specifying the reasons for needing it. Note that there is no prohibition against the FOIA administrator contacting the requester to make a special time arrangement – but here, of course, it takes two to make a deal. Prudence dictates that, if an arrangement is worked out, in order to avoid a future dispute, a confirmation letter with the relevant details should be written by the FOIA administrator to the person making the request.

Requests to receive records in electronic form may be advantageous for a variety of reasons. As noted above, states generally require a public body to comply with such format requests if the material can be readily and efficiently produced in this manner.

Particular statements or details must accompany a FOIA response.

Because FOIA exists to benefit the public, the required formats for responses tend to be fairly "consumer oriented" in what must be included.

State FOIA laws generally contain very specific instructions regarding exactly which details the public body must include when granting, denying, or granting a request in part.

The next issue is whether there are any particular statements or details that must accompany a FOIA response? There generally are. Because the FOIA exists to benefit the public, the required formats for responses tend to be fairly "consumer oriented" in what must be included. State FOIA language generally contains very specific instructions regarding the details the public body must include when granting, denying, or granting a request in part.

The FOIA response may require including such things as an explanation of the reason for a denial, a description of the material that has been rejected or redacted, an explanation of the right to appeal, and perhaps even a disclosure of the right to obtain attorney fees in a successful court case objecting to a denial.

One thought surely jumps out when considering the detailed response required for every FOIA request, namely that FOIA compliance imposes a substantial cost burden on the local government! Indeed, costs include personnel time, dedicated use of copy machines, experts to carefully separate exempt from non-exempt material, and the like. But the presumption implicit in the creation of the FOIA is important to consider here. Specifically, these costs and other requirements are necessary – and important – components of providing general government services to the public. To soften the burden, the legislature normally permits local governments to recover at least a modest part of the production expense, generally through a per-page fee to cover searching for, duplicating, and, if necessary, redacting the material. There may also be a limited reimbursement for the expense of determining whether records are exempt or non-exempt. Yet, again bearing in mind the purpose of the FOIA, the authorized reimbursement is typically insufficient to cover the full cost. In the big picture, this is a policy-driven cost issue that must be factored into the general budget for the cost of operating the government to serve the public. Although the direct benefit of providing access to records may accrue to only the few people who make requests, there is a bigger-picture assumption that this sunshine requirement, by generally making information available, provides indirect benefit to the public at large.

To ensure universal public access, some states provide a waiver of fees for persons unable to afford them, and also a waiver where production of the particular records is in the "public interest." On the latter point, it is worth noting that the most frequent requestors of FOIA materials from most governments are likely to be representatives of the media. On this score, many who work in media argue that it is *always* in the public interest for the media to keep the public informed, and thus they should *always* be granted a FOIA fee waiver. Historically, this claim for privileged access has been asserted under the First Amendment "freedom of the press" clause. In response to such claim, the Supreme Court of the United States has *not* been extremely generous in granting it.[2]

3. Appealing a Denial

If the public body denies – in whole or in part – a FOIA request for public records, the person making the request has a right of appeal. In some states, this may begin as an administrative appeal within the local government. Regardless, an aggrieved party may ultimately pursue relief in court, where the public is generally given favorable treatment, and courts err on the side of greater, rather than less access to public records. On the one hand, state legislatures frequently allow (or require) the grant of attorney fees (in full or in part) to a party that successfully secures a court order requiring production of a public record. Again, this favorable treatment is consistent with the goal of encouraging the public to become informed about and participate in the government process. On the other hand, it does place a heavy burden (and incentive) on the local government to get it right the first time.

C. FOIA Exemptions: What Records Are Exempt from the Production Requirement?

State legislatures have recognized that the disclosure of certain records would cause *harm*: either harm to an individual, or harm to the public.

As one well-recognized national treatise on municipal law puts it, a "balance [must] be struck between the public interest in disclosure, the privacy and reputation interests of affected individuals, and the government's interest in confidentiality."

The point that some records may be "exempt" has been mentioned several times already. Exemption issues are a vital part of the overall FOIA picture, and the subject of a great deal of the litigation that occurs under this law. It is a topic worth taking a close look at, including the *reasons* for the exemptions. In very general terms, state legislatures have recognized that the disclosure of certain records would cause *harm*: either harm to an individual, or harm to the public. As one well-recognized national treatise on municipal law puts it, a "balance [must] be struck between the public interest in disclosure, the privacy and reputation interests of the affected individuals, and the government's interest in confidentiality."[3] Consistent with this aim, state legislatures have included in their FOIA statutes very carefully worded exemptions from the broad policy requirement that all public records must be produced upon request. In an attempt to provide advanced notice to the competing interests, these exemptions are often very precise in their conditions or limitations.

FOIA exemptions vary from state-to-state, but many are derived from well-established norms and principles, adopted by state legislatures to provide logical protections for the public. For example, to uphold our public norm of respecting personal privacy, the legislature might allow redacting or with-holding certain personal details or documents, especially if not directly related to the topic of the FOIA request. Without such an exemption, an otherwise good faith FOIA request might cause an unwarranted invasion of a person's privacy rights. An exemption arising from an "established principle" is exem-plified by the "attorney–client privilege," which the FOIA allows to shield cer-tain materials produced during legal representation. And a "law enforcement" exemption clearly protects against harm to the public by preventing the forced disclosure of, for example, the inner workings of a public building security system, or the timing and location of planned police searches of unlawful sex-trafficking dens.

Of the numerous possible exemptions, each state legislature has exercised its own judgment on exactly which exemptions to recognize, and on how each should be treated in order to strike the right balance among competing inter-ests. While the purpose of this book is not to provide full details on all points of law in the country, it would be worthwhile for all public officials to learn a few of the most common statutory "exemptions" under the state's FOIA. After all, the disagreements over exemptions is one of the principle reasons for denying inspection or withholding copies of a public record.

As the reader wades into this "exemption" discussion, there may be a feel-ing that the waters are deep, and full of legal technicalities. But not to worry! Unless the reader is a FOIA administrator, there is no need to digest all the details. The key take-away is to understand the general purpose of these exemp-tions and recognize the basic flavor of legislative balancing between preventing harm on the one hand, and pursuing the goal of public access to records on the other hand. There will be no quiz at the end of this chapter.

1. Personal Privacy

The personal-privacy exemption is frequently asserted . . . and frequently lit-igated. The central issue focuses on the legally approved understanding of a "privacy right" which is entitled to protection. It calls to mind former U.S. Supreme Court Justice Stewart's take on obscenity: "I know it when I see it."[4] As with the definition of "public body," or "meeting," a dictionary definition alone falls short of providing a workable understanding of what is included in the term "privacy" that should not be invaded by producing a public record. Border skirmishes along the near and far edges of the definition find their way into courts, where the concept of an "unwarranted invasion of privacy" has been distilled down to *two essential components*.

First, as hinted by this section title, to fall within the exemption, the public record requested must involve facts or circumstances of a *personal* nature that would cause a privacy issue if disclosed. For example, records might be exempt if they would reveal intimate or embarrassing facts about an individual or disclose personally confidential information like a credit card number, the location of a family gathering, etc. Names alone have generally not been found to be of a "personal nature," but other specific information in a public employee's personnel file has a chance to qualify as being protected, especially if the information is unrelated to the inner workings of government.

The second key threshold for the privacy exemption is that disclosure must result in an *unwarranted invasion* – although there is certainly room for uncertainty about what might be "unwarranted." Courts evaluate this second factor by weighing the nature and extent of the personal invasion against the core purpose of the FOIA, namely the disclosure's potential to improve public understanding of government operations. Suppose a record in a department's files reveals the location in someone's home where valuables are kept. Disclosure of that record might on balance be "unwarranted," being a clear invitation to burglars while offering little or no information on the workings of the local government.

2. Attorney–Client Privilege

The principle of *confidentiality* between attorney and client has long been recognized as critical. A local government's legal counsel routinely provides legal advice and opinions to the public body through letters and other writings, explaining the rights and liabilities of the public body and its officials under any number of circumstances. The fact that the client is a "public body" does not eradicate the need for confidentiality. For example, if an attorney writes a letter to the governing board explaining the legal vulnerability of the community's position in a good faith dispute, a forced public disclosure of that letter would ruin any possibility for a productive negotiation with the adverse party. So, a writing that contains the legal opinion of the local government's attorney is generally exempt from disclosure.

Nevertheless, disputes can arise when someone argues that only *part* of an attorney's letter may contain a *legal opinion*, and that the rest should be disclosed as being purely factual in nature. A person making this FOIA argument probably has a strong case. If factual statements can be separated from a legal opinion, they should be made available to the public. So, if an attorney's communication contains no legal opinion, or includes a combination of facts and legal opinion, the factual statements might *not* be exempt from disclosure. The governmental entity can sometimes counter-argue that the facts are stated in such a way that they simply cannot be separated from the legal opinion. This can be a tough knot for the court to untangle.

Another potential dispute derives from the concept of "waiver." An attorney's opinion might already have been shared with persons or entities other than the public body client. Once such a sharing occurs, the law may consider the attorney–client privilege surrounding that opinion to have been "waived." In other words, why should the attorney–client privilege protect a record that was already offered voluntarily to someone outside the attorney–client relationship? Nuanced arguments can easily arise in this type of circumstance, and in many instances there will by varying results depending on the law of the particular state. For example, what should happen if a public body is a defendant in a lawsuit, and has a co-defendant in that suit, and the public body's attorney has been coordinating written legal opinions with the co-defendant's attorney to enhance their respective cases? Some courts recognize that there is a *common legal interest* that needs to be coordinated as part of a joint defense, and that the attorney–client privilege should protect it. This is just one more example of the tough "exemption" questions that can arise.

It is worth noting for comparison that a similar attorney–client exemption exists for the *open meetings* sunshine laws discussed in Chapter 2. If a local government's attorney is going to discuss a written legal opinion with the public body, it certainly makes sense that this be done in closed session to avoid violating the attorney–client privilege.

3. Law Enforcement

Records involving law enforcement are frequently the subject of FOIA denials. The interest protected from disclosure here is preventing danger to law enforcement personnel or diminished security for members of the public. The "law enforcement" exemption commonly covers such things as crime reports while an investigation is in progress, strategy discussions during law enforcement efforts, identity of confidential informants, and methods involving a particular surveillance. Other potential coverage might include communication codes, plans for the deployment of law enforcement personnel, or information concerning undercover officers. While the justification for this law enforcement exemption is clear and strong, state legislatures have stopped short of granting total insulation. Many states require the usual balancing of the value of exempting the information against the public's interest in receiving the information.

Balancing citizen interests with law enforcement plans and procedures under the FOIA parallels the balance needed in our civil society at large. On the one hand, we recognize the importance of protecting the community. We want our laws enforced and we want personal security. On the other hand, we value oversight by persons not engaged in law enforcement who focus on the protection of personal liberties and property interests. So, if the language of FOIA law enforcement exemptions appears complex, it may simply be a reflection of this underlying tension.

4.   *"Internal Deliberations Leading to Policy Formation"*

In our system of divided federal and state government, we have 50 individual states. Within the 50 states, the National League of Cities reports, there are some 3,000 counties. And within those counties there are approximately 40,000 cities, villages, and townships.[5] The virtue of these divisions was famously extolled by U.S. Supreme Court Justice Brandeis as creating "laboratories of democracy" which might "try novel social and economic experiments without risk to the rest of the country."[6] Local government officials engage in this "lab work" and experimentation daily as they develop solutions to the unique array of problems faced in their communities. And in doing so, they inevitably leave a trail of written and electronic records. State legislatures have concluded that officials might hesitate to communicate freely in the exploration of creative solutions if the ideas and opinions they express might be exposed to later criticism. So, provision has been made, at least in some states, to exempt the disclosure of *opinions* candidly exchanged by officials as they discuss new policy. The philosophy here is that protecting free expression will tend to encourage the highly important forthrightness needed in order to fully debate and achieve the best ideas for problem solving. But as with all the FOIA exemptions, this potential benefit must be weighed against the public interest in disclosure – the core purpose of the FOIA. At least some states have shown a general willingness to allow confidentiality of *ideas* and *opinions* during the "deliberative process," but have attached a variety of conditions requiring disclosure of *facts*.

5. "Records Made and Stored for Personal Use"

Public officials also have private lives, and inevitably leave a paper trail of personal records both on the job in their local government spaces and in their homes and other private spaces. Created and maintained for purely personal purposes, such records would seem to have no substantive connection to the workings of government and so ought to be exempt from disclosure. But where precisely is the line to be drawn separating "private" from "public"?

Where the record is *stored* might be relevant, but this factor has been rejected as the ultimate criterion in solving the private–public puzzle – and for good reason. Suppose a public official stores a document at home in a personal email file, but it was created as part of a function performed for the local government. The personal storage of the email is not a shelter, and the document might be subjected to disclosure as a public record.[7] By the same measure, a personal email stored on the government computer system might be found to retain its private character and *not* be subjected to disclosure.[8] The *most* relevant question appears to be whether the record was created, or kept, in order to accomplish an official *function* for the government.

D. Last Words

An informed electorate is an important goal for any democratic society. One of the functions of the 1ˢᵗ Amendment "Free Speech" Clause is to ensure that electors have access to information in the marketplace of ideas in order to inform themselves on the issues of the day. Consistent with these goals, the *core purpose* of the FOIA is to help the public understand government operations and activities. This is an important point for officials to consider when they are feeling the heavy burden of allocating personnel and resources to meet the requirements of this law. Using the local government website to inform the public about local FOIA policies helps to avoid surprises for everyone, and having a FOIA administrator who has a working knowledge in terms of answering basic questions about the FOIA, understanding "exemptions," and preparing responses will be invaluable in facilitating a cooperative relationship with the public and avoiding unnecessary litigation.

E. Now on to the Local Story

If this chapter has invigorated your appetite for practical legal guidance, you can continue the story by exploring the law applicable to your own particular form of local government, and the law of your particular state. Suggested storytellers include both your local government attorney and your state's local government association, which offers training for community officials. Your local story might begin with responses to these questions:

1. Under the laws of our state, what basic components must a FOIA request include, in order to be valid and compel a local government to produce public records?

   a. Must the request be made in writing?
   b. Can the request be to inspect the records, and then make copies of only those which are relevant, or is a person limited to making a request for copies?

2. Has our community designated a person to oversee our community's response to FOIA requests (a "FOIA administrator")?
3. How broad is the definition of "record" or "public record" which must be produced under FOIA? What characteristics must records have for FOIA to compel their release? For example, "prepared, owned, used, in the possession of, or retained by the local government?"
4. What "exemptions" from the obligation to produce records has the legislature recognized in our state, such as for "personal privacy," "attorney–client privilege," and the like? Is our FOIA administrator able to comfortably separate exempt from non-exempt records, and to seek assistance from the local government attorney or other experts, as needed?
5. When responding to a FOIA request:

   a. How much time does the community have to respond? What event starts the timer ticking? Can our FOIA administrator extend the time for any reason?

    b. What statements must be included in a response?

    c. To what extent may our community recover costs for searching, separating exempt from non-exempt, and copying?

6. If a FOIA request is denied in whole or part, what are the rights of the party making the request? Is there an administrative appeal before any person or body, or must an aggrieved party go to court?

7. In what circumstances will the court award attorney fees if the court orders records produced following a denial?

Notes

1. *United States Department of Defense v. Federal Labor Relations Authority*, 510 U.S. 487 (1994).
2. For example, *Houchins v. KQED, Inc.*, 438 U.S. 1, 9, 98 S. Ct. 258857 L.Ed.2d 553 (1978), held that: "This Court has never intimated a First Amendment guarantee of a right of access to all sources of information within government control." Of course, the media is entitle to receive records, even if there is no fee exemption.
3. McQuillin, The Law of Municipal Corporations (3rd ed), § 14:17.Records Subject to Inspection (accessed in 2020).
4. *Jacobellis v. Ohio*, 378 U.S. 184 (1964).
5. See https://www.nlc.org/number-of-municipal-governments-population-distribution (accessed in 2020).
6. U.S. Supreme Court Justice Louis Brandeis speaking in *New State Ice Co. v. Liebmann*, 285 U.S. 262 (1932).
7. *Adkisson v. Paxton*, 2015 WL 1030295 (Tex. App. Austin 2015).
8. *Howell Education Association v. Howell Board of Education*, 287 Mich. App. 228, 789 NW2d 495 (2010), leave to appeal to the state supreme court denied, 488 Mich. 1010.

Chapter 5

Federal Constitutional Limits on Local Governments

The issues presented in this chapter are at once the most interesting, the most challenging, and, in some instances, the most controversial. We trace a constitutional path along the ribbon of time stretching from the founding of the country all the way to the present, through a lens focused on the Bill of Rights and the Fourteenth Amendment. Local officials can find enrichment in understanding that these constitutional provisions secure critical protections of individual rights against actions of the government – including a local government.

The Fourteenth Amendment

Nearly a century after the founding of the country, the end of the Civil War ushered in both the need and the opportunity to finally address the national racial divide.

This translated into a most significant amendment of the Constitution intended to formalize essential points: slavery had indeed ended, and the "promissory note" securing full citizenship and voting rights for

---

African Americans was already past due. This gave rise to the Thirteenth, Fourteenth, and Fifteenth Amendments to the Constitution: formally declaring the end to slavery, providing citizenship and equal protection of law, and granting voting rights, respectively.

The Bill of Rights was originally adopted to protect individuals against actions of the *federal* government. The Fourteenth Amendment has been interpreted by the Court as making the bulk of the Bill of Rights to also protect individual liberties against actions of the *states*. This amounted to a seismic change in the Constitution itself – newly subjecting local governments many of the protections in the Bill of Rights.

Along this extraordinary path of some 230 years, the Constitution has provided stability. Yet there have been resounding changes in our society, requiring constitutional amendment and interpretation. Nearly a century after the founding of the country, the end of the Civil War ushered in both the need and the opportunity to finally address the national racial divide. This need and opportunity was met with obstruction. It became clear that the establishment of civil rights by force of law would be necessary, and this translated into the need to modify the Constitution in fundamental respects in order to formalize the essential points: slavery had indeed ended, and the "promissory note" securing full citizenship and voting rights for African Americans was already past due. This gave rise to the Thirteenth, Fourteenth, and Fifteenth Amendments to the Constitution: formally declaring the end to slavery, providing citizenship and equal protection of law, and granting voting rights, respectively.

In the fullness of time, the Fourteenth Amendment was interpreted by the Supreme Court to accomplish an ever broader effect. Specifically, the Court has interpreted this Amendment as incorporating most of the critical liberties stated in the Bill of Rights. Originally adopted to protect individuals against actions of the *federal* government, the Fourteenth Amendment has been interpreted by the Court as making the bulk of the Bill of Rights to serve as protections of individual liberties against actions of the *states*. This amounted to a seismic change in the Constitution itself – newly subjecting local governments to the protections in the Bill of Rights.

As the years passed, the Supreme Court recognized that our majoritarian system had the weakness of failing to fully recognize the rights of underrepresented minorities. In an attempt to cure this inherent shortcoming, about a century and a half after the founding, the Supreme Court adopted a more aggressive standard for reviewing legislation that appeared to shortchange minorities. In cases involving the constitutionality of legislation that substantially *impacted fundamental rights*, or *harmed minorities*, the Court began to apply what has become known as *closer judicial scrutiny*. The ramifications of this legal reorientation of constitutional law has resulted in important limitations on how local government power is exercised, and has altered the task of being a local government official.

The goal of this chapter is to provide a limited understanding of how the Supreme Court began to give certain liberties greater protection, and to summarize the methodology of the Court in granting this protection. While it is not feasible in this brief discussion to focus on the Court's interpretation of *all* of the rights and liberties in the Bill of Rights and Fourteenth Amendment, an attempt is made to provide local officials with a glimpse of how the Court attempts to enforce liberties associated with four of the monumentally important rights: due process, equal protection, free speech, and religious liberty – all individual liberties that regularly impact the business of local government in important ways.

A. Historical Background

1. Founding the Nation

At approximately the same time the Constitution was ratified, joining the states together as the "United States," ten amendments to the Constitution were also ratified in a single package known as the Bill of Rights. The purpose of the Bill of Rights was to guarantee to the people and the states that they retained significant autonomy from the federal government – that is, that the enumerated, or specifically mentioned, liberties embodied in the Bill of Rights could never be infringed upon by the newly created federal government. Free speech, religious freedom, and due process, among other rights, were expressly recognized as being protected. In addition, the Tenth Amendment spelled out that all power not expressly delegated by the Constitution to the federal government or expressly prohibited to the states would automatically be "reserved to the states respectively, or to the people." These guarantees provided the necessary spark that sent the nation on its way in the late 1700s.

It is incredibly important to keep in mind that, at the time of the adoption of the Bill of Rights and for approximately the first 75 years of our nation's history, the Bill of Rights only provided a protection of individual liberties from the exercise of *federal power*, and not on the use of power by the states and local governments. For example, the provision in the First Amendment, specifying that Congress shall make no law abridging the freedom of speech, protected the people's speech rights from being impaired by laws enacted by *Congress*. The Bill of Rights did *not* protect the people from laws enacted by *state* legislatures.

2. Post-Civil War

The expansion of liberty rights to also protect people from the actions of their own state governments (in addition to the federal government) began in 1868, when the Fourteenth Amendment was ratified. As the Bill of Rights and the Fourteenth Amendment have been interpreted by the Supreme Court over the years, the 1868 enactment of the Fourteenth Amendment made fundamental rights, including most of the liberties in the Bill of Rights, applicable *against the states*. There can be no doubt that the Fourteenth Amendment materially altered the constitution, and was a game-changer for the country.

3. Fourteenth Amendment and Local Governments

Understanding the protections provided by the Fourteenth Amendment is vital to appreciating the responsibility of local governments. Why? Because local governments are extensions of the "states" and, therefore, the liberties included within the protection provided through the Fourteenth Amendment shield individuals from the actions of local governments. This is of major consequence, and represents the basis of a good number of the federal constitutional claims filed against local governments seeking a vindication of individual rights and liberties.

4. "Fundamental" Rights

The material in this section may seem very legalistic and can be read at various levels, depending on the depth of understanding the reader would like to take away. The intent is to provide helpful historical background and context for issues that arise in local government, but a deeper understanding of constitutional law may also be discovered if desired.

"Fundamental Rights"

A special meaning has been developed in constitutional law for the term "fundamental right." The Supreme Court has recognized most of the rights and liberties in the Bill of Rights as being "fundamental." After all, they were expressly called out as special rights by proclaiming their undeniable existence in the first ten amendments to the Constitution.

This "fundamental" status means that neither Congress nor state legislatures may enact laws that transgress these rights unless there is a "compelling" reason. The Supreme Court has on several occasions invalidated state and local enactments that restrict "fundamental rights."

In addition to the fundamental rights specifically spelled out in the Bill of Rights, the Supreme Court has identified a limited number of additional rights and liberties for "fundamental right" status along with those stated in the Bill of Rights.

A special meaning has been embraced in constitutional law for the term "fundamental right." The Supreme Court has recognized most of the rights and liberties in the Bill of Rights as being "fundamental." It is easy to see why. After all, they were expressly called out as special rights by proclaiming their undeniable existence in the first ten amendments to the Constitution. This "fundamental" status means that neither Congress nor state legislatures may enact laws that transgress these rights unless there is a "compelling" reason. For example, because the First Amendment proclaims a free speech liberty, it is rare that the Court will permit a law to stand that restricts the content of a person's expressions. Indeed, the Supreme Court has on many occasions invalidated state and local enactments that restrict "fundamental rights."

In addition to the fundamental rights specifically enumerated in the Bill of Rights, the Supreme Court has identified a limited number of additional rights and liberties as being "fundamental." Despite *not* being enumerated in the Bill of Rights, these additional rights are given "fundamental right" status along with the enumerated rights. For example, although the Bill of Rights makes no specific mention of marriage or raising a family, the Court has long held that the right to marry and raise a family are fundamental rights. More recently, same-sex marriage was identified as a fundamental right, determined by a majority of the Court to involve a personal choice central to individual dignity and autonomy.[1]

So, the term "fundamental rights" includes many of the rights enumerated in the Bill of Rights, *plus* a limited number of unenumerated rights determined by the Court to have "fundamental right" status. With this understanding of "fundamental rights" in place, we now turn to a most powerful Court-made doctrine that transforms these fundamental rights into extraordinary individual protections.

The New Protection of Fundamental Rights

Beginning with a case decided in 1938, the Supreme Court began to look more deeply behind the words of certain laws passed by Congress and state legislatures to see whether these legislative bodies had a sufficient government reason to restrict "fundamental rights," and discriminate against racial and national minorities.

See *United States v. Carolene Products*, fn. 4

The story that explains how the Court determined to give these fundamental rights such potency begins in the late 1930s. Up to that point in American history, when laws were challenged, while the Court certainly guarded "free speech" and various other rights we now call "fundamental," they received the same treatment as laws affecting other rights.[2] For example, when a party challenged the validity of a local ordinance, the Court gave the local government the benefit of the doubt, and *presumed the ordinance to be constitutional.* A heavy burden was placed on the *challenging* party, who faced the near-herculean task of proving that the ordinance sought to achieve *no legitimate objective*; or, if there was a valid objective, the challenger had to show that the ordinance did not go about trying to achieve this objective in a *rational way*. Today, this standard of review by the Court is known as the "rational basis test." It is very favorable to the government, and the challenger has an extremely uphill battle to invalidate a law.

In 1938, the Supreme Court heard the case of *United States v. Carolene Products*, involving a challenge to a federal statute regulating milk products. Looking back, it was certainly not earth-shattering that the "rational basis" test was the standard the Court applied in deciding the case. However, although not germane to the *Carolene* case, the opinion included a now famous "footnote 4," in which Justice Harlan Fiske Stone, who wrote the opinion, presented a landmark idea. Specifically, in this otherwise unremarkable *Carolene Products* case that actually applied the customary rational basis test, a very remarkable footnote 4 conveyed a set of suggestions about how cases should be reviewed when particular types of laws are challenged. It was simply a recommendation on how certain laws challenged in future cases should be reviewed by the Court. Here are the types of laws the Court identified for *special treatment*:

> [L]egislation [that] appears on its face to be within a specific prohibition of the Constitution, such as those of the first ten amendments [of the Bill of Rights], . . . [or] legislation which restricts those political processes [minority representation] which can ordinarily be expected to bring about repeal of undesirable legislation [or] . . . statutes directed at particular religious, . . . or national, . . . or racial minorities, . . . [and] prejudice against discrete and insular minorities may be a special condition, which tends seriously to curtail the operation of those political processes ordinarily to be relied upon to protect minorities . . . [3]

In plain language, footnote 4 was identifying for closer court scrutiny those cases involving laws restricting such rights as free speech, freedom of religion and the right to vote, or laws discriminating against racial and national minorities. In these particular types of cases, footnote 4 proposed that the Court replace the long-established "rational basis" test with the following "heightened scrutiny:"

- ■ Laws being subjected to heightened scrutiny should not be presumed constitutional.
- ■ Rather than defer to the legislature that passed the law, the Court should take a more active role by determining whether an *adequate governmental interest* motivated the legislature to act.

In essence, the strategy of footnote 4 was: Where legislation has the effect of restricting fundamental rights or harming minority rights, there should be a lower presumption that the legislation is valid, and the government should be required to come into court and prove that there was a strong reason for passing the law. These recommendations of a single justice, as presented in footnote 4, began a transformation of how judges review cases, a practice that continues to reverberate to this date.

In view of the complication of this material, it is worth stating again that most of the rights "enumerated" in the Bill of Rights have been affirmed by the Court as being "fundamental." A number of additional rights have also been found to be deserving of special protection, and they too have been given "fundamental" status despite not being specifically mentioned in the Bill of Rights. Both types of fundamental rights, along with the protection for minorities under the Fourteenth Amendment, are afforded higher court review consistent with the strategy specified in "footnote 4," commonly known as "heightened scrutiny."[4]

5. The Bill of Rights and Fourteenth Amendment: A Closer Look

At the time of the Declaration of Independence, the American colonies were being mistreated by the federal government of England, which was headed by the king. The Declaration carefully explained the mistreatment being suffered, and proclaimed the rights of life, liberty, and the pursuit of happiness. Having suffered adverse treatment from an arbitrary English federal government, those seeking to establish our new nation wished to spell out in the Constitution the *protections of the people* from the new *United States* federal government. And that is exactly what the Bill of Rights was intended to accomplish. Prominent examples of such protections are found in the First Amendment, which prohibits the federal government from interfering with free speech and religion, and the Fifth Amendment, which guarantees due process, including a prohibition on the federal government from *arbitrarily* depriving people of their life, liberty, and property. As briefly discussed above, all of these guarantees in the Bill of Rights were originally protections only against actions by the new *federal* government.

When the Constitution was initially ratified, there were 13 sovereign states – the "united states," joined together to form a nation. As a condition to forming this federal entity, the individual states insisted upon a significant degree of *autonomy* as part of the arrangement. Despite the new union, each state was preserved as a distinct governmental entity in various ways. In particular, the original bargain that combined the states into one nation guaranteed that the individual states would retain significant *sovereign authority* over their respective *state affairs*. As we all know, one issue that some of the states were preoccupied with was the insidious view that some people could actually *own* other people – that *slavery* should be permissible. Although there were anti-slavery efforts made by many over the years, this appalling condition was allowed to persist until the conclusion of the Civil War, during which many soldiers lost their lives opposing slavery. Recognition of the degree to which slavery was an atrocity is found in the post-Civil War ratification of the Thirteenth, Fourteenth, and Fifteenth Amendments to the Constitution. These post-Civil War amendments did not merely abolish slavery; they also introduced *federal oversight of the states* on the protection of additional individual rights, including prohibiting discrimination, affording due process and protecting voting rights, respectively. No state would be permitted to retain autonomy to the extent that it could deny these critical rights to former slaves and others. So, the Fourteenth Amendment's formal prohibition of discrimination was expressly targeted against the *states* by prohibiting the use of *state* power against the people, as seen in this language from Section 1 of that amendment (with emphasis added):

> No *state* shall make or enforce any law which shall abridge the privileges or immunities of citizens of the United States; nor shall any *state* deprive any person of life, liberty, or property, without due process of law; nor deny to any person within its jurisdiction the equal protection of the laws.

In this critical step in the history of the United States, the Constitution continued protecting the rights of all people from actions of the *federal* government in the manner spelled out in the Bill of Rights, and newly began protecting the rights of all individuals from the actions of *state* governments.

Today, the Court reads the Fourteenth Amendment as protecting the people against action by state government that restricts any of the fundamental protections in the Bill of Rights, or any of the "unenumerated" fundamental rights. It is important to remain mindful that local governments are an integral part of the states, and therefore, all of these protections from action by *state* governments are by every measure protections of the rights of the people from action by *local* governments.

It is beyond the scope of this chapter to itemize and explore *every* liberty made applicable to the states through the Fourteenth Amendment. Rather, the focus here will be on the following liberties, chosen because they are routinely the subject of lawsuits involving local governments:

■ The due process clauses of the Fifth and Fourteenth Amendments
■ The equal protection clause of the Fourteenth Amendment
■ The free speech clause of the First Amendment, applicable to local governments through the Fourteenth Amendment and
■ The two religion clauses of the First Amendment, applicable to local governments through the Fourteenth Amendment.[5]

B. Due Process (Fifth and Fourteenth Amendments)

Guarantee of Due Process in the Fifth and Fourteenth Amendments:
No person shall be . . . deprived of life, liberty, or property, without due process of law.

1. Background

One of the greatest causes of citizen frustration is arbitrary government action; that is, action taken without an opportunity for discussion, or action taken for no legitimate reason. It is precisely this frustration that brought about our constitutional requirement for "due process." Long ago, during the rule of King Edward III of England, Parliament enacted several statutes to clarify the meaning and scope of the liberties provided by "Magna Carta," a constitution-like charter signed in 1354. "Due process," embedded in Magna Carta, restricted the arbitrary whim of the monarch by granting citizens the right to fair and principled decision-making. At the founding of the United States, these same demands of due process were enshrined in the Fifth Amendment, which applies to the federal government directly. Later, the Fourteenth Amendment was enacted, reiterating the due process demands of the Fifth Amendment as being applicable to the states (including local governments). These two amendments, major guardians of liberty, remain a unifying thread in our state and federal law. Public officials must follow a principled compass to ensure that they consistently meet the requirements of due process.

The Court has recognized two types of due process protections: *procedural* due process and *substantive* due process. They are both protections under "due process," but refer to two distinct guarantees.

2. Procedural Due Process

> The hallmarks of procedural due process are the requirements that government first give *adequate notice* to a person whose rights are to be impaired, describing the reason for the impending deprivation of rights, and then grant the person an *opportunity to be heard.*

Procedural due process is fairly straightforward. It presents a *procedural requirement* when a local government is going to deprive a person of an important liberty or property right.[6] The due process clause guarantees such a person a *fair government process* – before the right is deprived. What is a "fair process?" The hallmarks of procedural due process are the requirements that government first give *adequate notice* to the person whose rights are to be impaired, describing the reason for the impending deprivation of rights, and then granting the person an *opportunity to be heard*; that is, allowing the person to make a defensive presentation of the reasons why the deprivation should not occur.[7] The required formality of the process varies depending on the seriousness of the deprivation, and a greater discussion on this point can be found in the Supreme Court's opinion in the case of *Mathews v. Eldridge.*[8]

3. Substantive Due Process

> Substantive due process probes whether the government is achieving a *sufficient interest* to justify the deprivation of liberty or property anticipated to occur under the challenged action.

Substantive due process is less straightforward. It probes whether the government is achieving a *sufficient interest* to justify the deprivation anticipated to occur in the challenged action. A ruling that a local regulation violates substantive due process may well mean that the local government will be barred from enforcing its regulation, or taking other proposed action, "regardless of the fairness of the *procedure* used to implement it."[9]

The due process clauses of the Fifth and Fourteenth Amendments serve as protectors of *liberty* and *property* rights. In cases involving a deprivation of a *liberty* right, the Court's review may be more searching, as suggested by "footnote 4" of the *Carolene Products* case discussed above. The extent of the review will depend on the nature of the liberty right to be deprived. The Supreme Court has found a wide variety of meanings within this single word "liberty," among them the "freedom from bodily restraint . . . [and] also the right of the individual to contract, to marry, establish a home and bring up children, to worship God according to the dictates of [a person's] own conscience, and generally to enjoy those privileges long recognized . . . as essential to the orderly pursuit of happiness . . . "[10]

Some categories of liberty interests may receive a stricter review than others. If there is no "substantial impairment of a fundamental right," the court may use the *rational basis* test, which presumes in favor of the local government. (As discussed above, a "fundamental right" is typically one that is guaranteed in the Bill of Rights or specifically identified by the Court as being "fundamental," such as the right to marry.) Because it does *not* impair a "fundamental" right, one example of a regulatory impact that would receive the government-favoring "rational basis" review is an ordinance that prohibits a person from driving a car prior to reaching the age of 16, or unless such person wears corrective lenses. The right to drive a car is certainly not identified in the Bill of Rights, and the Court has not otherwise designated this right as being fundamental. In a due process challenge of this ordinance, the government-friendly rational basis test would apply, and the local government is most likely to prevail.

> If a local regulation substantially impairs the exercise of a fundamental right, it will be reviewed under the standard suggested in footnote 4 of the *Carolene Products* case, namely, the Court will discard the usual presumption that the local regulation is constitutional, and instead apply a *more exacting and searching judicial scrutiny* to determine whether there is a sufficiently compelling interest that justifies the law.

On the other hand, if a local regulation *does* substantially impair the exercise of a fundamental right, it may be reviewed under the standard suggested in footnote 4 of the *Carolene Products* case. With a *fundamental right* at stake, the Court discards the usual presumption that the local regulation is constitutional and instead applies a *more exacting and searching judicial scrutiny*. As mentioned above, "fundamental rights" include many of the rights enumerated in the Bill of Rights, such as the right of free speech, and also several "unenumerated" rights identified by the Supreme Court, such as the right to pursue a lawful occupation, acquire an education, get married or raise a family. The particular standards formulated by the Court for conducting this more exacting and searching review are of great significance, and are worthwhile for a local public official to know something about – at least in general terms.

It might be helpful to consider a hypothetical example involving a local government zoning ordinance. This will allow the illustration of comparative court review for ordinances that impair fundamental rights in relation to the review of those that do not. Begin with a garden variety zoning regulation that limits the use of property to non-commercial, purely residential purposes. So, this regulation "deprives" the property owner from using the property for commercial purposes. This amounts to a deprivation of a *social and economic* interest, not one of the fundamental rights. Accordingly, court review in this type of case will require a challenger to overcome a presumption of constitutionality by demonstrating that the restriction is arbitrary and unreasonable, having no relation to achieving a legitimate objective – the *rational basis* test.[11] The challenger will have an extremely difficult time meeting this tough test, and local governments prevail in most cases of this type.

Now consider a zoning ordinance that prohibits a resident from displaying in her bedroom window an 8½ by 10-inch political sign with a message that criticizes the government. This regulation places the local government into the realm of restricting the *fundamental* right of "free speech," enumerated in the Bill of Rights. Rather than applying the rational basis test, the court will apply a more searching review, commonly known as the "strict scrutiny" test. This test places a *heavy burden on the local government* rather than on the challenger, and the local regulation rarely passes this test.[12] Specifically, the *strict scrutiny* test applies when a court reviews an ordinance that deprives someone of a *fundamental* right. It gives *no* presumption of constitutionality to the ordinance. Showing merely a "legitimate" government interest is not good enough here. Rather, the government must demonstrate that there is a "compelling" interest for restricting the fundamental right. And even if the local government demonstrates a compelling interest for the regulation, the full burden is still not met. The local government must go on to show that the law attempts to achieve the compelling interest by the means that is *least restrictive* of the right being protected. That is, if the challenger can identify *any* alternative approach that would have been less restrictive, the local government is likely to lose. Merriam-Webster defines "compelling" as a forceful or irresistible drive or urge, or a cause under overwhelming pressure. That is a difficult standard to meet on its own, but to couple that with the second part of the test, the "least restrictive means" hurdle, results in a burden which is almost insurmountable. The chief lesson here is that it is rare that the government can regulate in ways that significantly restrict fundamental rights, such as, in this example, the display of signage based on the message expressed.

C. Equal Protection (Fourteenth Amendment)

> Guarantee of Equal Protection in the Fourteenth Amendment:
> *No state shall . . . deny to any person within its jurisdiction the equal protection of the laws.*

There was no requirement for equal protection of law in the original Constitution and Bill of Rights. It was the Fourteenth Amendment, ratified in 1868 after the Civil War, which proclaimed for the first time that "no state shall deny to any person within its jurisdiction the equal protection of the laws."

But what does "equal protection" mean? Here is a simplified answer. Start with assumption that local governments frequently distinguish how groups of people are treated – one group is treated in this way and another group is treated in that way. For example, say that a city creates a regulation specifying that a person under the age of 12 years old may not ride on the public transportation system without the company of an adult. This regulation would be creating a "classification" system by establishing two classes of persons: one class would be all persons under 12; the second class would be all people who are 12 and older. Then, the regulation affords *different treatment* to each of the classes – one class in a restrictive manner and another class in a more permissive manner. *Equal protection*, in the most straightforward sense, prohibits a local government (and the state itself) from creating a classification of people and purposefully treating one of the classes in an inferior manner *unless there is a sufficient reason for the different treatment.*

Equal protection does not provide protection based on whether certain rights are restricted. Rather, equal protection applies when the government is *intentionally discriminating* against one *class of persons* over another class without a justifiable reason.

The key to understanding equal protection is that it prevents a local government from *intentionally discriminating* against one class of people as compared to the treatment afforded to a comparable class if there is no valid justification. In most cases, classifications created by local laws will be subject to the government-friendly *rational basis test*. We are perfectly accustomed, for example, to government dividing taxpayers into classes – high income individuals, middle income individuals, and lower income individuals. The classes with higher income receive inferior treatment under the law: they are required to pay taxes at a higher rate. Likewise, we are accustomed to a system of classification for prospective motor vehicle drivers: a person in the class of individuals under 16 years old may not be licensed to drive, but a person in the class that is 16 years old and above can be licensed to drive – regardless of their driving skills. For these classifications based on income and age, two categories where differential treatment is likely to be motivated by practical rather than bad faith purposes, an ordinance will be evaluated under the favorable *rational basis test*.

Greater protection under *Caroline Products* footnote 4 arises when discrimination is focused on certain classes of persons, including classes based on race, national origin, and gender.

But now let us turn to equal protection review applied to ordinances that create classifications based on the categories of concern identified in footnote 4 of the *Carolene Products* case. These include categories where legislative majorities had historically passed laws that disregard the interests of minority groups. For equal protection purposes, the Court has held that *the type of review depends on whether the regulation creates a system of classification for inferior treatment based on one of five identified characteristics of people*. Stated again, the difference in treatment under equal protection (either *rational basis review* or *heightened scrutiny*) depends on the characteristics of the class of people being impacted by the ordinance, rather than on whether there is a fundamental right involved in the case. And for equal protection purposes, here are the *five types of "class" characteristics* that receive closer scrutiny under the equal protection clause:

- classes based on *race*;
- classes based on *national origin* (that is, the ordinance prescribes different treatment for persons with a place of origin outside the United States);
- classes based on *alienage* (that is, the ordinance prescribes different treatment for non-citizens of the United States);
- classes based on *gender*; and
- classes based on non-marital *children status* (that is, the ordinance prescribes different treatment for persons whose parents were not married at the time they were born).

The reality is that the Court has created even more complication on the equal protection subject.

We will attempt to avoid most of the additional complication, but it is worth knowing that there are two *levels* of "heightened scrutiny" under equal protection (rather than simply "strict scrutiny," which applies under substantive due process). Where a law purposefully discriminates against one class based on *race, national origin or alienage* (the first three of the five categories above) the court review will be based on the "strict scrutiny" standard. This is the highest level of scrutiny, and the same standard the Court uses under substantive due process to review a law that impairs the exercise of a fundamental right. (Those keeping score may recall that "strict scrutiny" requires the government to demonstrate that its challenged regulation was motivated by a *compelling government interest* and that the regulation uses the *least restrictive means* to accomplish the compelling interest.)

In addition to strict scrutiny, the second type of heightened scrutiny for equal protection purposes applies where a law discriminates against a class of persons based on *gender or non-marital children* classifications (the fourth and fifth of the five categories above). For a regulation that discriminates based on one of these classes, the court uses the "intermediate scrutiny" standard, a middle level not used in the due process context. This scrutiny is not as searching as strict scrutiny, but there is no presumption of constitutionality given to the law, and the government must come forward and demonstrate that there is a *significant* or *important* interest that it is pursuing by its regulation, and that there is a *substantial relationship* between the law and the important interest sought to be achieved.

It is worth reemphasizing that these five categories are the *only* types of class-based discrimination that activates heightened court scrutiny under equal protection. If the discrimination is based on *any other* class, such as economic status or age classifications, courts will apply the government-favoring *rational basis test*, and the ordinance will very likely survive the challenge.

Returning briefly to our ordinance hypothetical, if the local government ordinance imposes distinct treatment of two classes, but this time the distinction is shown to be based on race (rather than based on income or age), the strict scrutiny test may apply, with the likely result that the ordinance will be held to be invalid.

Another set of comparative examples may also be helpful to understand how the courts apply the relevant tests for an equal protection challenge, starting with the *rational basis test*. A good illustrative case is *New Orleans v. Dukes*.[13] The City of New Orleans concluded that there were too many "push cart food vendors" in the so-called French Quarter, and enacted an ordinance to reduce the number of vendors in order "to preserve the appearance and custom valued by the Quarter's residents and attractive to tourists." To accomplish the city's objective, the ordinance banned all vendors except those who had continuously operated in the French Quarter for eight or more years. Two vendors qualified. The effect of the ordinance was to create two classes of vendors: those who qualified with the time requirement and those who did not, and the latter group was given drastically inferior treatment by being entirely disqualified from continuing to operate in the French Quarter. One of the vendors who was disqualified challenged the ordinance under the equal protection clause. The Court applied the *rational basis test*, observing that,

> Unless a classification . . . is drawn upon inherently suspect distinctions such as race, religion, or alienage, our decisions presume the constitutionality of the statutory discriminations and require only that the classification challenged be rationally related to a legitimate state interest. States are accorded wide latitude in the regulation of their local economics . . . and rational distinctions may be made with substantially less than mathematical exactitude.

Predictably, the New Orleans ordinance was upheld because it was not subjected to closer scrutiny by the Court.

Now assume that the two vendors who qualified to remain in the City of New Orleans were white, and all the other vendors were either racial or national minorities. Implicit in the quoted language from the *Dukes* opinion, if the ordinance discriminated on the basis of race and national origin, the Court would have approached the case in a meaningfully different manner, removing the presumption of validity and imposing the more searching *strict scrutiny* test. In the *Dukes* case, under the rational basis test, the ordinance was upheld. If the ordinance were subjected to the weight of the *strict scrutiny* test, the likelihood is great that the ordinance would have been invalidated.

D. Free Speech (First Amendment)

According to the First Amendment guarantee of free speech:

Congress shall make no law . . . abridging the freedom of speech.

1. Background

Immediately prior to the Declaration of Independence in the 1700s, the ability of citizens to speak freely was restricted in significant respects. Statements critical of the government were forbidden – regardless of their truth! Under the law of *seditious libel,* anyone speaking critically about the government risked being charged with the *crime* of sedition (inciting rebellion against the state). In the colonies, seditious libel included criticism of the colonial governor. Further, any person desiring to publish and distribute written material required a *license* issued by the government. This type of pre-screening of written material by the government is known as a "prior restraint."

2. The Free Speech Protection: An Overview

In direct response to these speech restrictions imposed by England on the colonies, the very first amendment to the Constitution identifies the right of "free speech." Courts in the United States have made it their business to guard this central right jealously.

Although the First Amendment was intended to apply as a protection only against the actions of the *federal* government, the Fourteenth Amendment has been interpreted as making its guarantee of free speech applicable to the *states* (and, by extension, local governments) as well.

The First Amendment states that Congress (now interpreted to include state and local governments) *shall make no law* abridging free speech. Has the Supreme Court insisted that this command must be literally construed? Does the right of free speech mean that we can say anything, that we are totally unlimited in our speech? Fortunately, the answer to this question is "no." There have been a number of exceptions recognized by the Supreme Court to unbridled free speech. A few examples are expressions which are obscene, using speech to incite immediate illegal activities, child pornography, and speech that would amount to defamation. These types of speech have been deemed "unprotected" by the First Amendment; that is, the injunction that "Congress shall make no law" does not apply to these and a few other areas of speech which, on balance, have too great a potential to be harmful, such that the harm is not offset by the benefit that society would derive from giving them First Amendment protection.

Important to remember: The First Amendment "free speech" guarantee protects against *governmental* regulation, but does not apply to *private* rules and regulations.

Keep in mind that the First Amendment "free speech" guarantee protects against *governmental* regulation and does not apply to *private* rules and regulations. So, if a private retail business, for example, makes a rule for customers coming into the store that says "no political signs may worn on anyone's clothing in the store," this would not violate the First Amendment.

But what exactly is the benefit of protecting speech, particularly on subjects such as politics? One of the most important points is that, in order to intelligently vote and support candidates or issues, it is necessary to become educated on the important subjects of the day. The theory is that we are able to hold intelligent views only if we are *exposed to ideas on all sides of an argument*, and then be in an informed position to *formulate our own views*. But where do we get this exposure to ideas on all sides of an argument? The answer is through access to what has been called the *marketplace of ideas*. The First Amendment free speech clause allows all persons to speak their mind about politics – and most other subjects – in a public venue (such as a sidewalk or park). Going to a public venue to speak and listen is essentially going to the "marketplace." After being exposed in this marketplace to the views of people on all sides, we can then make an evaluation of what we find to be "the truth" – all without the necessity of a war, or even a physical fight. Many say that the Internet is actually a greater, and more efficient, marketplace than a public sidewalk or park. It certainly is easy to gain access to divergent views on the Internet marketplace – in some cases to a seemingly overwhelming extent! However, the Court has not yet formally decided that the Internet is a "public" venue where free speech is guaranteed.

> Under the First Amendment "free speech" clause, the Court will give high scrutiny to a government regulation that attempts to restrict the *content* of a person's expression.

A most important concept to grasp is a point that can have important bearing in case outcomes under the First Amendment. Specifically, the most "sacred" part of what is protected in speech is the *content* of what a person desires to express. Having the opportunity to access the marketplace of ideas means that the government cannot restrict this "content." Unless the government can meet the enormous demands of the "strict scrutiny" test by showing that there is a *compelling government need* for a restriction, and that the restriction has been couched in the *least restrictive terms*, the government simply cannot prohibit the free expression of a person's desired content (unless it is one of the forms of unprotected speech, such as obscenity). In other words, the government cannot restrict "what" we want to say. The legal meaning of "content" is broad, and encompasses the *ideas* that a person desires to express. Nor may a regulation prohibit "who" can make the expression. So a local ordinance may not say that certain people are permitted to speak at local parks, but others may not.[14] Nor can the government allow only certain *viewpoints* into the marketplace ("vote for Party X") while prohibiting the expression of opposing viewpoints ("vote for Party Y"). The key is that the government must keep the marketplace open to all ideas, without regard to popularity. It is worth repeating that when a government regulation targets the *content* of political or other protected speech, including viewpoint, the regulation has little chance of being upheld because it will be subjected to strict scrutiny.

3. Not All Speech Is Equal

Some categories of speech receive stronger protection than others. The objective of free "political" speech was at the forefront of reasons for protecting free speech. Indeed, political speech was probably most instrumental to the inclusion of the protection of speech in the First Amendment of the Bill of Rights. The point was that it had to be clear that criticizing the government was fair game. Supreme Court opinions have produced a hierarchy of the importance of various types of speech. In a 1942 case (that has not been overruled) the Court indicated that certain forms of speech have a *relatively low value*, such as expressions that are lewd, profane or insulting, which would likely result in a public disturbance if uttered in public. The Court indicated that such speech is of slight social value as a step to truth, so that any benefit offered is outweighed by the interest in order and morality.[15] More recently, in a case involving "hate speech," a separate opinion of a justice mentioned that the priority of various types of expressions looks like this (as of 1992 when the opinion was written):

- core political speech – highest, most protected;
- commercial speech and non-obscene sexually explicit speech – second-class expression;
- obscenity and fighting words – least protected.[16]

There is another important factor in determining whether a restriction, say in a local ordinance, will be invalidated by strict scrutiny. Namely, the Court will forego strict scrutiny if it concludes that the regulation does not *predominantly* intend to regulate the "content" of expression, and primarily has a *non-speech objective*. A brief example of a case on this should be helpful. A regulation in New York City was aimed at maintaining an acceptable level of noise being produced during performances on a stage located in Central Park. A predominant purpose was to protect an adjoining neighborhood from unreasonable disturbance. The performers on the stage wanted to control their own noise level and performance times, but this had proven unreliable. So, the city hired an expert sound engineer to control the noise in a way that would not harm the quality of musical expression being produced, while also protecting the adjoining neighborhood. In response to a "free speech" challenge, *the Supreme Court held that it was not the city's main purpose to interfere with the musical expression*. Rather, the city's predominant motive was to *protect the neighboring residents from harm*, and by hiring an expert the city had taken reasonable steps to avoid seriously impacting the content of the performers' speech. The Court did not apply strict scrutiny, and upheld the regulation.[17] This case provides an excellent example of what has been referred to as permissible "time, place, and manner" regulation that has only an incidental impact on free speech. In legal vernacular, this ordinance was allowed because it did not predominantly regulate content or subject matter. Loud noises, and performances occurring after the time limit, were banned to protect people from harm, and not to restrict the content of expression.

4. Free Speech Issues Relevant to Local Governments

First Amendment issues in a few areas of speech regulation are especially relevant in the local government context. Three will be briefly reviewed here.

First, in a case involving *sign regulation*, decided in 2015, the Court has made life particularly difficult for local government. This difficulty applies to all regulation of private signage, including ordinances applicable to signage on residential, office, commercial, and industrial properties, and even signage displayed for church purposes.[18] In the 2015 case, the Court described "content" regulation in such broad terms that a large number of local governments in the country have been required to rewrite their sign ordinances. Public officials need to consider what the predominant motive is in regulating signage and avoid regulations that attempt to restrict the *content* of signs to be displayed.

The second significant category is regulation focused on *adult entertainment establishments*. Here the Court's response has included some good news and some bad news for local governments. On the helpful side, the Court has concluded that adult uses, those offering erotic expressions, involve speech which is of *relatively low value*, and thus requires a lower level of protection. For this reason, local governments have been allowed regulate "adult uses" by showing that their ordinances regulating these uses are aimed at reducing related crime, such as prostitution or drug dealing that occur near such uses. The bad news is that the Court still finds that these expressions are protected by the First Amendment, albeit at a low level. So, a local *government is not permitted to totally exclude* uses offering adult expressions from the community. Uses that fall within this "second class" speech category include adult book stores, adult theaters, and topless or nude dancing facilities. Based on studies undertaken for the City of Detroit, an authoritative report concluded that when several of these uses are concentrated in close proximity, there is consistently a spike in crime. Clearly, if a local government attempts to regulate by completely prohibiting explicit sexual expressions, the regulation would be ruled an invalid attempt to prohibit the *content* of protected speech – even though the level of protection is relatively low. In *Young v. American Mini Theaters, Inc*, the Court accepted the proposition that a city may regulate *incidentally* by imposing a distance requirement between adult uses. This avoids the concentration of such uses that the Detroit studies showed are consistently a cause of crime. Thus, the *primary purpose* of the regulation is to address crime, even though it is clear that the regulation would have an *incidental* adverse effect on low-value-but-still-protected speech.[19]

A third area of "free speech" law which is often relevant for local officials involves a unique compromise the Court has forged in the protection of free expression in *government employment.* In this special setting, there are the following competing interests: on the one hand, the government has a legitimate interest in providing an effective and service-oriented workplace to serve the public; on the other hand, public employees should not be required to shed all of their protected speech rights at the door of city hall. These interests cross when a public employee is disciplined or fired *for making particular expressions.* So, what degree of protection for public employee speech should prevail? The Supreme Court concluded that the answer to this question depends on whether the particular expression of an employee involves a matter of "public concern."[20] If the expression is one of *public* concern, the employee must face only those speech restrictions necessary for the public employer to operate efficiently and effectively. But, where an expression of an employee relates only to matters of *personal* interest to the employee, including the employee's official personal duties, the government employer has a wider latitude in managing the public office – and disciplining the employee – without the court intruding in the name of the First Amendment.

E. Religion (First Amendment)

There are two First Amendment protections for religion:
Congress shall make no law:

■ *respecting an establishment of religion (the "establishment" clause); or*
■ *prohibiting the free exercise thereof (the "free exercise" clause).*

1. Background

The First Amendment protects religious rights in two related clauses which are on opposite sides of the coin: the establishment clause and the free exercise clause. The establishment clause prevents government from creating or *requiring* a religion, favoring religion over no religion or favoring one religion (or non-religion) over others, and the free exercise clause allows the exercise of one's religion of choice without a *substantial burden* being imposed by government. The Supreme Court has called the establishment clause a "co-guarantor, with the Free Exercise Clause, of religious liberty."[21] While they may at first appear unrelated, they actually work together in the interest of religious freedom.[22]

Clues as to the importance and motivation for these two clauses may be found in the beliefs and statements of James Madison, who would become a future president of the United States. He was *a primary author of the Bill of Rights.* Madison held very strong views about religion, seeing it on the one hand as a necessity for "civil society," but on the other hand as a quintessentially *personal* and *voluntary* quest, rather than something the government should sponsor or mandate, calling such actions by the government "an unhallowed perversion." Not surprisingly, given Madison's close involvement, the two religion clauses were written as the first among all the protections identified in the Bill of Rights.

In 1947, the Supreme Court commented that the two religion clauses were a reaction to the dramatic *religious persecution* that swept through Europe in the sixteenth and seventeenth centuries, where governments (monarchs) attempted to impose religious *uniformity by force.* This was a phenomenon that the founders strongly desired to avoid in their quest to preserve liberty. The Court also pointed out that the founders (we might suspect Madison in particular) desired to promote the *integrity of individual conscience.*[23]

2. The Establishment Clause

While it might be clear that the religion clauses were motivated by a desire to establish and maintain religious liberty, there have been changing rules on *precisely* what is meant by the constitutional command that laws shall not be passed "respecting an establishment of religion." There is no reason to expect that the Court has finished arguing about this subject. Local officials should stay tuned, as future cases will surely address this issue.

During the past several decades, Supreme Court opinions have created at least three tests for determining the validity of a law or policy challenged under the establishment clause. In very non-technical terms, these tests focus on *two criteria* for analyzing government action that impacts on religion: does the government action have a permissible *purpose*, and what is its *effect*. These tests have been applied in a variety of contexts, including situations in which government has provided aid for religious entities, rules, and actions involving the intersection of religion and public schools, and other circumstances in which the government has acted in a way that may give the impression that religion was being favored over non-religion, or that one religion was being favored over another.

There is no justification for an exhaustive analysis of all of these issues considering the scope of this book, and also considering the complexity and lack of clarity in the rules developed by various Supreme Court majorities through the decades. So the approach here will be to focus briefly on a pair of subjects where the establishment clause is particularly relevant to local government: first, saying a prayer at the beginning of a public meeting; and, second, placing religious symbols on public property, such as the display of religious symbols in front of city hall during the during holidays.

The first subject is prayer on the agenda at public meetings, which was the subject of a 2014 Supreme Court case arising in the town of Greece, a suburb of Rochester, New York.[24] The case challenged the town's practice of starting each meeting of the town board with a prayer – mostly led by representatives of the Christian ministry. In responding to the challenge of this practice, the majority of the Court felt like it was being placed in the untenable position of being asked to *censor* certain meeting presentations, or to decide *what prayers* were permissible. In either of these alternatives, the Court itself would become hopelessly entangled in the establishment of religion issue.

In the end, the Court held that the practice of the town did not violate the establishment clause. It was pointed out that in its first-ever session – shortly after approving the language of the First Amendment – Congress itself had voted to appoint and pay official chaplains. Both houses of Congress have maintained chaplains virtually uninterrupted ever since. In finding the practice to be constitutionally acceptable, the Court emphasized that interpretation of the establishment clause must take into consideration *historical practices and understandings.* However, the Court cautioned that while deference was being given to the historical practice of prayer at meetings, it is imperative that the *effect* of this practice may not cause members of the public to be coerced into favoring religion over non-religion or one religion over another. For example, a local government could not show favor for individuals that have chosen to participate in the prayer in relation to those who have chosen to abstain. In addition, the Court has drawn a sharp distinction between the practice of saying a prayer in the context of meetings with *mature adults,* as compared to the Court's *prohibition* on prayer in the public school setting where young, inexperienced individuals would generally be more *susceptible to indoctrination.*

The second subject that has created frequently litigated establishment clause issues is the placement of religious symbols on public property. This has included a range of symbols, from a display of the Ten Commandments in a courthouse to holiday displays associated with a particular religion such as Christmas trees and *crèche* scenes in front of city halls.

Over the span of time, the Court has struggled in the attempt to provide a cogent rule that would allow public bodies to predict the contours of permissible behavior within this context. The conflict among the Supreme Court justices on this issue was itself on "display" in the 1989 decision in *Allegheny County v. Greater Pittsburgh ACLU.* As mentioned above, the Court has developed at least three tests to apply to establishment clause cases, and in separate opinions by the justices, the facts of the *Allegheny County* case were analyzed under all three tests, with varying results. Very briefly, the facts encompassed two separate religious displays: (1) a *crèche* (nativity scene) at a county courthouse; and (2) a display in front of a government building that included a Christian symbol, a Jewish symbol, and a "neutral" salute to liberty. The separate opinions written in the case found the following. Under what might be considered the "strict separation" test, both displays on public property were deemed to be unconstitutional. Under what can be characterized as the "neutrality" or "endorsement" approach, the display with the nativity scene alone was deemed to be unconstitutional because it appears to favor only one religion, while the display that combined symbols was found to be permissible because it did not endorse a particular religion or favor religion over non-religion. And under the "accommodation" or "coercion" analysis, if there is an absence of coercion, "the risk of infringement of religious liberty by passive or symbolic accommodation is minimal," particularly considered in the context of the nation's historical traditions, which allow reasonable accommodations for holidays. Under this more liberal test, both displays were deemed acceptable.

In June of 2019, when the Court decided a new case involving a symbolic display, a coalition of justices supporting the historical analysis continued to hold sway.[25] The facts underlying this case began in 1925, after World War I, when a large "Bladensburg Peace Cross" was erected by a committee formed to give tribute to 49 area soldiers who gave their lives in the Great War. The completed monument consists of a 32-foot tall Latin cross that sits on a large pedestal, all located on public property. The American Legion's emblem is displayed at its center, and the words "Valor," "Endurance," "Courage," and "Devotion" are inscribed at its base, one on each of the four faces. Eighty-nine years after the dedication of the cross, a suit was filed, claiming that the memorial on public land was offensive, and that its presence there and the expenditure of public funds to maintain it violate the establishment clause of the First Amendment. To remedy this alleged violation, the plaintiffs asked a federal court to order the relocation or demolition of the cross, or at least the removal of the horizontal "arms" of the cross. The Court's majority view was that the religion clauses of the First Amendment aim to foster a society in which people of all beliefs can live together harmoniously, and the presence of the Bladensburg Cross on the land where it has stood for so many years is fully consistent with that aim. Through the passage of time, it acquired *historical importance*. The majority decision therefore concluded that the display, including the cross, does not offend the establishment clause. Rather, it carries special significance in commemorating the Great War, a symbol of the soldiers' sacrifice, and its design must be understood in light of that background. That the cross originated as a Christian symbol and retains that meaning in many contexts does not change the fact that the symbol took on an added secular meaning when used in World War I memorials.

Overall, the Court is looking at history and tradition, and is examining whether the government's actions and regulations are coercing adherence to a particular religion, or to religion over non-religion – an issue which is particularly important where children might be influenced. In addition, some on the

Court are analyzing facts from the angle that religion has been an important part of life in the country, which tends toward greater deference.

3.   *The Free Exercise Clause*

The second "co-guarantor" of religious liberty is the free exercise clause. At present, the Court seems to have settled on a much simpler formulation of rules for this clause as compared to the complications of its establishment clause pronouncements. Challenges under the free exercise clause are sorted into one of two categories: (1) laws and ordinances which are *neutral* and *general* applicability will be reviewed under the "rational basis" standard, which is very favorable to government; and (2) laws and ordinances that intend to *target religion* will be reviewed under the "strict scrutiny" standard, which is very *un*favorable to government. Both categories will be examined here, along with a federal law enacted by Congress to protect the free exercise of religion still further, known as the Religious Land Use and Institutionalized Persons Act (RLUIPA).

Recall from above that when a court reviews the validity of a local ordinance under the rational basis standard, the ordinance is *presumed* to be constitutional. The party challenging it has the burden of proving that the ordinance is *arbitrary* – meaning either that there is no legitimate objective for the ordinance, or that the ordinance does not go about trying to achieve its objective in a rational way. Under the rational basis test, the government prevails in an overwhelming number of cases. So *why* would this type of review, so lenient to the government, ever be used when an ordinance is being challenged as an interference with the *constitutional right* to freely exercise religion? The answer to this important question can be found in a 1990 Supreme Court case, *Employment Division v. Smith*, where a party claimed that it was improper to enforce a drug violation law against persons who are using a particular drug as part of a ceremony which is an integral part of their religion.[26]

The argument in the *Smith* case was that enforcement of the drug law created a *substantial burden* on the *free exercise* of the plaintiff's religion, in violation of the free exercise clause. Under the law in existence prior to *Smith*, the plaintiff's argument may well have prevailed. However, in the *Smith* case, the Court materially changed its interpretation of free exercise. Specifically, the Court observed that the *purpose* of the drug law being challenged in the case was directed at public safety, and had nothing to do with restricting religion. The law itself is absolutely "neutral" toward religion. The Court pointed out that the law is simply a *generally applicable* law that only *incidentally* interferes with religion. To accommodate this type of situation, the Court adopted a new rule that neutral, generally applicable laws on matters the government has the power to regulate (such as unlawful drug use) should be presumed reasonable. It is true that the drug law in question had the effect in limited instances of burdening religion. But that burden, the Court clarified, is purely incidental, rather than being the focus of the drug law. So, when a *neutral, generally applicable* regulation is challenged, the Court will apply the *rational basis test.*

Review of free exercise cases under the "strict scrutiny" standard occurs whenever the rule in *Smith* does not apply. As indicated in the *Smith* case, strict scrutiny will apply where the ordinance is *not* a generally applicable law that is neutral toward religion, but instead effectively *targets religion.* Under *strict scrutiny,* there is no presumption of constitutionality. The government must come forward to make the most difficult two-part demonstration: both that there is a *compelling* interest aimed at by the ordinance, and also that the ordinance seeks to achieve that compelling interest in a way that intrudes on the protected constitutional right less than any alternative would have. Under strict scrutiny, the government almost always loses.

Strict scrutiny may be seen in action in *Church of the Lukumi Babalu Aye, Inc. v. City of Hialeah*, a case heard some two years after *Smith.*[27] This case involved religious practitioners who used animal sacrifice as part of their worship. When they announced that they would be holding public services in the City of Hialeah, the city council adopted an ordinance prohibiting the religious sacrifice of animals. In its analysis of the case, the Court concluded that the city directly targeted this particular religion with its ordinance, which was neither generally applicable nor neutral. Therefore, strict scrutiny review applied, and the city lost the case.

4. The Religious Land Use and Institutionalized Persons Act (RLUIPA)

RLUIPA is a federal statute that imposes additional responsibility on local government to protect the free exercise of religion. Because this statute exists, a discussion of the constitutional interpretation of the free exercise clause does not adequately explain for public officials the full story on the "free exercise" subject. Being unhappy with the 1990 rule established by the *Smith* case, Congress "retaliated" by enacting an initial law with broad protection for the free exercise of religion, applicable to both the state and federal governments.[28] But in 1997, the Supreme Court invalidated Congress' retaliation by holding that the law was unconstitutional in its attempt to restrict the action of states.[29] Congress fired back by enacting a more narrowly targeted law. The Religious Land Use and Institutionalized Persons Act (RLUIPA)[30] is that law. It targets government decisions involving land use and those made in the institutional setting (such as in prisons).

There are two separate schemes of regulation in RLUIPA that impose local government responsibility. The first RLUIPA requirement imposes the rigorous *strict scrutiny* standard on local land use decisions on *specific properties* that result in a *substantial burden* on the free exercise of religion.[31] Perhaps the most litigated issue under this part of RLUIPA is the meaning of "substantial burden." The Supreme Court has not weighed in on this issue, and there are varying definitions among the federal circuits on what must be demonstrated in order to show that the government decision causes a substantial burden on the free exercise of religion. The second type of RLUIPA land use regulation is known as the *equal terms* requirement, and is designed to prohibit discrimination against religious assemblies as compared to other similar land uses. The rule here is that no government shall impose or implement a land use regulation in a manner that:

■ treats a religious assembly or institution on *less than equal terms* with a non-religious assembly or institution;
■ discriminates against any assembly or institution on the basis of religion or religious denomination; or
■ totally excludes religious assemblies from a jurisdiction, or unreasonably limits religious assemblies, institutions, or structures within a jurisdiction.[32]

F. Last Words

The Bill of Rights and Fourteenth Amendment can be examined from two perspectives. Viewed from the perspective of "the people," these constitutional amendments provide our most important *guarantees of liberty*. Viewed from the perspective of government, the amendments *limit* the actions and regulations of federal and state (including local) government officials in ways that must be recognized as they carry out their day-to-day duties. The precise nature and extent of the liberties protected in these amendments, and the manner in which the Supreme Court has chosen to review government regulations impinging on them, is not well known outside of legal circles. Similarly, it is not commonly known that the Bill of Rights was intended to protect the people solely from actions of the *federal* government, and that the Fourteenth Amendment, as it has been interpreted by the Court, changed forever the federal–state relationship in the country by transforming a good part of the Bill of Rights into protections of the people from regulation by *state* government as well. As a consequence, the actions and regulations of *local* officials must conform to the fundamental limitations found in the Bill of Rights and the Fourteenth Amendment, including the people's rights to due process, equal protection, free speech, and freedom of religion.

G. Now On to the Local Story

If this chapter has invigorated your appetite for practical legal guidance, you can continue the story by exploring the law applicable to your own particular form of local government, and the law of your particular state. Suggested storytellers include both your local government attorney and your state's local government association, which offers training for community officials. Your local story might begin with responses to these questions:

1. Are there state constitutional provisions that establish parallel *state* protections for the same or similar rights as those in the Bill of Rights and Fourteenth Amendment?
2. Do state *statutes* exceed the limitations contained in the Bill of Rights and Fourteenth Amendment by imposing even more obligations on local governments and officials, creating additional protections, such as for handicapped persons and against discrimination in the area of public employment?

Notes

1. *Obergefell v. Hodges*, 576 U.S. 644, 135 S. Ct. 2584, 192 L.Ed.2d 609 (2015). Additional fundamental rights that have been identified by the Court, including the right to marry and rights associated with parenting.
2. In reality, for a limited period beginning with the case of *Lochner v. New York*, 198 U.S. 45, 25 S. Ct. 539 (1905) and continuing into the 1930s (a period that can be associated with the rise of the United States in the world business arena), the Court frequently substituted judgment for the Congress and state legislatures with regard to the wisdom of economic regulations said to interfere with contract and property interests. This practice abruptly ended with the Court's decision in *Nebbia v. New York*, 291 U.S. 502, 54 S.Ct. 505 (1934).

3. *United States v. Carolene Products Company*, 304 U.S. 144, fn. 4 (1938).
4. See n. 1 above.
5. Although there are a considerable number of local governments in the country that face claims concerning the meaning of the 2nd Amendment guarantee of the right to bear arms, and the corresponding question of gun control, the technicalities and nuances of these subjects will not be addressed here.
6. It also applies when government is going to deprive a person of "life," which thankfully is not a frequent subject in the context of local government law.
7. There are some instances when due process is deemed to be satisfied if the hearing is provided after the deprivation occurs.
8. 424 U.S. 319, 335 (1976).
9. *Daniels v. Williams*, 474 U.S. 327, 331 (1986).
10. *Roth v. Board of Regents*, 408 U.S. 564, 572 (1972).
11. *Village of Euclid v Ambler Realty Co.*, 272 U.S. 365 (1926).
12. See *City of Ladue v Gillio*, 512 U.S. 43 (1994).
13. 427 U.S. 297 (1976).
14. *Reed v. Town of Gilbert, Ariz.*, 576 U.S. 155, 135 S. Ct. 2218, 192 L.Ed.2d 236 (2015).
15. *Chaplinsky v New Hampshire*, 315 U.S. 568 (1942).
16. *R.A.V. v. St. Paul*, 505 U.S. 377 (1992).
17. *Ward v. Rock Against Racism*, 491 U.S. 781 (1989).
18. See *Reed v. Town of Gilbert* (n. 14).
19. *Young v. American Mini Theatres, Inc.*, 427 U.S. 50 (1976).
20. See *Connick v. Myers*, 461 U.S. 138 (1983) and *Garcetti v. Ceballos*, 547 U.S. 410 (2006).
21. *School District of Abington Township v. Schempp*, 374 U.S. 203, 256 (1963) (Concurring Opinion).
22. Redlich, Attanasio, and Goldstein, *Understanding Constitutional Law*, (3rd edn, LexisNexis, 2005) Ch 17, p 689.
23. Choper, et al., *Constitutional Law: Cases, Comments, and Questions* (12th edn, West, 2015) Ch 8, pp 1208–1209 (2015)/
24. *Town of Greece v. Galloway*, 572 U.S. 565 (2014).
25. *American Legion v. American Humanist Association*, __ U.S. __, 139 S. Ct. 2067, 204 L.Ed.2d 452 (2019).
26. *Employment Division v. Smith*, 494 U.S. 872 (1990).
27. *Church of the Lukumi Babalu Aye, Inc. v. City of Hialeah*, 508 U.S. 520 (1993).
28. Religious Freedom Restoration Act of 1993 (RFRA), 42 U.S.C. 2000bb ff.
29. *City of Boerne v. Flores*, 521 U.S. 507 (1997). The *City of Boerne* decision left the statute intact as applied to the federal government.
30. 42 U.S.C. 2000cc ff.
31. 42 U.S.C. 2000cc(a).
32. 42 U.S.C. 2000cc(b).

Chapter 6

Law-Making Powers of Voters

A study of political history in the United States will confirm that the drafters of our Constitution rejected the establishment of a "monarchy" as the form of our new government. But they also rejected creating a "direct democracy." At the close of the Constitutional Convention of 1787, as Ben Franklin left Independence Hall on the final day of deliberation, he was asked what form of government *had* been created. By all accounts, Franklin's reply was that it is "a *republic*, if you can keep it." Essentially, the government framework established for the country was *not a democracy*, where all electors vote directly on each piece of legislation, *but a republic*, where the people elect "representatives" who enact laws on behalf of their electors and the country.

> Roughly 100 years after the U.S. Constitution was ratified, a group promoted "initiative" and "referendum" as *direct democracy* solutions to the perceived problem that interest groups and lobbyists had too much power in the country's representative form of government.

Some hundred years later, in the late 1800s and early 1900s, there was a *populist* reform movement that expressed concern about interest groups and lobbyists having excessive power over state and local government policy. This movement implicitly questioned the functioning of our representative form of government, and whether we *should* "keep it." To remedy the situation, reformers proposed placing greater "democracy" directly into the hands of the people. One of the consequences was the creation in many states of what might be called a new layer of "direct democracy" sown onto the fabric of the representative form of government.

> The use of initiative and referendum remains an option in many states today, authorized either by state constitution or legislation, or both. The breadth of authority varies from state-to-state, but it may extend to creating or amending ordinances, and amending local charters.

This new democracy layer included authorizations granting electors the direct powers of "initiative" and "referendum."[1] Initiative is the power of electors to directly place on the ballot a proposal for new legislation not advanced by the legislature. Referendum is the power of electors to directly place on the ballot and vote on the option of rejecting legislation recently passed by the legislature. In some sense, considering the state system of government in the big picture, these powers might be deemed the establishment of an additional "check and balance" on the legislative branch of government.

Adding these powers was not aimed at *replacing* the firmly entrenched republican form of government, but the intent was to add a new layer of power over the existing system. Today, by using the process of "initiative," members of the public at the state and local level can effectively sidestep their own elected representatives by initiating new laws and submitting them for direct popular vote. Similarly, through the "referendum" process, the people can, by filing a petition, bring about a popular vote to accept or reject new laws passed by elected legislative representatives.

The use of initiative and referendum remains an option in many states today, authorized either by state constitution or legislation, or both. The breadth of authority varies from state-to-state, but it may extend at the local level to ordinances as well as charters. In certain areas of the country, such as on the West Coast, ballot propositions at the state and local level are utilized extensively, advancing extremely impactful changes. The use of this direct democracy format has not occurred without vigorous discussion on the merits of this added dimension stitched onto the fabric of governance. Some of the questions raised in this discussion seem to parallel the reasons for establishing the direct democracy arrangement in the first place: too much power given to interest groups and the disproportionate influence of money. Of course, supporters of the use of this direct democracy approach suggest that these problems, such as the adverse influence of money, are already entrenched in the representative form of government, albeit less transparent to the public.

A.   Local Initiative and Referendum: When Is It Valid, and What Details Should a Local Official Focus On?

Federal and state constitutions provide no *implied* or *inherent* right to use initiative and referendum, so they require authorization from the state. In some states, there is a direct authorization in the state constitution. In other states, the state constitution may authorize the legislature to provide for initiative and referendum by state law. In still other cases, the legislature may include the authority as part of the enabling law for local charters, permitting local use of initiative and referendum for making amendments to the charter or for initiating and reviewing ordinances. The policy favoring these tools is sufficiently great in some states that *unless forbidden by the state constitution* a state legislature may confer the power on local governments to give their citizens the power of local initiative and referendum even in the absence of an affirmative constitutional authorization.[2]

1.   The Subject Must Be Legislative Action, Not Administrative Action

One of the central features of these direct democracy powers is that they apply solely to *legislation*. They generally do not allow taking or undoing *administrative* action.

The local initiative and referendum powers are limited to initiating and reviewing charters and initiating and reviewing *legislative* actions that are within the authority of the local government. *Administrative* actions are generally *not* subject to initiative or referendum, with certain outlier exceptions. Complicating this rule, the legislative-administrative distinction can create a close decision or "gray area" that will require judicial intervention to resolve. For example, if a state has authorized the power of local referendum for ordinances, *zoning* enactments may be submitted for popular vote if a valid petition is filed for such purpose because the enactment and amendment of a zoning ordinance represent *legislation*. But when a property owner and the local government are engaged in litigation, they may reach a settlement by entering a *consent judgment* that changes the land use authorization on the owner's property. Should this change of use authorization by way of lawsuit – which has the equivalent result to zoning – be subject to referendum because the zoning statute prescribes legislation as the means of changing zoning regulations? Or should it not be subject to referendum, because a consent judgment is not "legislation"?

Local government action is generally considered *administrative* if it will merely carry out law or policy already in existence, as compared to *legislation* that makes new law or declares new policy. Another general rule of thumb (always subject to exceptions) is that actions which are to be effective on a *temporary* and *special* basis are considered administrative, while actions with a more *permanent* and *general* effect are typically regarded as legislative.

When a challenge is presented, the decision on whether a resolution or ordinance is legislative or administrative becomes a matter for judicial determination. Often, however, considering that "pure democracy" is being exercised, courts may defer on determining the validity of a proposed initiative or referendum until a vote of the people is taken. (If the vote fails, the court is spared the need to make a ruling). As always, there are exceptions to such judicial deferral. For example, an initiative proposing a vote of the people to compel the local government to take an *administrative* action could immediately be ruled invalid, as it is beyond the scope of the initiative power.

2. The Power of Initiative

If permitted by state law or constitution, the power of *initiative* may be used to amend existing local legislation or charter, or to create an entirely new ordinance or charter provision. If an initiative ballot proposes a new ordinance that *has a legal defect "on its face"* (meaning its validity can be determined even without applying the ordinance to a particular situation) a court may cancel the initiative, as the ordinance would be invalid whether passed or rejected. On the other hand, if the only legal objection to an ordinance proposed by ballot initiative is that it might have an unconstitutional *effect* when applied, the courts may allow a public vote, and determine constitutionality only if the measure passes.

Whether a particular initiative is permitted may depend on whether and how the legislature has authorized the power to be exercised. For example, a particular local initiative may not be permitted if the proposal involves specific powers granted by the state legislature *directly to the governing body* of the local government, rather than more generally to the local government. Likewise, the people, acting with the power of direct democracy, may not enact an ordinance that exceeds the scope of the local government delegation of authority from the state legislature, or that otherwise conflicts with state or federal law.

Needless to say, creating an entire ordinance by initiative can be tricky business, particularly in the absence of debate and deliberation. There is an old saying (although its author can't be traced with any certainty) that, "Laws are like sausages: It's better not to see them being made." This adage almost certainly arises from that part of legislating in which give-and-take occurs, ultimately resulting in some sort of compromise. The significance of this is that, in the enactment of law using the process of initiative, there is little or no opportunity for competing parties to get together for the purpose of discussing and compromising on differences, or for the purpose of discovering unintended consequences. Ballot initiative battles all come down to a "yes" or "no" vote. This is likely to translate into a "win" or "lose" outcome rather than a compromise.[3] Recent state marijuana laws are a prime example. The process of initiative was employed to amend state law in several states to legalize medical marijuana, with lengthy and complicated pre-made statutes being placed before the voters, who could only respond with a "yes" or "no."

3. The Power of Referendum

The use of *referendum* applies after the legislative body has passed a law. So a petition seeking a referendum vote may be filed only in response to the passage of legislation. In other words, at the local government level, the purpose of the direct popular vote proposed to be taken is to allow the electorate to pass on legislation which has already been enacted by the local legislative body. When a referendum petition is filed, this action generally has the effect of *suspending* the operation of the target ordinance. Assuming the petition meets the specifications of the state statute or local charter (whichever is applicable) the legislative body is prohibited from undermining the referendum process before a vote is taken by passing another law which is substantially the same as the one suspended. In some states, once a referendum petition is filed, the legislative body has the opportunity to save the local government the time and expense of an election by simply repealing the legislation targeted for referendum.

If the legislative body does not repeal the measure, the clerk of the local government will need to confirm that the petition meets all the governing requirements (such as petition form, and minimum number of valid signatures), and then schedule the referendum vote to be held at a special or regular election held by the local government. Once the referendum vote is taken, if there is a majority vote to defeat the measure, the legislation passed by the legislative body will be deemed void. At that point, the legislative body may not simply "try again" to pass the same or similar enactment voided by the referendum vote. However, the legislative body is not prevented from passing new legislation on the same subject matter if it acts in good faith, with no intent to circumvent the effect of the successful referendum. The new enactment must be sufficiently different from the one voided by the referendum, perhaps taking into consideration some of the objections raised during the referendum process.

B. Customary Procedure for a Local Initiative or Referendum

The process provided for exercising the initiative and referendum powers varies from state-to-state. It is typically spelled out by state constitution or statute for proposals relating to state law and local legislation, with the exception that initiative and referendum procedure at the local government level may be governed totally or partially by local charter. Those pursuing the use of these powers must follow the required steps, with strict compliance being required in some states and a more liberal interpretation allowed in others. In all events, the law may require the use of a particular petition format containing mandatory language in various provisions – and in some cases requiring a precise size of paper, with a specific font and font size.

Here are some customary initiative and referendum procedures at the local level:

■ The state or local government provides a list of requirements for filing a petition, written in understandable language.

- To be valid, a petition must utilize the specified format and be signed, including a specified minimum number of signatures of registered voters.
- The circulator of the petition must verify the completed petition and file it with the local government clerk, who will inspect it to ensure compliance with the form and signature requirements.
- If the proposition in the petition is too lengthy to fit on the election ballot, a specified process will be used to reduce the proposition to an approved summary (although the full language of the proposition must be made available).
- The clerk will publish a notice of the date on which the proposition will appear on the ballot, along with the language of the proposition to be on the ballot.
- On the appointed date, the proposition will be submitted to the electorate on the ballot.
- The electorate will vote "yes" or "no" on the proposition and thus determine whether the particular measure is accepted or rejected.

Different treatment is given among the states on whether a person signing an initiative or referendum petition may later withdraw his or her name. If a state does not expressly provide for this situation, the typical resolution is to allow withdrawal of a name up to the time that the petitions and signatures are formally inspected and approved by the local government clerk.

C. Limitations on Direct Democracy

The powers of local initiative or referendum may be granted to the people by state constitution, statute or charter. Regardless of source, there is typically no right to petition for action that might threaten the immediate preservation of public health, peace, safety, or existing public institutions.

As discussed above (but it is worth repeating) the powers of initiative or referendum are typically not applicable to *administrative* actions. Under the administrative umbrella are matters such as emergency police legislation, salaries of officials, and utility rates. Ordinances that approve contracts, rather than specifying regulations, may not be subjected to these powers.

Likewise (unless authorized by statute), referendum is not available to accomplish the reduction of a local government *budget*, and the powers of initiative and referendum are not applicable to *appropriation* ordinances essential to render a statutory budget system effective.

D. Last Words

At the establishment of the United States, the concept of "direct democracy," with electors themselves voting on each law, was intentionally excluded from the new government's structure. Rather, the Constitution established a republic, in which electors vote for representatives who vote for or against laws on their behalf. A little more than 100 years later, a populist reform movement successfully amassed a multi-state buy-in for adding a layer of "direct democracy" to supplement the law-making structure of the government. That new layer consists of "initiative," the power of electors to directly place on the ballot a proposal for new legislation not advanced by the legislature, and "referendum," the power of electors to directly place on the ballot for popular vote an effective "veto" of legislation recently passed by the legislature. It appears that these powers of direct democracy will remain part of the structure in many states, at least for the foreseeable future, and they have already made a considerable difference. This is true not only at the state level, but also at the local level, where ballot propositions allow the public to enact, or "veto," charter provisions and ordinances. In some instances, the power of initiative is being used full circle, not merely to check the state legislature or local government, but to overturn legislation enacted by a previous ballot initiative! Wherever these powers of direct democracy are enabled by state constitution and law, now and in the future, they are likely to be potent tools.

E. Now on to the Local Story

If this chapter has invigorated your appetite for practical legal guidance, you can continue the story by exploring the law applicable to your own particular form of local government, and the law of your particular state. Suggested storytellers include both your local government attorney and your state's local government association, which offers training for community officials. Your local story might begin with responses to these questions:

1. Are the powers of initiative and referendum authorized in our state? If so, are they authorized by the state constitution, by statute, or both?

2. If initiative and referendum are authorized:

   a. Can these direct democracy tools be used only to create or challenge legislative enactments, or is ours one of the few states that allow their use for administrative action as well?

   b. Can ballot propositions be used to create or review state-level legislation? If so, when a valid petition for a new proposition has been filed, what action may the state legislature take in response?

   c. Can the state legislature or local government *amend* new legislation or ordinances created by initiative? If so, does it require a two-thirds or three-quarters majority vote in the legislature, or a similarly heightened voting standard?

   d. Are both of these direct democracy tools available to create or review local charter provisions?

   e. Can ballot initiatives and referenda be used to create or review local ordinances? If so, are they authorized under state law, or under individual local charters?

   f. There has been national debate on whether state ballot propositions are too easily influenced by money and abused by interest groups. Is this a valid concern with regard to the use of initiative and referendum to create or review local charter provisions and ordinances, or has the state addressed this in some manner?

3. In some states, zoning ordinance amendments enacted by the local legislative body are subject to oversight through the power of referendum, but the overwhelming rule is that the power of initiative is not permitted to enact new zoning provisions. Is this the rule in our state?

Notes

1. See Mandelker *et al.*, State and Local Government in a Federal System (7th ed., LexisNexis) pp. 1020–1021.
2. McQuillin, The Law of Municipal Corporations, § 16:47 (3d ed.) (accessed in 2020).
3. See, for example, *City of Cuyahoga Falls v. Buckeye Community Hope Foundation*, 538 U.S. 188 (2003).

Chapter 7

Fair Housing

Providing access to decent housing for all, free of discrimination, has long been an important objective in the United States, an objective that has escaped full realization in spite of considerable attention.

Traditionally, for purposes of providing an adequate assurance of lawful and decent housing, communities often understood this to involve local government enforcement of zoning and construction code regulations. While such enforcement continues to be relevant, it has become well-recognized that lawful and decent housing requires more comprehensive action in order to resolve the problem of housing segregation that remains in our country. Perhaps the most pervasive additional effort at addressing this issue is embodied in a federal law known as the Federal Fair Housing Act (42 U.S.C. 3601 *et seq.*) which broadly declared in 1968 that it is "the policy of the United States to provide, within constitutional limitations, for fair housing throughout the United States." In 1988, the Fair Housing Amendments Act expanded its protections.

The Federal Fair Housing Act (or "FHA") will be the focus of this chapter. The discussion will first consider an historical context, focused on the first half of the 1900s, when the problem of housing segregation took a turn for the worse during the two World Wars, as well as the period after World War II, when the problem was exacerbated as metropolitan areas were created throughout the country. We will then focus on three specific areas of activity in which local governments can become targets for legal action under FHA regulations, thus making the FHA relevant to local officials. The discussion will finally turn to a review of court decisions which discuss the manner in which claims are made against local governments, and reviewed by the courts, under the FHA.

A. Housing Segregation in Historical Context

The best starting point in seeking a clear understanding of the issues at stake for local governments under the FHA is an explanation of key legal and factual circumstances prevailing in the years following the ratification of the Fourteenth Amendment in 1868, extending through the first half of the twentieth century.

1. "Separate but Equal" – Early Interpretation of the Fourteenth Amendment

> Under the 1896 Supreme Court decision in *Plessy v. Ferguson*, the "separate but equal" doctrine approved separation treatment of economic and social activities by race.

As discussed in Chapter 5, the Fourteenth Amendment is multi-dimensional in its creation of rights. But precisely what rights in terms of prohibiting discrimination were intended to be formally granted by the Fourteenth Amendment? Today, it is easy to take as a constitutional given that no distinctions in treatment under the law should be based on race. In the late 1800s, there were differences of opinion on this point, even among the members of the Supreme Court.

History leaves no doubt that a universally understood purpose of the Fourteenth Amendment, coupled with the ratification of the Thirteenth and Fifteenth Amendments, was to provide full equality with regard to fundamental *civil* rights. This was made clear in a criminal case that arose only a few years after the ratification of the Fourteenth Amendment, *Strauder v. West Virginia*.[1] The case involved an African American defendant convicted of murder in a state whose law prohibited blacks from sitting on juries in such cases. The Supreme Court overturned the conviction and invalidated the law, reasoning that "the true spirit and meaning" of the Civil War amendments was securing "to the race recently emancipated the enjoyment of all the civil rights that under the law are enjoyed by white persons."

But not all rights are fundamental *civil* rights. In the social and economic spheres, Southern states began enacting the now-infamous "Jim Crow" laws, which created a system of racial *separation* in various walks of life.

The Supreme Court was called on in 1896 to decide *Plessy v. Ferguson*, a challenge to the constitutionality of Louisiana's Separate Car Act of 1890, which required "equal, but separate" train car accommodations for white and non-white passengers.[2] Plessy was of mixed race and refused to leave the coach designated for "whites only." It was this historic case that declared it *lawful* under the Fourteenth Amendment for a state to provide for "separate but equal" social and economic accommodations. As we look back today at the effect of the *Plessy* decision, it seems shocking. Nonetheless, the "separate but equal" doctrine survived for nearly six decades.

In the context of property law, the Civil Rights Act of 1866 (42 U.S.C. § 1982) declared that: "All citizens of the United States shall have the same right, in every State and Territory, as is enjoyed by white citizens thereof to inherit, *purchase, lease, sell, hold, and convey real and personal property*."[3] A very few years later, the Fourteenth Amendment made all persons born or naturalized in the United States "citizens of the United States." But these orders for civil rights relief were not enforced in a manner to successfully avoid housing discrimination in the first half of the 1900s. Indeed, the Civil Rights Act of 1866 was held to prevent discrimination *by the state*, however, it was not until 1968 that the Supreme Court held that it applied to prohibit *private* discrimination.[4] And private discrimination in housing was widely practiced in the first half of the 1900s.

In the 1948 Supreme Court decision in *Shelley v. Kraemer*, the Court held for first time that the Fourteenth Amendment was violated by state court enforcement of private restrictive covenants that prevented persons "not of the Caucasian race" from occupying land on a particular street of St. Louis.

This half-century period also witnessed official city involvement in segregated housing. For example, in 1917, the Supreme Court in *Buchanan v. Warley* invalidated a city ordinance in Louisville, Kentucky that *required segregated housing* in certain neighborhoods.[5]

Finally, in the 1954 decision in the landmark school segregation case entitled *Brown v. Board of Education*, the Supreme Court overruled the separate but equal doctrine (after World War II).[6]

The point here is that during the entire first half of the 20th century, from 1896 to 1954, both the Civil Rights Act of 1866 and the Fourteenth Amendment *appeared* to pave the way to fair housing. Yet there is no escaping that the realization of this civil right fell severely short during this period. Rather, the nation under *Plessy's separate but equal doctrine* was experiencing a wholesale separation of the races in social and economic matters until 1954 (and beyond), and the Court's interpretation of 1866 fair housing civil rights protection short-circuited adequate relief to prevent private housing discrimination. It was during this window of time that significant housing segregation would have inevitably taken root.

2. The "Great Migration" in the Era of "Separate but Equal"

The "Great Migration" is a name given to the large-scale movement out of the South of some *five to six million individuals*, largely southern blacks. The path of their migration led to northern and western cities during the two World Wars, chasing promises of new jobs and a new life. However, the timing of these Migrations puts them in the first half of the 1900s, which as just discussed was the era of the *Plessy v. Ferguson* "separate but equal" doctrine. This means that the large demand for new housing that would have occurred in the destination cities during the Migrations would have coincided with widespread separate but equal segregation.

During the two war periods, urban manufacturing was exploding with demand for new workers, and the major industrial centers reached out across the nation with job advertisements. In the initial period during World War I, major destinations of the "migration" included Chicago, Detroit, Pittsburgh, and New York City. By World War II, the exodus continued from south to north but also began to include the west coast: Los Angeles, Oakland, San Francisco, Portland, and Seattle.[7] This second wave of Great Migration included a significant number of southern whites as well as blacks.

The motivations for migration were a combination of the desire to escape the oppressive conditions then prevailing in the South, along with the promise of jobs and greater prosperity in the North and West.[8] Some sectors of the economy grew so desperate for workers that employers offered to *pay* prospective workers to relocate north.[9]

The full scale and consequence of the Great Migrations was not widely known or appreciated at the time. But the local impact was significant. In

St. Louis, Missouri, for example, the early arrival of tens of thousands of new job-seekers worried European immigrants, who held fears that the new workers would be willing to accept lower wages.[10] In 1917, a serious race riot occurred in neighboring East St. Louis.

As World War II continued to be fought, in June of 1943, with the "separate but equal" doctrine still in place, and the second the Great Migration occurring, racial tensions reached a new peak. Race riots broke out in the city of Detroit, Michigan:

> On June 20, 1943, a fight broke out between African American and white Detroiters spending their Sunday on Belle Isle, the city's large park in the middle of the Detroit River. Fighting spread to the [City's] mainland, and rumors crisscrossed the city, stoking racial tensions that had been running high and threatening to boil over into violence for months.
>
> Many factors contributed to the tension that was finally released during the 1943 Race Riots. With America's entry into World War II, Detroit's auto factories were converted to manufacturing material for the war effort. As a result, Detroit experienced a large population influx of people from around the country to fill the jobs created by the War's demand. Between 1940 and 1943, *Detroit's population increased by about 500,000—roughly a third of its previous population.* Many of the newcomers were white southerners who often brought a tradition of discrimination against African Americans with them. Blacks also flocked to the city, and frequently there was competition for jobs.[11]

Of course, it cannot be suggested that the fundamental problem of segregated housing in urban America can be attributed to the Great Migrations. There were other material influences, including racism. But as we look back, it is clear that there was a significant housing demand associated with the extensive movement from the South to the North and West during a period in which segregated accommodations were a way of life, owing at least in part to the separate but equal doctrine. It is likewise clear that the Court remained reluctant to apply federal civil rights law to private housing transactions at a time when parties were widely engaged in discriminatory practices. These circumstances, taken together, would have created an enflaming set of conditions that likely contributed significantly to the housing issues that gave rise to the enactment of the FHA.

3. *Exacerbation of Segregation by Post-World War II Movement to the Suburbs*

> There was an exacerbation of segregated housing based on a post-World War II movement of people from older cities to newly developing suburban areas surrounding the cities.

In the years after the end of World War II, a major new "migration" of people began. Residents emigrated from older urban areas to newly developing and expanding "suburbs" surrounding the cities. This movement became a long-term trend, facilitated by improved automobiles used by those who moved to the suburbs to access jobs and other activities in urban downtowns.[12] The trend was further encouraged by the advent of the interstate freeway system and improved state roads, greatly extending the viable work-commute distance. This new suburban development – residential and commercial – was further aggravated in the 1960s by an activity known as "redlining," which involved the *official identification of areas within cities that would receive inferior mortgage lending and related financial treatment*, often corresponding to areas of housing classified on the basis of race. "Redlining" was one of the discriminatory practices that would be expressly prohibited by the 1968 enactment of the FHA.

A well-known 1975 opinion of the New Jersey Supreme Court, *NAACP v. Township of Mount Laurel*, recounts the exit of people and real estate investment from older urban communities and the corresponding birth of "metropolitan" regions surrounding the older cities.[13] Many motives are attributed to this suburban exodus: some worthy, such as the natural appeal of newer housing opportunities, and some unworthy, such as racism. Associated with this suburban movement was the creation of a zoning pattern *designed to attract high-end housing*. The Court in *Mount Laurel* concluded that, on the one hand, there was a legitimate goal for this zoning, namely the fostering of high tax base intended to fund police, fire, library, and school resources. Yet, on the other hand, this tax-base goal would be achieved at the inappropriate expense of low and moderate income families, who were left with substandard housing in the older urban communities. Policy motives aside, it was clear that anyone without the financial resources to own automobiles and purchase suburban homes would be left behind. Many low and moderate income people were effectively trapped in the older urban areas, where nearly two-thirds of all non-white families lived in neighborhoods marked by substandard housing and urban blight.[14]

The ultimate consequence of the post-World War II "metropolitanization" movement was a further perpetuation of the segregation problem – and further justification for the enactment of a national fair housing act.

4. The Modern Urban Migration

A Contemporary Issue

Modern revitalization of cities leading to *gentrification*.

Another contemporary "migration" has created a controversy over housing segregation, namely the recent movement of people back into cities. For decades, many older urban cities have faced serious issues aggravating the affordable housing problem. There has been a loss of population, a lack of investment in affordable housing, along with a tax base decline. All of these problems are intertwined. Related to these factors, limited urban services budgets have had to accommodate relatively high demand for fire and security services.

Accordingly, governments in central cities have long viewed city improvement, revitalization, and restoration as an *antidote to urban blight*. Revitalization projects promise benefits such as renovated buildings and properties, better safety, fire suppression, security, integrated neighborhoods, economic development, and a general rise in tax base as a result of new development.

The strategy of eradicating blight through urban renewal projects has a long history.[15] Indeed, for many years, both government programs and public-private strategies have sought adequate financing to remove substandard buildings and seed new growth zones. Creative zoning and planning efforts have aimed for long-term city returns by attracting private investment in renovation.[16]

Even so, meaningful success stories were elusive until fairly recently, when a wave of new demand for an "urban lifestyle" arose among the younger "modern" working population. This appears to have tipped the scales in favor of sustainable urban renewal in older cities across the country.

Revitalization projects in older cities seems uniformly appealing – calling up images of specialty coffee shops, yoga studios, juice bars, loft-style condominiums with roof gardens, jogging strollers, Montessori schools, and a substantial step up in tax base for the city. But who will ultimately occupy the older cities which are being revitalized? The short answer is that the entrepreneurs who are the agents of revitalization must, to some degree, seek an influx of *new* purchasers and tenants who have adequate incomes to buy or rent the redeveloped properties, needed to finance revitalization. To many of the people living in the local neighborhoods prior to redevelopment, the results may appear more like a barbed-wire "Keep Out" fence after revitalization occurs. This is the phenomenon of "gentrification."

Gentrification is a common and controversial topic in urban planning because it involves favorable objectives, but at the same time undermines the overarching goal of providing affordable and integrated housing. So, the results of revitalization in older cities are "good news" to some, and "bad news" to others. Ideally, revitalization can offer a "win-win" objective, offering new employment and recreation opportunities for all residents, boosting city tax revenue enough to improve city-wide urban services, and providing the opportunity for an integration strategy that avoids a wholesale displacement of low and moderate income residents from the neighborhoods in which they had been living. This requires great foresight, and making fair housing a priority. Two opposing (yet both rational) viewpoints must be reconciled.

- Argument in favor: To some, gentrification simply occurs as an expected outcome of urban revitalization in which neighborhoods improve through a renewed interest in restoring older housing stock that can draw new residents and businesses. It represents change, but change for the better: the revitalization of an economically distressed or depressed neighborhood. Indeed, the residents of an area being moderately gentrified may benefit from the process.
- Argument in opposition: To others, gentrification means evicting and excluding. Those with lower incomes may be forced to relocate their families and their businesses – if alternative habitable space is available at

all – because of the resulting increased rents or taxes. Gentrification might translate into an eviction mandate for the entire redeveloped area.[17]

The Supreme Court has begun to hear cases involving attempts to "upgrade" communities and address the fair housing issue.[18] Presumably, it will take time for these cases to develop a cohesive avenue of relief that takes into consideration both the need for revitalization as well as the adverse consequences of unchecked gentrification.[19]

B. Local Governments are Targets under the FHA

> There is potential local government liability under FHA in connection with the following activities:
>
> ■ planning and zoning;
> ■ providing municipal services; and
> ■ accommodating people with disabilities.

The principal regulatory targets of the FHA appear to be private real estate sellers, landlords, and lenders. In a nutshell, the FHA forbids discrimination in the sale, rental, and finance of housing. State and local governments are tied to these private actors by language forbidding "any law of a State, a political subdivision, or any other such jurisdiction that purports to *require or permit* any action that would be a discriminatory housing practice under this [Act]."[20]

Indeed, local governments have very much become one of the marks for legal action under the FHA – and predominantly through a provision that does not expressly identify them as intended targets. In what might be referred to as "catchall" language in the Act,[21] the FHA makes it unlawful to refuse to sell or rent after the making of a bona fide offer, or to refuse to negotiate for the sale or rental of, *or to otherwise make unavailable or deny*, a dwelling to any person because of race, color, religion, sex, familial status, handicap, or national origin. The Supreme Court has accepted the proposition that Congress intended to create local government responsibility by inserting this catchall language.[22] A local government may become the target of an FHA action for *otherwise making unavailable or denying* a dwelling to any person belonging to one of the *protected classes*: race, color, religion, sex, familial status, handicap, or national origin.[23]

Given the significant *liability* that may be imposed under the FHA, it is important for local government officials to understand the sort of circumstances which could open the door to litigation against their communities. There are at least three broad categories to recognize.

1. Planning and Zoning

States delegate to local governments the authority to exercise planning and zoning power through state planning and zoning enabling acts.[24] Most local governments within metropolitan areas receive and exercise this power.

The standard format for exercising planning and zoning power begins with creating a "comprehensive plan," often referred to as a "master plan." This plan divides the community into zoning districts that are calculated to meet unique local needs for housing, commerce, industry, and recreation, with the districts arranged so as to promote and protect public health, safety, and general welfare. The highest priorities in the exercise of planning and zoning are the protection of local residential neighborhoods and the promotion of quality of life for residents.

Courts have found that certain local governments have made insufficient provision in their plans for housing accessible to low and moderate income users. There might be too little land zoned for such uses as apartments, or there might be other regulations, such as large lot size, that push the purchase price of housing units beyond the affordable range. In either case, it may be alleged under the FHA that housing for one or more classes that are protected in the act (chiefly racial and national minorities) are "made unavailable" as a result of local regulations.

A related holding (not under the FHA) was the 1975 case, *NAACP v. Township of Mount Laurel*, discussed above. The New Jersey Supreme Court essentially held that, in the developing communities surrounding older urban areas in New Jersey, there is an obligation to make provision for a proportionate share of low and moderate income housing.[25] The *Mount Laurel* case was filed as a challenge to validity of the township's zoning. If filed today, the Mount Laurel case would probably rely on the FHA.

For a more subtle example of potential local government liability under the FHA, assume that a developer has been approved for government grants to provide needed housing for low income racial and national minorities. The developer contacts the local government, seeking a rezoning to allow construction of low income housing, say in the form of apartments or a mobile home park. Assume the local government has knowingly neglected to include much low income housing in its zoning plan, believing that customary lending conditions would make it impossible to finance affordable low income housing even if permitted. Yet now, owing to special grants, this developer can realistically make ends meet to provide needed housing for racial and national minorities. The only hurdle is a rezoning to allow apartment or mobile home park use. When the necessary public hearing is held on the developer's request for rezoning, residents living near the proposed project show up to object, urging that the rezoning for low income housing be allowed somewhere else in the community, or in a neighboring community. If the local government listens to these residents and rejects the proposed rezoning – even if it intends to consider a rezoning elsewhere in the community – a lawsuit could be filed under the FHA catchall clause, asserting that the local government is "*otherwise making housing for minorities unavailable*" in the community.

2. *Municipal Services*

In the case of new or revitalized development, the feasibility of a housing project may depend on the availability of municipal services, such as public sewer or water. It could be argued, then, that a local government decision to deny extension of public utility service for a low income project needed in the community would "make housing unavailable."

So, if municipal sewer or water service is required in order to construct needed affordable housing for a protected group, such as racial or national minorities, and if such service is rejected, the courthouse door may be open to a claim under the Fair Housing Act. A claim does not always translate into liability. (See the discussion of legal standards later in this chapter). But denial of municipal services may be reviewable under the FHA catchall clause of 42 U.S.C. § 3604, to determine whether the denial does in fact "make housing unavailable."

The court's willingness to find a Fair Housing Act violation may come into sharper focus if sewer and water service has been granted to a proposed upscale housing project but rejected for a proposed affordable housing project nearby, with no rational explanation. On the other hand, the case might fail under the FHA if the service which has been denied is proposed for renovation of an *existing* affordable housing project – because the project's housing is already "available." This scenario should not be entirely discounted, however, in light of a reading of the FHA by the Ninth Circuit Federal Court of Appeals. In *Committee Concerning Community Improvement v. City of Modesto*, it was concluded that "the [FHA] language does not preclude all post-acquisition claims."[26] The court explained that the FHA prohibits discrimination "in the terms, conditions, or privileges of sale or rental of a dwelling, or *in provision of services or facilities* in connection therewith," citing § 3604(b) and regulations enacted by the department of Housing and Urban Development. It acknowledged, however, that other courts have rejected post-acquisition claims under the FHA.[27]

3. *Accommodating People with Disabilities*

By including "handicap" as a basis for discrimination in the 1988 amendment to the Fair Housing Act, Congress sought to allow people with disabilities to participate in mainstream living to the extent reasonably feasible.

Local officials will find that the FHA definition of "handicap" is very broad. It includes persons with an unofficial record or reputation of impairment as well as those officially certified. The definition also covers any physical or mental impairment "which substantially limits one or more of such person's major life activities."[28] It does not, however, include illegal use of or addiction to a controlled substance as defined by federal statute (unless the person asserting an FHA claim is in recovery).

The FHA provides a very special remedy for handicapped persons. Specifically, such a person is entitled to a *reasonable accommodation* in the rules, policies, practices, or services when necessary to provide an equal opportunity to use and enjoy a dwelling.[29] This FHA guarantee imposes a responsibility on the local government, as well as their zoning boards and other specific entities.[30] As an example, consider what sort of "reasonable accommodation" might be required if a state licensed care facility is proposed within an area zoned as single-family residential. Many states consider such facilities to be "single family housing," provided the number of occupants is within the maximum head count specified by law, often six handicapped occupants. But a care facility might argue that it is not economically feasible to operate at such a small scale. Consequently, denying a reasonable accommodation on the maximum headcount would, in effect, "make housing unavailable" in single family residential zones for any person requiring a care facility to live.

When may a local government take the position that a proposed accommodation is not "reasonable?" Unfortunately, the standard for making this determination is fact-sensitive and not uniformly interpreted throughout the country. Among cases where courts have found that a requested accommodation was *not* reasonable, the most common trait appears to be that granting the accommodation would create an *undue financial or administrative burden.* Other objections upheld in court have been similar: granting the proposed accommodation would undermine the regulatory scheme, would impose an undue hardship or burden on the entity making the accommodation, would require more than a moderate change, or would amount to a fundamental change.[31]

The burden of proof is upon the party claiming entitlement to the accommodation. But local governments beware: local ordinances may need to include appropriate *procedures and standards* for processing requests for reasonable accommodations, in order to safeguard against an appearance of having *arbitrarily* granted or denied a request.[32]

C. Asserting and Reviewing a Fair Housing Act Discrimination Claim Against a Local Government

1. Overview

Discrimination claims involve complex legal analysis. From a practical perspective, however, two primary approaches have been recognized by courts for marshaling the FHA machinery to target local government actions: "disparate treatment" theory, and "disparate impact" theory.

- *Disparate treatment*: The traditional approach has been to assert discrimination based on disparate *treatment* under the Fair Housing Act, 42 U.S.C.A. § 3604. The claimant must demonstrate that a determination to deny a housing project by the local government was the product of *actual discrimination.* This means there was *purposeful* discrimination *with animus against a protected group* as a significant factor. This can be very difficult to prove.
- *Disparate impact*: A recently approved approach is more flexible. It seeks to prove a violation based on a disparate *impact*, so a claimant need only demonstrate the *effect* of the local government's action,

regardless of intent. A claim of disparate impact alleges that local government practices have had a *disproportionately adverse effect* on members of a class protected under FHA (such as racial and national minorities) and that the difference was not justified by any legitimate rationale. This method, which focuses on 42 U.S.C.A. 3604(a), was approved in 2015 by the Supreme Court in *Texas Dept. of Housing and Community Affairs v. Inclusive Communities Project, Inc.*[33]

2. *Making a Claim of Disparate Treatment*

To succeed in a *disparate treatment* claim under the FHA, the claimant must show that a local government imposed *purposefully different treatment* based on the claimant's membership in a protected class, resulting in the unavailability or denial of housing.

It is extremely challenging for a claimant to prove that adverse treatment was *purposeful* and also *due to claimant's membership* in a protected class. After all, what evidence can a claimant show in court to *prove* the inner thoughts of local government officials? The Supreme Court recognized this dilemma some time ago. In an effort to level the playing field, it created a methodology known as the "burden-shifting procedure," which relieves the claimant of the need to *fully prove* that a decision was intentionally class-based. Instead, the claimant need only show that an *animus against a protected group* existed and that it was at least an *important factor* in the decision. (For example, it is enough if the claimant shows that the local government decision was a *knowing acquiescence* to race-based *citizen opposition* to the developer's proposal.)[34] The burden then shifts to the local government to show that its decision was based on a legitimate purpose unrelated to the discriminatory animus.

A U.S. District Court in New York pointed out the following for the claimant's initial ("prima facie") burden of proof:

> "Discriminatory intent may be inferred from the totality of the circumstances." Relevant factors include: "[t]he impact of the official action whether it 'bears more heavily on one race than another,'" "[t]he historical background of the decision," "[t]he specific sequence of events leading up to the challenged decision," "[d]epartures from the normal procedural sequence,"

"[s]ubstantive departures, . . . particularly if the factors usually considered important by the decision maker strongly favor a decision contrary to the one reached," and "contemporary statements by members of the decision making body, or reports."[35]

3. *Making a Claim of Disparate Impact*

Rather than attempting to prove actual local government *intent* to discriminate, the claimant may instead file a *disparate impact* challenge, asserting that a local government decision had a disproportionately adverse *effect* on members of a class protected under FHA (such as racial and national minorities) unjustified by a legitimate rationale. In approving the use of this approach to establish liability, the Supreme Court has held that disparate-impact claims are consistent with the Fair Housing Act's central purpose of eradicating discriminatory practices within the housing sector of our Nation's economy. (Here the Court referred to an earlier New York case, which invalidated a zoning law that had prevented construction of new multifamily rental units.[36])

Although the Court has approved the use of disparate impact theory in FHA cases, it has also established what might be considered "hurdles" to achieving success with a complaint. Specifically, the Court has cautioned that "disparate-impact liability *does not displace valid governmental policies.*" To prevent paralysis of normal and necessary government functions by potential disparate impact claims, the Court has stated a number of *limitations* on the successful use of the disparate impact theory. While these parameters may sound like abstract and subjective pronouncements, because this area of law is relatively new, there are very few factual applications that would assist our understanding. So the following standards for evaluating the potential for use of disparate impact liability is about as much as can be reliably provided at this point:

▪ Disparate impact *alone* is not sufficient. Liability should not be imposed based solely on a showing of *statistical impact disparity*. The FHA is not an instrument to force housing authorities to reorder their priorities. Rather, the aim is to ensure that those priorities can be achieved without *arbitrarily creating discriminatory effects or perpetuating segregation.*

- A disparate-impact claim that relies on a statistical disparity *alone* must fail. There is a *"robust causality requirement"* to proving discrimination under this theory. There must be a showing of government policy or practice *causing* the disparity. Local government may not be held liable, for example, for a racial imbalance it did not create. Neutral government policies, goals, and purposes do not violate FHA requirements under disparate-impact theory unless they create or perpetuate "artificial, arbitrary, or unnecessary barriers.
- A *valid interest* can justify the decision or policy despite the impact. Government may avoid liability by stating and explaining the *valid interest* served by the challenged decision or policy. Zoning officials often make decisions based on a mix of factors that contribute to quality of life and represent legitimate governmental concern. Two types of factors may be relevant:

  - *Objective* factors, such as cost and traffic patterns; and
  - *Subjective* factors, such as preserving historic architecture.

As in disparate *treatment* cases, the "burden-shifting procedure" applies to disparate *impact* cases. Once plaintiffs have made their initial ("prima facie") case by showing that a local government decision caused a discriminatory housing effect, the burden shifts to the government to demonstrate that its actions furthered a legitimate, bona fide governmental interest. If the government makes this showing, the burden shifts back to plaintiff to prove the existence of a viable alternative practice to achieve the government's goals that would have less disparate impact.

D. Last Words

The broad focus of this chapter has been on the extensive history and perpetuation of housing discrimination during the first half of the 20th century, leading to the enactment and enforcement of the Federal Fair Housing Act in 1968. The FHA was predominantly directed to private real estate sellers, landlords, and lenders, seeking to address discrimination in the sale, rental, and finance of housing. However, state and local governments have been implicated by the courts when they are found to have taken certain actions prohibiting housing availability for racial and national minorities and others protected under the Act.

It is important for local officials to understand the various contexts in which local government might be targeted by legal action under the FHA, as outlined in this chapter. However, it is also worthy of recognition that Congress made provision for local governments to be recruited as a partners, rather than targets in the fight to cure segregated housing. Specifically, under 42 U.S.C.A. § 3616, the FHA provides for cooperation between the federal government and the state and local agencies administering fair housing laws:

> The Secretary [of Housing] may cooperate with State and local agencies charged with the administration of State and local fair housing laws and . . . utilize the services of such agencies and . . . reimburse such agencies and their employees for services rendered to assist him in carrying out this subchapter. In furtherance of such cooperative efforts, the Secretary may enter into written agreements with such State or local agencies.[37]

It is suggested that there is great potential for seeking affirmative resolutions to long-term housing segregation through federal partnerships with local agencies as laboratories of experimentation.

E. Now on to the Local Story

If this chapter has invigorated your appetite for practical legal guidance, you can continue the story by exploring the law applicable to your own particular form of local government, and the law of your particular state. Suggested storytellers include both your local government attorney and your state's local government association, which offers training for community officials. Your local story might begin with responses to these questions:

1. Is there a state agency responsible for promoting or ensuring fair housing? Are there other state-sponsored programs with this goal?
2. Does our state have laws intended to address "exclusionary zoning" as described in this chapter?

3. Does our state have "accessibility" laws that prohibit discrimination by requiring special accommodations in housing? If so, do these laws create legal obligations for local governments?

4. Does our local zoning ordinance include *procedures and standards* for processing requests for reasonable accommodations, in order to safeguard against an appearance of having *arbitrarily* granted or denied a request for a "reasonable accommodation" under the FHA for care facilities in residential neighborhoods?

Notes

1. 100 U.S. 303, 306 (1879).
2. 163 U.S. 537 (1896).
3. This Civil Rights Act was enacted under the authority of the Thirteenth Amendment, and later reenacted under the Fourteenth Amendment.
4. *Jones v. Alfred H. Mayer Co.*, 392 U.S. 409 (1968).
5. 245 U.S. 60 (1917).
6. 347 U.S. 483 (1954).
7. Stephanie Christensen, The Great Migration (1915–1960), Blackpast.org (December, 2007). https://www.blackpast.org/african-american-history/great-migration-1915-1960/; Great Migration – Black History – HISTORY.com, History.com (retrieved April 9, 2017); "The Great Migration" (PDF). Smithsonian American Art Museum; Wilkerson, Isabel. "The Long-Lasting Legacy of the Great Migration" Smithsonian (retrieved October 3, 2019); and The Second Great Migration, http://www.inmotionaame.org/print.cfm;jsessionid=f830444661458729315793?migration=9&bhcp=1 (accessed in 2020).
8. *Id.*
9. *Id.*
10. Jeannette Cooperman, St. Louis Magazine (October 17, 2004) https://www.stlmag.com/news/the-color-line-race-in-st.-louis/ (accessed in 2020).
11. Detroit race riot of June, 1943, 2012 Post by Johanna Russ was the Archivist for the American Federation of State, County, and Municipal Employees (AFSCME) from 2008 until 2013, contained in Walter P. Reuther Library, Wayne State University, http://reuther.wayne.edu/node/8738 (accessed in 2020).
12. *Texas Dept. of Housing and Community Affairs*, above.
13. *NAACP v. Township of Mount Laurel*, 67 N.J. 151, 336 A.2d 713 (1975).
14. *Id.*
15. A prominent example of blight removal and urban renewal can be found by reading one of the Supreme Court's landmark eminent domain cases, decided shortly after World War II, *Berman v. Parker*, 348 U.S. 26 (1954).

16. See the broad discussion about "gentrification" across may cities (and internationally), and the numerous references at https://en.wikipedia.org/wiki/Gentrification#Atlanta (accessed in 2020).

17. See generally, Eric M. Larsson, J.D., 165 Am. Jur. Proof of Facts 3d 205 (2017, with 2019 update).

18. *Texas Dept. of Housing and Community Affairs v. Inclusive Communities Project, Inc.*, 135 S. Ct. 2507, 192 L. Ed. 2d 514 (2015).

19. Existing strategies are discussed at https://www.scag.ca.gov/Documents/ComprehensiveGuideToLocalAffordableHousingPolicy.pdf (accessed in 2020).

20. See 42 U.S.C. 3615.

21. 42 U.S.C. 3604.

22. *Id.*

23. Most recently discussed in *Texas Dept. of Housing and Community Affairs v. Inclusive Communities Project, Inc.*, 135 S. Ct. 2507, 192 L. Ed. 2d 514 (2015).

24. See Chapter 9 of this book for a more detailed discussion of planning and zoning.

25. See, for example, *Huntington Branch, N.A.A.C.P. v. Town of Huntington*, 844 F.2d 926 (2d Cir. 1988) , judgment aff'd in part, 488 U.S. 15, 109 S. Ct. 276, 102 L. Ed. 2d 180 (1988) (which would need to be read with the criteria provided in *Texas Dept. of Housing and Community Affairs v. Inclusive Communities Project, Inc.* in 2015).

26. 583 F.3d 690, 713–714 (9th Cir. 2009).

27. The Court cited *Cox v. City of Dallas*, 430 F.3d 734, 745 (5th Cir. 2005) as a court rejecting post-acquisition claims under FHA.

28. 42 U.S.C. 3602(h).

29. 42 U.S.C. 3604(f)(3)(B).

30. *Smith & Lee Assoc. v. City of Taylor*, 13 F.3d 920, 924 (1993), appeal following remand, 102 F.3d 781 (6th Cir. 1996); *Larkin v. Michigan Dep't of Social Services*, 89 F.3d 285, 289–290 (6th Cir. 1996)

31. *Oconomowoc Residential Programs, Inc. v. City of Milwaukee*, 300 F.3d 775, 784 (7th Cir. 2002); *Davis v. Echo Valley Condominium Association*, __ F.3d, No. 18–2405 (6th Cir. 2019); *Bryant Woods Inn, Inc. v. Howard County*, 124 F.3d 597, 604 (4th Cir. 1997); *United States v. Marshall*, 787 F. Supp. 872, 878 (WD Wis 1991).

32. Smith & Lee, *above*, 13 F.3d at 929–930.

33. 135 S. Ct. 2507, 192 L. Ed. 2d 514 (2015).

34. *Mhany Management, Inc. v. County of Nassau*, 819 F.3d 581 (2d Cir. 2016).

35. *Rivera v. Incorporated Village of Farmingdale*, 784 F. Supp. 2d 133, 146–147 (E.D.N.Y. 2011); also see *Sanghvi v. City of Claremont*, 328 F.3d 532, 536 (9th Cir. 2003), *cert. denied*, 540 U.S. 1075 (2003); *Weldon v. Kraft, Inc.*, 896 F2d 793, 797 (3d Cir. 1990) (citations in the opinion were omitted).

36. *Town of Huntington, N.Y. v. Huntington Branch, N.A.A.C.P.*, 488 U.S. 15, 18, 109 S. Ct. 276, 102 L. Ed. 2d 180 (1988).
37. The concept of such cooperation has been discussed favorably in the past, and it would make sense to recruit local governments as cooperative partners rather than naming them as defendants in lawsuits. See *Banks v. Perk*, 341 F. Supp. 1175 (N.D. Ohio, 1972), affirmed in part, reversed in part 473 F.2d 910.

Chapter 8

Financing Local Government

How do local governments raise the money necessary to operate? One thing is clear: the manner in which local governments secure revenue is carefully regulated under state law. After all, local governments secure funding as custodians on behalf of members of the community, and they are relied upon to use that funding to provide basic products and services needed by members of the public every day – streets, police, fire, emergency response, parks, drinking water, and sanitary sewage disposal, to name a few. But officials have something very important going for them. Local governments can do what private entities can only dream of doing: they can send property tax bills to property owners, with an enforceable expectation that the bill will be paid. And there are other sources of revenue available as well.

Local governments have no inherent power to raise revenue; they must secure money in the manner allowed by state constitution or law. This chapter will explore some of the basic sources of revenue that local governments rely on to pay their bills for operations and improvements. The following selected sources of revenue will be examined:

- general property taxation;
- special assessment;
- special property taxation for dedicated purposes;

- fees, franchises, and special service taxes and fees;
- borrowing money by the issuance of municipal bonds.

This list of revenue sources represents a substantial part of the picture of revenue potential for most local governments. Local income taxes are imposed in some local governments, but no attempt will be made here to cover this topic due to their unique nature and uneven application throughout the country. In addition, while there are many very significant state and federal schemes for "sharing" revenues with, and providing grants to, local governments, these arrangements will not be addressed either. It is not that they are unimportant. In fact, revenue sharing and grants to local governments can represent a significant share of total revenue for many communities. But, these sources are generally not within the control of local government officials, and of equal importance, the formulas and calculations for revenue sharing and grants reveal that they do not always fall into logically explainable categories. They are typically bundled as part of larger spending packages manufactured by mysterious political negotiations by state and federal legislators and officials. Nonetheless, public officials should be aware that these types of funding exist, even though not discussed here.

Because the subject of local government revenue sources involves the extraction of money (property) from individuals, important constitutional provisions come into play, such as due process. Therefore, in order to ensure that fundamental constitutional protections of property owners are observed, most state money-raising regulations are very detailed and include procedures protective of private property rights. Unfortunately, this subject can be dry, and potentially produce periodic boredom on the part of the reader. The good news is that this chapter is not intended as a detailed treatise on the subject of finance, and a vigilant effort has been made to provide straightforward and understandable explanations in a concise summary of revenue sources, with the goal of making officials aware of their existence and their basic features.

A. General Property Taxation

The oldest and largest single source of local government revenue is the *general property tax*. This is a tax levied on private property – not persons – with the amount of the tax being proportional to the property's value. Because this revenue source taxes "according to value," it is often referred to as an "*ad valorem*" tax.

Under long-standing principles of law, the subject of "property" is divided into two basic categories: "real" property, which can be said to include land and things attached to the land, and "personal" property, such as motor vehicles and household possessions. In a commercial setting, personal property also includes various types of machinery and equipment. For a variety of reasons, *real* property taxation will be the main focus of the discussion here.

Because so much is at stake for both the local government and individual property owners, real property taxation is carefully devised. Here are a few important highlights:

1. Assessing the Value of Individual Properties

The general property tax is based on the *fair market value* of each property to be taxed, with a formula applied to determine *assessed* value or *taxable* value which is used to calculate the tax.

Fair market value is the price at which a buyer and seller would arrive after an arm's length private sale negotiation. In slightly more detail, it is the price at which the property would be sold on the open market between a willing and knowledgeable seller and a willing and knowledgeable buyer, with the assumption that the property has been exposed on the open market for a reasonable period of time.

The general property tax is based on the *value* of the taxed properties. So, it is obviously necessary to figure out what each piece of private property is worth. Assessing property value is a highly specialized exercise, and is undertaken by individuals known, unsurprisingly, as "tax assessors." The ultimate task of the assessor is to determine "fair market value." This is a term of art with a particularized meaning, although state law may refer to the same value in the property taxation regulations using terminology such as "true cash value."

"Fair market value" is the price at which a buyer and seller would arrive after an arm's length private sale negotiation. In slightly more detail, it is the price at which the property would be sold on the open market between a willing and knowledgeable seller and a willing and knowledgeable buyer, with the assumption that the property has been exposed on the open market for a reasonable period of time. Examples of sales that are *not* considered to be "arm's length" would be those from one family member to another, or mortgage foreclosure sales where the property is not actually placed on the open market – that is, a foreclosure sale represents a "forced" sale that is scheduled for a single day, with the typical buyer being a mortgage lender who typically offers to purchase for the amount owed on the outstanding mortgage obligation.

Value in the market setting is influenced by general economic conditions, as well as many other factors attributable to the property being assessed, such as its location, zoning, size, and surroundings, among other relevant facts and circumstances. Various valuation methods are applied in assessing value, with one of the most common methods being to ascertain the recent sale price of other *comparable* properties, and then adjust for size, location, surroundings, etc., to adapt the sale price to the actual property being assessed. Once this value is determined, many states multiply it by a fraction (such as 50 per cent) to arrive at the "assessed value," which is used in the tax-calculation process.

After the assessment process, but before property owners are provided with their actual tax bills, it is customary for local governments to give the owners of the assessed property the opportunity to disagree with the valuation arrived at by the assessor. For this purpose, the local government may send each owner a notice indicating the assessor's opinion of value for the coming year. In some states, this notice is sent only if there has been change in value from the prior year. Upon receipt of the assessment notice, the owner is given a specified amount of time appear at a tribunal established by state law to seek a reduction in the amount of the assessment, and then perhaps challenge that tribunal's determination in court.

2. *Property Tax Exemptions and Limitations*

Certain properties will be relieved from the obligation to pay general property taxes because the state legislature has determined that their particular use or user qualifies for an *exemption*. The most common exemptions are for educational institutions, places of religious worship, various government-owned properties, and charitable organizations. Whether a particular property qualifies under the law for an exemption is a regular subject of litigation.

In addition to tax exemptions, tax *limitations* have been established in a few states such as California and Michigan. Rather than totally exempting properties, tax limitations place a temporary "cap" on the taxable value of certain properties. For primary residences, and perhaps other selected properties, a temporary limit is established by law on the *amount of increase* in property tax from year-to-year. So long as the same individuals or families continue to own the property, the amount of property tax owed compared to the previous year cannot increase by more than the amount set by law, regardless of any spike in the actual market value of the property. This type of limit is essentially a *political* decision which has the effect of reducing the state's tax base in order to protect low, moderate, and fixed-income persons from being taxed "out of their properties." In the handful of states where tax limitation exists, it was accomplished by citizen-initiated ballot propositions to amend the respective state constitutions.

As years pass within a local government subject to a tax limitation, some properties in the community will change hands, while others will continue to be owned by the same person or family. When properties change owners, the protection of the limitation law resets, at which point their taxable value accelerates to the full market value (assessed value) in an event called "uncapping." The inevitable outcome over the course of several years is that owners who have held their properties continually may end up paying dramatically lower taxes than recent purchasers of comparable properties. This disparity was challenged in *Nordinger v. Hahn*, decided by the U.S. Supreme Court in 1992.[1] The plaintiff in that case was paying five-fold more in property taxes than some of her California neighbors with comparable homes. Some might view this as inequitable, but the Supreme Court upheld the tax-limitation formulation on the basis that the state was achieving rational and reasonable goals, including the avoidance of rapid housing turnover, and the prevention of the displacement of lower and fixed-income people from their homes due to the inability to pay their ever-increasing property taxes.

Getting back to the general property tax process, the overall "tax base" for a local government is the total assessed valuation of all properties, less any relevant tax exemptions, and with tax limitations being factored. Tax base becomes important when the local government undertakes the budgeting process, and sets the rate of taxation for the year, two subjects that will be visited next.

3. Budgeting and Setting the Tax Rate

Another important step in the property taxation process is setting the *tax rate*. The assessed value of individual properties (subject to exemptions and limitations) is multiplied by the tax rate to determine the dollar amount of respective tax bills.

The property tax *rate* is customarily expressed in dollars of tax owed per 1,000 dollars of taxable assessed property value (or some comparable formula). In some states, local governments may have their maximum chosen for them. The maximum rate of taxation in a city may be fixed by charter, and the rates for townships and counties may be set by state law.

In setting the tax rate, some local legislative bodies will select the maximum amount permissible by law or charter. Others may attempt to reduce the burden on taxpayers by setting the rate lower than the maximum authorized. But how does a local legislative body know when it is prudent to approve a lower rate, considering bills for services will still come due? Is it simply a matter of pleasing taxpayers (voters) and hoping that things will work out? The answer requires a brief tour of the *budgeting* process.

The annual ritual of *budgeting* provides a methodology for projecting the amount of revenue that will be needed for the next fiscal year. Of course, the available supply of money must take into consideration at all sources of revenue. Property taxes are generally the most important component of local government finance. But, as mentioned at the beginning of this chapter, there are other revenue sources (several of which will be discussed below). All sources of funding will need to be factored into the budgeting process. For example, let's say that the local government budget predicts that one million dollars will be needed to operate the government in the next year, and it estimates that $500,000 will be collected from sources other than general property taxation, such as fees, franchises, revenue sharing, and grants from the state. This tells those engaged in the finance process that it will be necessary to set a property tax rate at an amount which, when multiplied by the available tax base, will produce enough tax revenue to cover the remaining $500,000 (perhaps with some sort of added amount for contingencies). Naturally, if this produces a required tax rate that is outside the limits established by law or charter, the community will need to either go back to the drawing board on its planned expenses for the year, or explore an additional revenue source.

The budgeting process typically begins with the preparation of a proposed budget by the chief administrative or financial officer, such as the city mayor, city manager, town manager, or township supervisor. Once the administrative officer meets with department heads and others, and completes a tentative budget, it goes to the legislative body (such as the city council, county commission, or township board) for review, public hearing, and approval.

The final budget predicts the amount of money that must be raised from all sources in order to keep the government running in the desired manner during the next fiscal year.

4. Enforcing the Property Tax Obligation

There is an obligation on the part of property owners to pay property taxes, enforced under provisions of law that ultimately allow the government to hold a "tax sale" on those pieces of private property for which the property tax obligation has not been paid. The mandatory process leading up to a tax sale requires one or more notices of the delinquency, and an opportunity for the owner to satisfy the obligation prior to the sale. Beyond these basics, the laws of individual states provide a variety of processes required before a tax sale may be used to satisfy the property tax obligation.

B. Special Assessment

> "The principle underlying a special assessment to meet the cost of public improvements is that the property upon which they are imposed is peculiarly benefited, and therefore the owners do not, in fact, pay anything in excess of what they receive by reason of such improvement."
>
> See United States Supreme Court in
> *Norwood v. Baker* (1898)

While general property taxation is the mainstay for financing the local government as a whole, "special assessment" financing is a distinct mechanism for funding public improvement projects that uniquely benefit *particular areas* within the community. In a nutshell, where there is a public improvement project that will provide *special benefits* or "uncommon advantage" to a definable area within the community, if authorized by state law, a local government may create a "special assessment district" and collect annual assessments in relation to each property in the district for a period of years to provide funding for the project. Typically, the local government will *borrow* the money to advance payment for the project by selling municipal bonds. The money borrowed from the purchasers of the bonds is then repaid in annual install-ments of principal plus interest while the bonds are outstanding. The duration or life of the bonded indebtedness is normally limited to the useful life of the improvement, and the period of years for special assessment installments will typically correspond with the life of the bond debt. The special assessment installments repay the principal amount borrowed from the bond purchasers, plus interest.

Very common "special assessment" projects are improvements to streets, roads, sidewalks, and utility systems. An important condition for using special assessment financing is that the improvement project must provide special benefit or uncommon advantage *predominantly to properties within the defined area* of the community, as it is those properties which will be called upon to pay the bill for the project. While the project may incidentally, or gener-ally, benefit properties outside the "assessment district," or provide some gen-eral benefit to the community at large, it is the special benefit or uncommon advantage that justifies the obligation of the properties within the district to be responsible for paying for the project.

The rules for establishing and administering special assessment financing are provided by state law, and perhaps local charter. However, there are added intricacies and conditions for special assessment creation established by the federal Internal Revenue Code and related Treasury Regulations. Importantly, Congress has authorized certain tax benefits for the purchasers of municipal bonds which provide favorable tax treatment on the interest earned on the bonds issued for public projects, such as public sewer and water systems and public roads. Of course, Congress has also established special *requirements* that must be met in order to be entitled to the benefits, as will be further addressed later in this chapter.

An important step in each special assessment financing arrangement will be the local government's determination of the *extent* of special benefits or uncommon advantage the improvement project will provide to each respec-tive property within the assessment district. This is a crucial determination because the maximum amount a property owner may be called upon to pay, that is, the amount of the assessment against each particular property, must be *related to the benefits received* by the respective property as a result of the project. The precise relationship between the maximum assessment and the benefits from the project, as well as the criteria for determining the extent of "benefits," varies from state-to-state. For example, in one or more states, the total amount of assessment charged to a property must have a direct relation to the *increase in value* of that property as a result of the project. In other states the benefit is not strictly limited to an increase in value, and may also include a *special service* provided to the property as a result of the project. In certain states, the special benefit or uncommon advantage may take yet other forms, including *relief of the property from a burden, creation of special adaptability* in the land, or an improvement which *allows the land to continue being used.*

Summing up, a special assessment differs from general property taxation in fundamental ways. Where general property tax is collected to support the community at large, and is calculated according to the overall value of each property being taxed, a special assessment pays for an improvement within a defined *part* of the community, and the amount of payment by each property owner is based on the value of special benefits that accrue to the respective property as a result of the project. Overall, the theory is that the total amount of special benefits or uncommon advantage received by a particular property will be roughly equal to the total amount charged to the property in the form of assessments. Therefore, again in theory, no property owner will suffer a loss, but each owner is made whole, with a fair balance between the value of benefits or advantages on one side of the equation and the amount of the assessment payments on the other side of the equation. It was an appreciation of these points that led the U.S. Supreme Court, in 1898, to observe that: "The principle underlying special assessments to meet the cost of public improvements is that the property upon which they are imposed is peculiarly benefited, and therefore the owners do not, in fact, pay anything in excess of what they receive by reason of such improvement."[2]

This hypothetical may help illustrate the basic arrangement involved in a special assessment. Assume that it will cost $100,000 to pave a street on which 10 homes have frontage and will receive a special benefit. The local government will borrow $100,000 by selling municipal bonds to advance the money necessary to pay the design engineer and the paving contractor for the project. If each home on the street will receive roughly $10,000 in special benefits as a result of the paving project, then over the life to the special assessment district's existence, each home will be assessed and required to pay annual installments totaling $10,000 to cover the cost of the project. Of course, this is a simplistic example because there will be other expenses associated with the project, including interest payable to the bond purchasers while indebtedness to them is outstanding. But overall, this illustrates the methodology for borrowing money for a project and using special assessment financing to pay the money back.

It must be recognized that special assessment payments are not voluntary, and proposed projects and assessments are not uniformly embraced by the affected property owners, regardless of the promised benefits. So, under some statutory schemes, a special assessment arrangement will be conditioned on a demonstration that *at least a majority* of property owners to be assessed are in support of the project and special assessment financing. Where this type of requirement applies, the owners of property within a proposed special assessment district will have input on whether special assessment financing may be used for a particular project. This type of input is treated differently from state-to-state, and sometimes depends on the type of local government (city, township, etc.) imposing the special assessment.

On the subject of imposing special assessment financing despite objecting property owners, one justification is that, in its absence, many projects would simply not get done. Additionally, if special assessment financing did not exist, a limited number of property owners may well get stuck voluntarily financing the whole project even though many other owners would benefit. While it may appear to be harsh to require objectors to pay a share of a project against their will, there is some comfort in recognizing that improvement projects are generally in the public interest *and* result in special benefits that will accrue to all owners, including those who are required to pay against their will.

Once special assessment financing has been lawfully established, if a property owner fails to pay an assessment on the established schedule, state law customarily grants the local government a lien (security interest) in the property of those not making payment. Ultimately, continued non-payment may result in the delinquent property being sold to pay the assessment. This is analogous to a "tax sale" of delinquent property to satisfy an unpaid property tax.

Before leaving this subject, there is cause for caution on the use of special assessment financing to fund road or utility improvements associated with *proposed new development*. This caution might best be explained by a hypothetical. Let us say a new shopping center project is proposed, and that the feasibility of the development will depend on extending public utilities to serve the improved property. Assume that the cost of the utility improvements is so great that the developer is unable to advance the money in cash, and consideration is being given to funding the utility improvements by special assessment financing and the sale of municipal bonds to raise the front money. The local government would repay the money borrowed for the project from the proceeds received from special assessment installments. If we assume that the shopping center would be the main property bene-fited by the project, this means that repayment of the bond purchasers will *rely* on the collection of special assessment installments principally from the shopping center property. If these installments are not paid by the shop-ping center, the local government's remedy will be to sell the shopping center property in order to pay the bond purchasers. *And here is the cause for caution*: while there might be great optimism for the shopping center project at the time it is proposed, if the economy goes into recession, and the project is never constructed, the raw land (where the shopping center was intended to be constructed) may have little value, especially during difficult times. The result would be that the local government could get stuck with the obliga-tion to repay the bond purchasers, and have no recourse for recovering such payment from the property due to its lack of value. So it bears repeating that extra caution is warranted when municipal bonds are being considered as the means of borrowing money for a project, where the ultimate source of funds for repayment of bond purchasers is a project that has yet to be constructed.

C. Special Property Taxation for Dedicated Purposes

Beyond authorizing the *general* property tax to fund general operations of the local government, state law may also authorize a "special *ad valorem* tax" for additional, specifically dedicated purposes. (Recall that "*ad valorem*" refers to tax imposed on a property "according to its value" and is really just a technical term for our familiar system of value-based property taxation.) In some states, these "special" property taxes must be approved by voters, and will remain in effect only for the limited period of time approved.

Special property taxation is also frequently used along with municipal bonds, allowing the local government to advance the money for the cost of a project or service, with the entire community being taxed to fund repayment of the money borrowed from bond purchasers. Generally speaking, because all property in the community is taxed, money raised by this method of finance will be expended for the benefit of the community at large, as compared to special assessment revenue expended only for a specially benefited part of the community.

In states where local governments have a ceiling on *general* property taxation, a dedicated tax can be used to enable specific additional services that would not otherwise fit within the budget. For example, a special tax could be imposed to fund or supplement police and fire services, improve library services, or pay for parks and recreation expenditures. Again, some states require voter approval to impose a dedicated *ad valorem* tax in excess of the general property tax ceiling.

Special property taxation can also be used to finance public improvement projects, similar to a special assessment financing, but with the advantages that a dedicated *ad valorem* tax can be used for projects with a community-wide scope, and there is no need to determine special benefits or uncommon advantage for individual properties. For example, a local government may determine that it would be appropriate to establish a community park system that would require the acquisition of large properties and need a substantial park staff. Or perhaps there is a desire to update the library system with electronic media. Revenues from currently available sources may be inadequate to cover the needed expenditures, even after including potential fees or charges for use of the intended facilities. Subject to any taxpayer approvals that may be needed in the particular state, the local government may propose a special property tax dedicated exclusively to funding the desired project.

Funding by special property taxation may also be an option for two or more local governments acting together to provide an improvement or service, such as a regional transportation system. Such a project may be difficult (or inequitable) for one community to undertake alone, but feasible when attempted in combination with one or more other local governments. Again, if authorized by state law, the participating local governments may each propose to establish a property tax dedicated exclusively to funding a proportionate share of the transportation service.

D. Fees, Franchises, and Special Service Taxes and Fees

Local governments also enjoy the benefit of charging fees, requiring franchises, and imposing taxes and fees in special services areas, to the extent permitted under state law. These revenue sources are distinct from property taxes and special assessments.

1. Regulatory Fees

Regulatory fees represent an important source of review used to provide services and facilities enjoyed by particular members of the community.

The actual amount of a regulatory fee need not be based strictly on special benefits received, but must be fairly allocated among those paying the fee.

The fees collected are limited for use in funding the particular service or facility for which the fees are imposed, and may not be used to fund general government services.

Regulatory fees are an important and very legitimate source of revenue when imposed in permissible amounts provided by state law. The justifying concept for regulatory fees is that there are certain government services and facilities which are used by only a limited number of residents at a particular time. They generally do not directly benefit most taxpayers, and the relevant service provided is not limited to a defined area within the community. Under these circumstances, local governments may charge fees to those receiving the benefit of the direct service.

A familiar example of this arrangement would be a municipal golf course. Though a golf course arguably provides beneficial green space for the community at large, only some residents will enjoy the primary benefit of actually using it. So, it may be appropriate to charge a fee to the active users of the golf course to cover at least a portion of the overall cost of the golf course operation. A broad application of the "fee" concept can also be found in the typical building department of a local government. The need for and direct benefit from operating a building department will accrue to those few property owners in the community who are improving property at a given time. Again, a general or indirect benefit will accrue to the community at large by ensuring that buildings and improvements are safe and durable. But the direct service provided by the building department will go to those engaged in the improvement or development of their properties. Therefore, the theory is that those who are voluntarily engaging in the improvement of their properties and receiving the direct services should pay building permit and inspection fees to help defray the costs of operating the building department. The amount of permit or inspection fees may not be established with the view of making a profit. Fees must be used in offsetting the expenditures required to provide the service.

Other significant local government departments also utilize regulatory fees. Public sanitary sewer and public water systems generally establish fees for the services provided. These systems might be considered "enterprises" that operate exclusively on fee revenues, independent from other funds raised by taxation in the community. Typically, the fees charged by utility systems are calculated by experts to ensure that the fee amount paid by each respective user is reasonably related to the proportionate amount of service demanded by that user, and also to ensure that the aggregate amount of fees collected from all users does not exceed the cost of establishing, operating, and maintaining the particular program.

The actual amount of a regulatory fee need not be based strictly on special benefits received, but must be related to the relative benefit of respective users, and be calculated based on the overall cost of the service. In practice, calculating the fees to charge users is not an exact science due to the large number of variables involved, but the calculation must be made based on the sound discretion of the local legislative body setting the fee. An ordinance or resolution setting a regulatory fee is usually deemed valid as long as there is a *reasonable relationship* between the amount of the fee charged and the proportionate cost of providing the service to respective users.

This point has already been stated, but it is worth repeating that, in setting the amount of a fee for a particular service, it is critical to keep in mind that the revenues generated by fees may *not* be redirected to other departments or services in the local government. A regulatory fee might be invalidated as an unauthorized tax if a significant portion of the revenue it generates is used for general government purposes, rather than to fund the particular service for which the fee is imposed.

2. Franchise Fees

Franchise fees are another source of revenue for the local government that may be imposed to the extent authorized by state law. Briefly, franchise fees are revenues derived from granting franchises or privileges to companies doing business in the local community. Good examples are gas, electric, or communications services that pay a franchise fee for the use of public rights-of-way for the placement of their pipes and lines.

3. Special Service Taxes and Fees

Some states provide for additional revenue sources that might be characterized as hybrids, referred to as *special services taxes*,[3] or in some states as *special service fees*.[4] These hybrid revenue sources have characteristics of a special assessment, but do not require the local government to make detailed determinations of special benefits to each property. Rather, these taxes or fees are levied on properties in a contiguous part of the community which are provided with special services. As in the case of special assessment projects, which may result in general benefit outside the area being charged, the local government must draw a line around the area that will pay the tax or fee, and those outside the line are not be required to pay the tax or fee even though they may receive an incidental general benefit.

■ For a *special service tax* to be approved, the taxed properties must be *actually or potentially benefitted* by the service provided in the program. However, an important feature distinguishing this revenue regime from special assessment is that the amount of the tax imposed is determined based only on the *cost of providing the service*, with no need to estimate *special benefits received*, which can involve expensive and contested determinations. The area to be served by the program is a contiguous district within the local government referred to as a *special service area*. "Special services" may include a variety of programs provided by the government for the area to be taxed. Again, like special assessments, the costs and expenses of providing the special services are covered from the revenues collected as taxes levied on the properties within the service area.

The requirement that taxed properties be *actually or potentially benefitted* means there must be a reasonable expectation that services will make the area to be taxed a better place to live and work, and it can be reasonably determined that properties are capable of receiving direct benefits – even if the benefit is "potential." On the other hand, if there are characteristics of the property itself that prevent the receipt of the services, such as a limitation based on the permitted uses of the property under zoning, the tax will not be permitted.

■ For *special service fees*, the local government must determine that those being charged the fee are benefited, but the amount of a special service fee is, like the special service tax, calculated based on a reasonable relationship to the overall cost of the service. Mathematical exactitude is not required, and the particular mode adopted in assessing the fee is generally a matter of local legislative discretion.

E. Borrowing Money by the Issuance of Municipal Bonds

Simplified Picture of Money Flow When Bonds Are Used to Fund a Project

Municipal bonds sold to purchasers → Sale proceeds used to fund project

Taxes or special assessments collected each year → Repay bond purchasers

---

Many frugal individuals resist borrowing money to purchase things. They prefer to "pay cash" for what they need and use. Local governments in the past operated on a similar track by setting money aside in a designated fund over a period of time until enough was accumulated to make a desired purchase. Modernly, however, consistent with the wide use of personal credit cards in our society, it has become routine for local governments to *borrow* money by issuing *municipal bonds* in order to advance sufficient cash to undertake new projects and services. The indebtedness created from this borrowing is repaid over a period of years from general or dedicated taxation, special assessment, and other sources of revenue.

Borrowing by the issuance of municipal bonds is also common in connection with local government activities that produce a *stream of revenue*, such the operation of a utility system. The securities issued for such revenue-producing enterprises are commonly called *municipal revenue bonds* because repayment of the principal borrowed, together with interest, is expected to be realized from the revenue generated by the local government enterprise. Such revenue might derive from one-time fees for connecting to the system, periodic fees for the ongoing use of the system, or both.

Municipal bond finance has become a large and important part of the overall local government funding picture. This type of borrowing has enabled significant projects throughout the country. While there is *no inherent right of a local government to borrow*, state laws and constitutions generally provide clear authority for this purpose.

As a practical matter, municipal bond borrowing is, by and large, accomplished through agents of the local government who specialize in bond financing. As agents for local governments, these experts enter the *municipal bond market*, which provides a forum for tens of thousands of state and local governments to raise money for public purposes such as water and sewer systems, transportation systems, street and highway improvements, and public building construction. The federal and most state governments encourage the use of this bond market by relieving the purchasers of these municipal bonds from paying income tax on the interest earned. Importantly, this allows municipalities to find buyers even for bonds issued at relatively low interest rates. Because many bond-funded projects undertaken by local governments are of large magnitude, even a small interest-rate advantage will result in a significant savings in terms of the cost to finance the projects. This savings means that projects can be done more efficiently, or they may be more extensive than would otherwise be feasible.

It is worth noting that tax exemptions apply only to bonds issued for *government projects or purposes*, as compared to bonds issued to finance *private activities*, or for *private purposes*. By way of example, bonding to finance a public street would clearly be a government project or purpose, and bonding to finance construction of a private street within a condominium project would probably be considered financing for a private purpose. If a project, after bond issuance, is deemed by the Internal Revenue Service to be for a private activity or purpose, the tax advantage on interest income is likely to be lost – which has the further likelihood of triggering claims against the local government (and perhaps others) by the purchasers of the bonds.

In addition, although a full explanation of this point would be quite extensive, it is important to at least mention that local governments issuing municipal bonds may also have liability in the event the expected source of revenue to pay the bondholders becomes unavailable – such where the property in a special assessment district has insufficient value to support the special assessment payments (discussed above). The degree of liability depends on the extent and type of credit pledged by the local government to the repayment of the municipal bonds. In the unlikely (but not unheard of) worst case scenario, private property owners throughout the issuing community may be called upon by special tax assessment to contribute toward the payment of the bonded indebtedness.

F.   Last Words

Local government finance appears not only on ledgers and balance sheets, but on buildings, roads, sidewalks, parks, and other physical places. The work of local officials in planning, budgeting, and being creative with finance, is directly related to the safety, function, and aesthetic quality of the community. General property taxation is customarily the largest single source of ongoing revenue, but there is little room for creativity in this department. Knowledge is power with regard to other potential revenue sources. Making productive use of the revenue tools available has the potential of raising the value of private property in the community. This in turn has the effect of increasing the potential revenue available from the general property taxation of private properties. So, there are tangible benefits to becoming familiar with the possibilities of financing through the use of special assessments, special property taxation for dedicated purposes, service fees and borrowing through the issuance of municipal bonds. Gaining a working knowledge of these revenue mechanisms takes a real effort, but translates into making the community a better place to live, work, and play.

G.   Now on to the Local Story

If this chapter has invigorated your appetite for practical legal guidance, you can continue the story by exploring the law applicable to your own particular form of local government, and the law of your particular state. Suggested storytellers include both your local government attorney and your state's local government association, which offers training for community officials. Your local story might begin with responses to these questions:

1. Is general property taxation our community's primary source of revenue?
2. Property tax calculations generally do not use full fair market value. The formula varies from state-to-state, with some using 50 per cent of the fair market value, perhaps with one or more other adjustments. What is the formula used to arrive at the valuation that is used as the basis for calculating property tax in our state?
3. When the value assessed for an owner's property is scheduled to increase, the owner is typically given notice, followed by an opportunity to contest the increase. What process do property owners in our community

have available to contest a proposed increase? Is there a special tribunal to resolve disagreements, or does the property owner simply head to court?

4. Does the state apply a tax limitation to protect longtime homeowners from being "taxed out of their homes?" (This would presumably take the form of a "cap" on the amount of annual increase in the valuation used to calculate the property tax – regardless of the amount of increase in fair market value.)

5. To use special assessment financing for public improvements, must the local government secure a majority (or greater) vote of property owners in the district?

6. Does the state allow our local government to impose a dedicated "special property tax" to finance a community-wide project or service? If so, is voter approval required in advance of imposing such a tax?

7. What are our state's rules regarding regulatory fees? Are there any special limitations or requirements before fees may be imposed, or on how the amount of the fee must be calculated?

Notes

1. 505 U.S. 1 (1992).
2. *Norwood v. Baker*, 172 U.S. 269, 19 S. Ct. 18743 L. Ed. 443 (1898).
3. See *Coryn v. City of Moline*, 71 Ill.2d 194374 N.E.2d 211 (1978).
4. See *Bloom v. City of Fort Collins*, 784 P.2d 304 (Colorado, 1989).

Chapter 9

Background and Importance of Zoning

Being a good steward of land use development within a community is a core component of a local official's work. The Supreme Court has emphasized the importance of this role, noting that the "regulation of land use is perhaps the quintessential state activity."[1] Justice Thurgood Marshall put it this way: "[Local land use control] is one of the primary means by which we protect that sometimes difficult to define concept of quality of life."[2] A local government's land use decisions physically, functionally, and aesthetically impact the community – often for the long term. It is one of the greatest opportunities local officials have to leave a lasting mark on the community's character.

Two chapters are devoted to local land use control. With the goal of providing local officials with a basic but meaningful understanding of the subject, this chapter and the next will trace the subject across three types of control methodologies, touching in this chapter on "traditional" *pre-zoning* controls, and then taking a deep look at *zoning*, the most prominent form of local land use regulation. The next chapter will follow with a discussion of several *non-zoning* control measures.

In this chapter, the focus will be upon:

■ pre-zoning land use controls:

   ■ controls fashioned by the courts in traditional "nuisance" actions;
   ■ controls created by private parties entering into "covenants;"

■ land use control by local "zoning" regulation.

A.   Pre-Zoning Land Use Controls

Pre-zoning land use controls are included as part of this discussion not simply because they remain in use by private parties and local governments, but also because they are the foundation from which modern regulations developed. An appreciation of these historical tools will allow a more complete understanding of the regulations that local officials are called upon to enact and administer today.

1.   The Law of Nuisance

The law of nuisance is predominantly *court-made law*, where court decisions build upon one another on a case-by-case basis. When these cases are examined cumulatively, they form a "system" of land use control under the governance of the court.

"I should be free to make the most productive use of my land, so long as it doesn't damage yours." This statement is a good characterization of one of the most fundamental land use controls applicable for more than a century after the founding of the United States. During this period, the country retained a predominantly agrarian character. Most property owners were farming and ranching on large parcels, using few machines or chemicals, and living in homes located far from neighbors. Productive use of each property could typically be maximized without creating an *unreasonable intrusion* upon the use and enjoyment of surrounding properties.

During this agrarian period, an idealistic notion prevailed that private property rights deserve exceptionally high priority, and that every person has a fundamental right to use private property for any lawful purpose so long as he or she does not visit *nuisance* conditions upon neighbors. This view that individuals should use what belongs to them without harming what belongs to others has ancient roots in English common law.

Precisely what type and degree of interference with the use of one property should be considered to be an actionable "unreasonable intrusion" on a neighboring property? The large part of the answer to this was formally provided by the law of "nuisance."

Nuisance law waits for a particular dispute to arise. If attempts at peaceful resolution fail, the aggrieved party starts a lawsuit, and a court becomes the arbiter. The nuisance system allows the court to consider all of the particular facts and circumstances relevant to the property dispute, and then fashions a customized solution. Through the course of court opinions over the years, principles developed for determining when an intrusion is serious enough to warrant court intervention. So, the law of nuisance is predominantly *court-made law*, where court decisions build upon one another on a case-by-case basis. When these cases are examined cumulatively, they form a "system" of land use control under the governance of the court.

While nuisance law is no longer the predominant means of land use control, it is by no means dead. Local governments retain the authority in the appropriate circumstance to assert that an owner is causing a public nuisance in order to resolve a land-use dispute, and private owners may bring nuisance claims against one another.

> The party claiming that a nuisance condition exists must prove that the alleged wrongdoer is causing a *material intrusion* of a *non-physical character*, and that such action is *unreasonable*. The court must ultimately determine whether a nuisance condition exists, and if so, exercise discretion to fashion a remedy to stop the nuisance from continuing.

The determination on whether the claimant is entitled to relief in a typical nuisance case depends on the *specific facts*. The party claiming that a nuisance is occurring must prove that the alleged wrongdoer is causing a *material intrusion* of a *non-physical character*, and that such action is *unreasonable*. Ultimately, the court determines whether a nuisance is occurring and, if so, must exercise its discretion to fashion a remedy to stop the nuisance from continuing.

Life in the United States began to change dramatically during the industrial revolution. Development caused the formation and expansion of urban, and later metropolitan, areas. In a more urban environment, people and activities come into closer proximity, and the industrial revolution brought instruments of industry and transportation that began to have greater nuisance-like impacts – loud noise, dust, smoke, odor, vibration, and potential for danger to both adults and children. As characterized by the Supreme Court in 1926, there were suddenly far more circumstances in which activities amounted to "a right thing in the wrong place, like a pig in the parlor instead of the barnyard."[3] Because there was a greater frequency of conflict, and considering that the problematic activities tended to be more complex in nature, the traditional nuisance system, requiring a new lawsuit for every conflict, proved fundamentally inadequate to address life in the modern city. The situation cried out for a new and more proactive system of land use control, such as "zoning."

2. Private Covenants

> There are two types of parties to a covenant: *benefited* parties and *burdened* parties.
>
> The benefited party is given the right to enforce a *restriction on the use property* by the burdened party.
>
> Perhaps the most common form of covenant is used to restrict the use of land for residential purposes, and prohibit more intense uses.

Another traditional "system" of land use control, which continues to be used robustly, is the establishment of private *covenants*. This form of control arises out of private agreements voluntarily entered into between parties, predominantly incidental to the sale and purchase of real estate. There is good authority for saying that covenants represent a "traditional" means of land use control – they evolved from a 1583 decision in England.[4]

Today, many are familiar with the most frequently used form of covenants, generally known as *deed restrictions*, which are customarily established at the time a *subdivision* is created. Covenants are also created incidental to conveyances or leases involving only a limited number of properties which have not been made part of a formal "subdivision."

There are two types of parties to a covenant: *benefited* parties, and *burdened* parties. A benefited party is given the right to enforce a *restriction on the use of property* by a burdened party. Perhaps the most common form of covenant is the "residential use only" restriction, used to prohibit more intense uses. In recent years, covenants requiring all or part of the burdened property to remain in an *undeveloped* state have also been used to conserve land for aesthetic purposes or environmental preservation.[5]

In the typical covenant arrangement, each property owner is *both* a benefited party and a burdened party. That is, the benefit-burden relationship is *mutual*. Any party to the covenant may enforce the restriction, but at the same time all parties to the covenant must abide by it. For example, let's assume that Alicia owns 10 acres of land. She divides the property into two 5-acre parcels and sells one to Dennis and retains the other 5-acre parcel for herself. Alicia's intent is to build a home on her parcel, and she wants to ensure that the parcel conveyed to Dennis is also limited to residential use. So, as part of the conveyance to Dennis, Alicia creates a covenant requiring Dennis's property to be solely for residential use, and prohibiting it from being used for all other purposes. Now, if Dennis has his wits about him, he will refuse to complete the purchase of the respective 5-acre parcel unless Alicia's property is also restricted solely for residential use. Assuming that Alicia agrees to this arrangement, Alicia will be a benefited party, able to enforce the residential restriction against the burdened party, Dennis. And Dennis will also be a benefited party, able to enforce the residential restriction against the burdened party, Alicia. This mutual set of rights and obligations also applies in the larger subdivision context. All purchasers of lots in the subdivision are benefited, able to enforce the deed restrictions against all other lot owners in the subdivision. All purchasers of lots in the subdivision are also burdened, and have a duty to comply with the deed restrictions, which are enforceable by all other lot owners.

To be fully functional, a covenant must apply to *future owners* of the benefited and burdened properties. The truth is that a covenant would have considerably less value if it could not be enforced by and against subsequent owners. After all, the protection afforded by the covenant would otherwise be effective only during the period that the original owner is in possession (which could be a very short time indeed!) The determination of whether a covenant applies to future owners is made based on the *intent* of the parties in the creation of the covenant. If an intent to apply to future parties exists, then its application will "run" with the land itself, and the fact that a property has been passed to new owners will not free the future owners from the benefit and burden of the covenant. In such cases, the covenant can be referred to as a *"covenant running with the land."* This type of covenant was first approved by England's Lord Chancellor Cottenham in 1848, deciding the landmark case of *Tulk v. Moxhay.*[6] In other words, this tool has also been around for a long time.

Land use controls imposed by covenant take a wide variety of forms. As mentioned, "residential use only" is perhaps the most common. But merely perusing a modern set of subdivision deed restrictions will reveal that there are numerous other controls incorporated into them. By way of examples, deed restrictions typically restrict the placement of a house to at least a minimum distance from the street, restrict lots from being less than a minimum area and width, and prohibit construction of a home without a garage – and in many cases prohibit construction unless the garage is attached to the house.

It is essential for the covenant to be *recorded* in the government office where deeds and related documents can be found by purchasers. Recordation accomplishes the all-important function of placing the purchaser *on notice of the existence and terms of the covenant.* In the absence of recordation, the purchaser is likely to have no idea the covenant even exists, and this may result in the covenant being unenforceable against a future purchaser – who is likely to acquire the property without notice of the covenant.

B. Land Use Control by Local Government Regulation

How did "nuisance law" and private "covenant" law serve as foundations for zoning law?

Nuisance law is designed to stop land uses which are occurring on one property which are harmful to other properties. Government regulation, such as zoning, seeks to *anticipate* conflicting uses likely to result in nuisance or other adverse conditions, and proactively prevent the conflict from occurring in the first place by separating the conflicting land uses before a nuisance ever arises.

Covenants are designed to provide land use restrictions in order to make life more compatible among properties over time. Local government regulation frequently seeks to do the same thing.

The preceding section discussed two important traditional land use controls that predate local government involvement: "nuisance law" and private "covenants." We are now turning to *land use control created by local government regulation*. While quite distinct in terms of creation, it is clear that modern controls were a natural outgrowth of the traditional schemes. Nuisance law is designed to stop uses from occurring on one property which are harmful to other properties. Government regulation, such as zoning, seeks to anticipate the uses that would result in nuisance or other adverse conditions that would be harmful to neighbors, and *proactively prevent the conflict from occurring in the first place*. Covenants running with the land are designed to provide land use restrictions in order to make life more compatible among properties over time. Local government regulation frequently seeks to do the same thing. In other words, the longstanding law governing "nuisance" and "covenants" served as a conceptual foundation for local government regulation.

Local officials are likely to encounter one or more occasions on which making land use control decisions becomes a *political* challenge. Indeed, these decisions can have important long-term impact on lives and properties, which can be a daunting prospect. On the bright side, involvement in land use governance provides the opportunity for officials to leave an enduring positive mark on the community. This opportunity might involve far-sighted planning decisions and management, or perhaps the introduction or application of innovative zoning which is designed to achieve previously unimagined community development, or a pioneering effort to provide new housing alternatives to serve the broader community.

The balance of this chapter will be devoted to local zoning, enacted under governance of a state zoning enabling act. Zoning is perhaps the most important land use regulation under the control of local governments.

C. Zoning Regulations

1. Brief History and General Background

U.S. Supreme Court Justice Thurgood Marshall: "[z]oning has been observed as being one of the primary means by which we protect that sometimes difficult to define concept of quality of life."

Of the various regulations available for local land use control, the zoning power is perhaps the most pervasive and well recognized. Zoning regulations have been enacted in all, or nearly all metropolitan areas, meaning that this form of land use governance directly impacts a substantial portion of the country's population. Again referring to U.S. Supreme Court Justice Thurgood Marshall, zoning has been observed as being one of the primary means by which we protect that sometimes difficult to define concept of quality of life. It is worth devoting considerable attention to this subject for a number of reasons. It provides the basis for local officials to make a difference in their communities. It has the potential of impacting lives and properties, both positively and negatively. And the potential for litigation involving zoning decisions is an inescapable factor that must be assessed in local government decision-making. Local officials can have a substantial positive influence in all of these areas.

Through the 19th century, land use control issues were handled on a case-by-case basis under nuisance law, or addressed by private covenants, as discussed above. However, in the early part of the 20th century, under the pressures brought to bear by the industrial revolution, and based on the occurrence of intense, high-impact urban land usage in cities throughout the country, the need arose for a more *comprehensive and planned approach to land use control*. In its 1926 landmark decision approving the exercise of the zoning authority, *Village of Euclid v. Ambler Realty Company*, the Supreme Court concluded that land use control in our cities had fallen into disharmony, and comprehensive community planning as a basis for land use regulations like zoning and subdivision regulations represented the appropriate solution.[7]

As the 1900s progressed, population in major cities grew by leaps and bounds, with corresponding increases in the intensity of land usage and development. Because there were no effective rules on where industrial uses were permitted in relation to residential neighborhoods, housing was becoming more directly exposed to harmful impacts. New machinery, equipment and vehicles were fostering all manner of industrial effects and dangers, such as traffic, noise, heat, odors, dust, fumes, and the like. Interestingly, even retail businesses were being adversely impacted by heavy industrial uses. Imagine a slaughterhouse in an urban area opening for business in the immediate proximity of a restaurant or fine jewelry establishment. High rise buildings were facilitating even greater intensity and changing the dynamics of air and light availability to nearby uses. These and other circumstances were effectively crying-out for the land use control mechanism that became "zoning."

In 1916, due in part to the attraction of jobs and the intensity of immigration through the international port in the city, New York was one of the focal points of population concentration and industry-induced disharmony. To achieve more effective land use organization, the City enacted a city-wide Zoning Resolution, the first of its kind (though several other cities had experimented with more localized controls). In the years following New York's pioneering effort, experimentation with zoning accelerated across several states, prompting the United States Department of Commerce in 1924 to promulgate a model state zoning statute, commonly referred to as the Standard State Zoning Enabling Act, which resulted in considerable uniformity of zoning regulation in the country.

Rather than waiting for nuisance conditions to arise from industrial and other uses being developed and operated in a haphazard fashion, zoning allows local governments to anticipate potential nuisance conditions and *proactively organize the location and relationship of uses and regulate for nuisance avoidance.* Zoning became an extraordinary force for protecting neighborhoods from direct industrial impacts, providing a more favorable environment in which to rear children and fostering a high quality of life.

Local zoning ordinances are formulated by applying community planning principles to divide the municipality into *land use districts* which are drawn on a *zoning map* in an organized fashion. A core feature of zoning is the layout of *uniform land use districts*, with each district being designated to authorize a particular type of use, including residential, office, commercial, or industrial. For each district, the zoning ordinance will specify a list of specific uses that are permitted. Ideally, these land use districts are organized with spatial relationships that promote safer, healthier, and more convenient conditions in which people live, work, and recreate. Crucially, residential districts are separated from industrial districts in order to avoid nuisance-like conflicts from harming occupants of the residential districts. Likewise, all of the districts are arranged to promote quality of life. A set of regulations applicable to each zoning district is then established.

From a legal standpoint, the use of the zoning tool is authorized under the "police power," which is the government power to protect and promote the public health, safety, and general welfare. Under the Tenth Amendment to the United States Constitution, "The powers not delegated to the United States by the Constitution, nor prohibited by it to the States, are reserved to the States respectively, or to the people." The Constitution does not delegate the police power to the federal government. Therefore, it is considered as being exclusively reserved to the states. In turn, state legislatures throughout the country have delegated to their respective local governments the authority to exercise the zoning power.

The attractiveness of the zoning authority in the 1920s resulted in widespread adoption in major cities. This phenomenon quickly ran headlong into the Great Depression, which seriously dampened land development through World War II. When the war was over, however, a resurgence occurred, and zoning had a significant impact on post-war development.

Post-World War II zoning innovated the practice of prescribing for most zoning districts a list of uses that would be *permitted only if express approval is granted based on the exercise of considerable administrative discretion*. This new concept of *discretionary zoning* allowed communities to list uses that might or might not be permitted within a zone, depending on the application of various subjective criteria and flexible standards, such as whether a proposed use would be "compatible with the surrounding neighborhood," or would "foster a stable tax base." To pursue such a discretionary use, often referred to among the states as a "conditional use," "special exception use," or "special land use," a property owner must make a special application and receive express permission from the local administrative body (such as the planning commission) based on a public review of the proposal. In a residential zoning district, for example, an elementary or nursery school might or might not be compatible with a neighborhood depending on such things as property size, building design, utility requirements, and traffic patterns.

An all-important issue relating to this type of discretionary zoning is whether the *standards* provided in the ordinance for decision-making by administrative officials are *specific enough*. Indeed, if the standards are too broad, and give officials excessive discretion, decisions under the ordinance can no longer be considered to be reliably guided by standards in the ordinance. Officials become empowered to say "yes" or "no" to the proposal based on extraneous factors, such as whether the proposed use – or the applicant – fits the image of what the officials want in the community. For example, if the standard for approval is "whether the proposed use would be in the best interest of the community," each member of a planning commission might have a different reason for voting to approve or deny. The "actual" reason for denial might be based on a dislike for two-story homes, or worse, dislike for certain racial or ethnic minorities. Having meaningful standards in the ordinance to guide decision-making is critical.

2. Comprehensive Planning: A Constitutional Necessity

In 1924, the Department of Commerce created a model state zoning statute, officially known as the Standard State Zoning Enabling Act.

One of the important features in this model act was the directive to establish zoning "in accordance with a comprehensive plan."

The model act clarified that "no zoning should be done without such a comprehensive study."

The comprehensive plan was the inventive genius that allows the use of zoning to plan the community by separating conflicting uses, which ultimately protects people from dangers and creates better places to live.

One of the most insightful visions that has permitted "zoning" to be successful, and which provides its meaningful contribution to the promotion of healthy, safe, and functional communities, is the concept of dividing the community into *uniform zoning use districts*. The intent of this formulation is to arrange separate residential, office, commercial, and industrial use districts to serve the ultimate needs and interests of members of the community. Certainly, this aspirational formulation sounds like a positive model. But just how could this idealistic goal be realized in each local government? What is the methodology for transferring the goals of the model into various use districts so as to create the completed jigsaw puzzle known as the zoning map? The answer to these questions is revealed through the inventive genius of the "comprehensive plan," now referred to in many states as the "master plan."

As zoning was beginning to be widely used in the 1920s, the United States Department of Commerce promulgated a Standard State Zoning Enabling Act,[8] as mentioned above. Recognizing that the exercise of "zoning" was a new phenomenon, and also that the mechanics of this exercise are certainly not self-evident, the Standard State Zoning Enabling Act was intended as a model to educate and standardize the exercise of this new power in states throughout the country. The Act made provision for the establishment of *uniform zoning districts* for each class of use or type of building. One of the important features in the model act was the directive to establish zoning ordinance regulations, including the division of the community into use districts, "in accordance with a comprehensive plan." The model act clarified that "[n]o zoning should be done without such a comprehensive study."[9]

Recall that earlier land use control had been based on the concept of court-made nuisance law, in which individuals could use their private property in the manner and up to the limit that it caused harm to others. The concept of zoning called for the planning of communities in a way that didn't wait for harm to actually occur, but proposed to *anticipate* the impacts from the interaction of various types of uses. Based on this formulation, the intent of zoning is to *proactively prevent nuisance-type harm from occurring in the first place by separating incompatible uses*. Harm would be prevented, for example, by prohibiting industrial uses of property in a residential neighborhood. This was a new exercise of government authority that seriously interfered with the broad use rights property owners had been accustomed to under the law of nuisance. Indeed, industrial uses – and even commercial uses – would be prevented from locating in residential districts even prior to there being any evidence on the ground that actual harm would occur. So naturally, this exercise of zoning authority was deemed to be totally unwarranted by real estate developers, who immediately challenged zoning as an unconstitutional infringement on property rights. This challenge ultimately had to be sorted out by the United States Supreme Court.

When this "landmark" case reached the Supreme Court, *Euclid v. Ambler Realty Co.*[10] represented a classic constitutional showdown. Ambler Realty Company perceived a clear trend of industrial development in Cleveland, Ohio. There was good evidence that such development would migrate along the path of major highway and rail infrastructure, and into the small neighboring Village of Euclid. Ambler Realty acquired land in the village along the anticipated path of development. However, the legislative body of the village, desiring to preserve its predominantly residential character, utilized the newly introduced zoning power to divide the community into separate use districts. A portion of the Ambler Realty property was designated for industrial use, but a large part was restricted for residential use. This exercise of zoning had the effect of reducing the value of the Ambler Realty property by 75 per cent of what it was estimated to have been in the absence of the zoning "intrusion." Ambler Realty's constitutional challenge on the use of zoning power reached the Supreme Court in 1926.

The Court upheld the village's zoning, accepting that the organization of the community into planned use districts forms an important basis for achieving legitimate state objectives, predominantly the protection of residential neighborhoods, and that the village's exercise of zoning authority was reasonable and rational, thus satisfying the constitutional mandate of due process. However, in reaching the conclusion that zoning was permissible under the Constitution, the Supreme Court cautioned that, while it was approving the validity of limiting the usage of private property under this new "zoning" authority, there were important limits. If a future party challenging the validity of a particular zoning exercise were able to prove that the ordinance as applied to a particular property was "clearly *arbitrary and unreasonable,* having *no substantial relation to the public health, safety, morals, or general welfare,*" the ordinance could be declared unconstitutional. In other words, the Court declared that a community couldn't simply draw arbitrary lines on a map and haphazardly designate use restrictions with no rhyme or reason. The location of districts must be based on a plan that achieves legitimate objectives. The 1924 Standard State Act clarified by footnote that use of a *comprehensive plan* "will prevent haphazard or piecemeal zoning," that is, it will prevent the arbitrary use of zoning power.

Comprehensive planning remains a major fortification for the exercise of zoning. The required contents of a local government's comprehensive plan are generally dictated by state law. The essence of the plan should take into account the *location and relationship* of use districts, the *types of land uses* to be permitted in the respective districts, and an explanation of the legitimate objectives sought to be achieved by these land use patterns. The plan should also examine how these uses are to be provided with services, including details to enable planning and engineering for schools, streets, parks, water, and sewage facilities, fire and police protection, and other public services. The incorporation of all of these considerations protects the resulting zoning, undertaken "in accordance with the plan," from the claim that a local government is exercising the zoning power in an arbitrary manner. In general, the ideal situation is that a comprehensive plan will provide the underlying basis for the exercise of zoning power, and the zoning ordinance will give effect to the plan.

3. Flexible Zoning Mechanisms

After World War II, local governments increasingly utilized new zoning mechanisms granting officials considerable *discretion* in approving and denying both small and large land use proposals. Three such mechanisms that remain in common use are *"planned unit development," "cluster development," and "conditional use"* authorization, sometimes referred to as *"special exception use"* or *"special land use"* authorization.

The *planned unit development* (PUD) authorization is frequently used to mix single family residential units with other residential and non-residential components in a single development. Yes, it is a mix of uses not simply in one zoning district, but in a single development. The PUD would not have been in the wildest dreams of those in the 1920s who initially advanced the use of the police power to divide the community into grids with uniform zoning districts. One of the most important assumptions in the early grid zoning arrangement was that single family neighborhoods could not be encroached upon by other uses. So, PUD represents a profound transformation from that earlier model. With PUD, which applies on a development-by-development basis, the rule of "flexibility" replaces the inflexibility of the earlier the grid pattern. The specific degree of flexibility in a PUD will depend on the authorization in the respective state's zoning enabling acts and local government zoning ordinances. Some states permit a broad form of PUD, where local governments can opt to allow any combination of land uses (residential, office, commercial, recreational) in a single development.

The key to making a PUD workable is the application of planning principles to achieve compatibility among uses, along with creative engineering to ensure that each use in the mix is sufficiently protected from unreasonable impacts. In the best of worlds, the particular mix of uses will have a positive synergy that could not otherwise be achieved. Local officials should be aware, however, that PUDs can be very complex. In addition to planning and engineering guidance, the local government attorney should be involved at all critical stages of the review and approval process to make sure that the final PUD product is what was "advertised" to the community. Among other things, legal assistance is important to assure that the approval documentation includes a development process with an enforceable means of assuring adequate utility and other services for the entire project, especially one that is built in phases.

Cluster development authorization is another tool offering unique advantages for the developer as well as the public. Using the cluster approach generally results in the *same overall density* of development on a property, but restricts the physical improvements – and disruption of the land – to a defined portion of the property. A typical cluster residential development can be illustrated by the following hypothetical. We start with a thirty acre parcel of property. Under a traditional development design, the homes, roads, and utilities would be spread over the entire property. With the typical cluster approach, the same number of homes, along with the roads and utilities, are "clustered" onto a portion of the property, say ten or fifteen acres, with the balance of the land, including habitat, forests, wetlands or other sensitive areas, remaining undeveloped (and permanently restricted to ensure preservation). The developer's interests are advanced by achieving the same number of homes to sell, and by reducing the expenses for grading, roads, and utilities. The public's interests are advanced by preserving open space and natural resources.

"*Conditional Use*" or "*Special Land Use*" authorization is generally conditioned on the developer making a demonstration to administrative officials that certain *subjective requirements* are met. The types of requirements considered during local review of a project will vary not only from state-to-state, but from community-to-community within a state. Examples of the standards applied in determining whether to approve a discretionary use include *compatibility* with land uses in and adjacent to the development, *intensity* of use, the *impact* on traffic safety and environmental resources, and demand on *public facilities and services* (utilities, streets, police, and fire). To reiterate, reviewing a proposal under these variables is quite a *subjective* matter, permitting the exercise of considerable discretion by administrative officials. The discretionary approval process might be applied in determining whether to approve buildings with a height greater than otherwise permitted, or a particular type of use within a zoning district. Many zoning ordinances will list a number of "conditional uses" in each zoning district, with such uses being permissible only if discretionary approval is granted based on a demonstration that subjective standards have been met.

4. Administrative Zoning Boards and Commission

Once in place, the land use policies in the zoning ordinance must be *administered*. This means that the stated regulations and maps of the zoning ordinance must be *applied to specific properties* in the community. This job is performed by *administrative* boards, commissions, and officials designated in the zoning ordinance. The basic administrative mission is to judge whether land use proposals submitted for consideration comply with the intent and merits of policies established in the zoning ordinance by the legislative body.

a. The Planning Commission

Important administrative functions are performed in most states by local government "planning commissions," referred to in some states as "planning boards" or "zoning commissions." The members of this body, over time, typically develop a deep understanding of the zoning ordinance and policies of the legislative body, as well as the physical and functional layout of the community. It might be said that they become the *citizen zoning experts* of the local government, and are in a position to make insightful administrative decisions and provide valuable recommendations to the legislative body.

Although there is a variation among states on the precise functions of the planning commission, here are some of the essential jobs often performed by this body:

- ■ preparing and amending the community's comprehensive plan ("master plan" in some states), or recommending the plan and amendments to the legislative body, depending on whether the legislative body has reserved final decision-making for itself;
- ■ conducting public hearings, and making recommendations to the legislative body, on zoning ordinance amendments;
- ■ conducting reviews and hearings on applications for land uses that require discretionary approval, such as conditional uses. Depending how this function is delegated in the zoning ordinance, the planning commission may itself be the approving body for such uses, or its role may be to make recommendations to the legislative body;
- ■ conducting reviews and hearings, and making decisions, on applications for site plan approvals for the development of individual properties – often required for all improvements other than single family residences; and
- ■ conducting reviews and hearings, if delegated by state law and local ordinance, involving approval of subdivision plats and condominiums.

b. The Zoning Board of Appeals

The "zoning board of appeals," sometimes referred to as the "board of zoning appeals," or the "board of adjustment," is another administrative body that performs tasks indispensable for successful zoning administration.

In the preparation of comprehensive regulations for the entire community, it is a virtual certainty that there will be isolated properties that simply do not meet the generally applicable minimum standards in the ordinance. For example, the zoning ordinance may specify a minimum lot size of 10,000 square feet in area for a single family residence. There may well be vacant properties that existed at the time the ordinance was enacted that have perhaps 9,500 square feet in area. Such a property does not meet the requirement for the minimum total area of a residential building site. Similarly, there will be isolated properties that do not meet other requirements, such as a minimum lot width, or that would be unable to meet building setbacks from lot lines if a customary home were placed on the property.

One of the key powers delegated to the zoning board of appeals is the authority to essentially "fix" problems of technical compliance as long as justice is done to surrounding properties and the problem that needs fixing was not created by the property owner seeking relief. Such a "fix" is actually known as granting a *"variance"* that permits a property to be developed without strictly conforming to particular zoning ordinance requirements. The applicant for variance relief must demonstrate that the proposed development meets a short (but meaningful) list of requirements specified by state law, local ordinance, or both. One important rationale for this variance-granting power is the recognition that, in the absence of such authority, the owners of isolated properties that fail to comply with the strict letter of the zoning ordinance would have no other recourse but to file claims in court alleging that the ordinance prohibits reasonable use of their properties. In this respect, the administrative authority to grant variance relief permits the zoning board of appeals, using a relatively streamlined process, to sidestep the burdens of costly litigation. This avenue of relief is beneficial for both the property owner and the community.

The zoning board of appeals may also be given the authority to hear and decide appeals in cases of property owners who allege that a zoning official has wrongly interpreted or misapplied the zoning ordinance. Again, this authority provides a means – though not a guarantee – of avoiding litigation.

c. Administrative Decisions Based on Discretionary Standards

> It is especially important for planning commissioners and other administrative officials to understand the requirements imposed by law on administrative decisions which are made by applying subjective criteria, requiring the exercise of administrative discretion.

There is an important distinction between governmental actions and decisions which are "legislative" in character, and those which are "administrative" in character. Because land use controls are often the subject of court challenge, it is important for local officials to have a basic understanding of the distinction between the two types of decisions. In this regard, it is especially important to understand the requirements imposed by law on administrative decisions which are made by applying *subjective criteria*, requiring the exercise of *administrative discretion*.

Legislative officials are *elected to make public policy* for the community. Making public policy includes *establishing the rules in the ordinance* that must be applied by administrative officials. Legislative officials are directly answerable to voters for the decisions they make. If voters are displeased with the policy decisions made by legislative officials, their remedy is at the ballot box.

Administrative officials are not elected, so are not directly answerable to the voters. They are *appointed to apply the policies made by the legislative body*, such as when administrative officials review an application for development on a particular property, and determine whether the proposed development meets the relevant policies established in the ordinance by the legislative body. When acting in that capacity, it is important to remain mindful that *administrative officials are not permitted to adopt a new rule each time an approval for development is sought*. Making the rules is a legislative function.

The process of administrative decision-making can be very challenging, particularly where decisions must be made based on *subjective criteria*. For example, it is very common for zoning ordinances to require that conditional uses be "compatible with the surrounding neighborhood."[11] Deciding what "compatible" means takes officials into a gray area, with plenty of room for the exercise of *administrative discretion*. This requires the formation of opinions – and opinions among officials may differ. Needless to say, decision-making in this context can easily find its way to the courthouse.

There are *two critical requirements* that officials should recognize with regard to decisions that require the exercise of discretion:

1. The legislative body must provide adequate standards *in the ordinance to guide administrative officials.*

The first important requirement is that there must be *adequate standards provided in the ordinance to apply in making discretionary decisions*. This means that, when a decision on a proposed project is made, administrative officials must be able to find clear enough guidance in the ordinance that the decision is actually based on the *policy dictated by the legislative body*, and not based on whether the administrative officials like or want to approve the proposal. Stated in other words, administrative officials must be provided with enough guidance to *understand the intent of the legislative body*.

For example, a court in the State of Washington rejected the standards for administrative decisions under a city's zoning ordinance. In the words of the court:

> Because the commissioners themselves had no objective guidelines to follow, they necessarily had to resort to their own subjective "feelings." . . . [They] enforced not a building design code but their own arbitrary concept of the provisions of an unwritten [aesthetic ideal]. . . . This is the very epitome of discretionary, arbitrary enforcement of the law.[12]

In non-legal terms, the standards will typically be *adequate* if they provide the basis for making *consistent* decisions on various proposals. The standards will be *inadequate* – and too subjective – if the administrative board or official can make *opposite decisions* on two substantially identical proposals. When this is possible, neither the applicant nor the decision-maker has been provided with sufficient guidance. If there are inadequate standards, the administrator can make a decision based on whim – or worse, based on some improper reason such as the appearance or background of the applicant.

Another textbook example can be found in a case from Maine, where a local ordinance had used extremely broad terms when it delegated to the zoning board the authority to grant approval of a development proposal. This ordinance indicated only that a proposal up for review should be approved so long as it would not be detrimental to the neighborhood or adversely affect the health, safety, or general welfare of the public. The court declared that the legislative body cannot delegate authority in terms that are *so discretionary that the zoning board is essentially making legislative decisions every time it decides a case*. Terms that are too broad "permit the [administrative] board to determine what unique or distinctive characteristics . . . will render [the proposal] detrimental or injurious to the neighborhood."[13] Those "unique or distinctive characteristics" must instead be provided by the legislative body, identified in the language of the ordinance with enough particulars to inform administrative officials of the policy they are to administer – rather than allowing the administrative officials to effectively make new policy in every case.

2. *Administrative officials must make* findings of fact *that explain why the specific proposal either meets or fails to meet the standards of the ordinance.*

The second necessary ingredient for valid administrative decision-making involves *connecting the subjective standards* of the ordinance *to the specific facts* on a particular property. When officials make an administrative decision using discretionary standards, they must recite the *specific facts about the proposed project* that result in it meeting or not meeting the standards in the ordinance. The easy thing to overlook in carrying out this obligation is that, no matter how clearly the administrative official or body has the facts *in mind* when making the decision, it won't pass muster in court unless those facts are actually *stated* in the decision (that is, made part of the written minutes) and identified as the basis for the decision.

Abstractly, this doesn't sound like a difficult requirement to comply with. But experience reveals that this is typically one of the steepest learning curves for administrative officials. It is not sufficient for the officials to conclude in their decision that the applicant has met, or failed to meet, an ordinance standard. Rather, administrators must *articulate, in the meeting minutes of the decision, the fact-based reason why the standards are met or not met.*

A case in Michigan made this point clear when it reversed the determination by a zoning board of appeals that an applicant had shown "unnecessary hardship" and was thus entitled to a variance. The court's analysis started with a question:

> What, then, are the reasons for the Board's finding the broad standard of 'unnecessary hardship' to be satisfied? No one knows. No reasons are given. In other words it boils down to this: there is unnecessary hardship because there is unnecessary hardship, and, because there is unnecessary hardship, the standard (of unnecessary hardship) is satisfied. . . . [many] courts . . . require not merely conclusions, but a statement of the basis for the board's findings of 'unnecessary hardship' . . . set forth in factual detail, thus preventing arbitrary, unguided action.[14]

As an illustration of this same point,, suppose that the administrative commission must determine whether a development is "compatible with the surrounding neighborhood." A *valid* motion granting approval might include the following *factual* substantiation:

> The proposal is approved for the reason that the proposed development is compatible with the surrounding neighborhood *considering the following facts:* the applicant proposes the same use as is already present in the neighborhood, and the improvements and architectural style of the proposal are very similar to other nearby structures.

When a court is presented with a challenge of an administrative decision, the judge's function is not to second-guess the administrator's conclusion. Rather, the reviewing court should *review the record* to focus on two principal issues: (1) whether the ordinance provides adequate standards for making consistent fact-based decisions; and (2) whether the administrative official(s) reasonably applied the standards of the ordinance to the specific facts of the case, as reflected in the minutes. If the court finds these two bases covered, it will be much more inclined to conclude that the administrative decision was on proper footing.

D. Last Words

Zoning is the most powerful land use control tool. In the 1920s, its use began to flourish. Due to the new concentrations of population in the great American cities, and the significant adverse land use impacts caused by the instrumentalities of the industrial revolution, zoning sprang out from the inability of nuisance law to adequately respond to threats to public health, safety, and general welfare. Without a doubt, zoning created a much greater imposition on private property owners as compared to nuisance law, which allowed owners to use private property for any otherwise lawful purpose, so long as it did not cause nuisance conditions on neighboring property. Zoning essentially makes all property owners sacrifice a portion of the land-use freedom permitted under nuisance law. Under the zoning regime, all properties are classified in one of a number of zoning use districts and, with certain exceptions, each property is saddled with the obligation to conform to the uses permitted in its classification. The Supreme Court concluded in 1926 that this sacrifice required by zoning is a reasonable trade-off for preventing widespread nuisance, given the new complexity of modern society. The simple point is that, while each property owner sacrifices, such owner is spared the burdens that would naturally result if their neighbors' use of property were not restricted in the manner required by zoning. All uses, including residential, office, commercial, and industrial, are protected from materially incompatible uses being allowed to locate around them. So, while zoning creates burdens, it also creates corresponding indispensable advantages. There may be a better land-use control system, but we haven't discovered it yet.

E. Now on to the Local Story

If this chapter has invigorated your appetite for practical legal guidance, you can continue the story by exploring the law applicable to your own particular form of local government, and the law of your particular state. Suggested storytellers include both your local government attorney and your state's local government association, which offers training for community officials. Your local story might begin with responses to these questions:

1. Has our community followed the post-World War II trend in land-development regulation by the widespread inclusion in the zoning ordinance of uses that may be approved under *discretionary* standards? If so, does this include:

    a. "Conditional," "special," or "special exception" land uses?
    b. Planned unit developments that permit mixed uses within a single development?
    c. Cluster zoning, permitting higher density development on part of a property while requiring preservation on the balance of the property?

2. Does our state (under its statutes and court decisions) allow relatively broad discretionary standards for land use approvals (such as the requirement for a proposed use to be "consistent with the pattern of development in the neighborhood"), or must the standards narrowly restrict the exercise of discretion?

3. If our state allows the use of planned unit development, are individual developments limited to a relatively narrow set of uses that may be included (such as single family residential plus recreational use) or is it within the judgment of local governments to determine the combination of uses (such as single family residential, multi-family residential, office, and commercial uses)?

4. The "zoning board of appeals," sometimes referred to as the "board of zoning appeals," or the "board of adjustment," is delegated the authority to grant "variances." A variance permits development on a property that falls short of the technical requirements stated in the zoning ordinance. In our community, what must a property owner demonstrate in order to be entitled to approval of:

a. A "non-use" variance, allowing development despite the total area or other dimensions of the property failing to meet the zoning requirements?

b. A "use" variance, allowing development for a use not otherwise permitted in the zoning district? (Not all communities grant "use" variances.)

5. Do our local government boards, commissions, and officials make detailed findings of fact to explain and substantiate their administrative decisions?

Notes

1. *Federal Energy Regulatory Commission v. Mississippi*, 456 U.S. 742, 767, n. 30 (1982).
2. *Belle Terre v. Boraas,* 416 U.S. 1, 13 (1974).
3. *Village of Euclid v. Ambler Realty Co.*, 272 U.S. 365, 388, 47 S. Ct. 114, 71 L. Ed. 303 (1926).
4. *Spencer's Case*, 77 Eng. Rep. 72 (KB 1583). Anyone having an interest in the history of covenants after *Spencer's Case*, is encouraged to read the Maryland case entitled *Gallagher v. Bell*, 69 Md. App. 199, 516 A.2d 1028 (1986).
5. In many instances preservation objectives are accomplished using "conservation easements," rather than "covenants," but the two types of restrictions are, for practical purposes, are nearly the same.
6. 41 Eng. Rep. 1143 (Ch. 1848).
7. *Village of Euclid*, above, at 393.
8. See Emerson, *Making Main Street Legal Again: A SmartCode Solution to Sprawl*, 71 Mo. L. Rev. 637, 652 (2006).
9. The distributed copy of the Standard Act is available online at https://www.govinfo.gov/content/pkg/GOVPUB-C13-18b3b6e632119b6d94779f558b9d3873/pdf/GOVPUB-C13-18b3b6e632119b6d94779f558b9d3873.pdf. (accessed in 2020). In addition, in 1926 the U.S. Department of Commerce released A Standard City Planning Enabling Act, which was a model statute to guide community planning and preparation of master plans by local governments.
10. *Village of Euclid*, above.

11. The courts in some states insist on clear guidance being provided to administrative officials, and the requirement for a conditional use to be "compatible with the surrounding neighborhood" may be found to be too subjective in nature to provide sufficient guidance.
12. *Anderson v. City of Issaquah*, 851 P.2d 744 (1993).
13. *Cope v. Inhabitants of the Town of Brunswick*, 464 A.2d 223 (Me. 1983).
14. *Tireman-Joy-Chicago Improvement Ass'n v. Chernick*, 361 Mich. 211, 214, 218 (1960).

Chapter 10

Non-Zoning Land Use Controls

Building on the discussion in the last chapter of "traditional" land use controls and "zoning," this chapter will discuss local government engagement with "non-zoning" regulation. The intent is to cover a few frequently encountered non-zoning subjects:

- construction and maintenance codes;
- subdivision and condominium regulation;
- environmental regulation;
- regulation of signs and billboards;
- historic preservation regulation;
- overview of other non-zoning regulations.

A. Construction and Maintenance Codes

Most would agree that it is in the public interest to regulate the manner and quality of building construction and maintenance. Even as technological advancement continues to add new options and complexity, we continue to embrace uniformity and efficiency. So, as of the late 1990s, many states have determined to defer to *model international codes* for building, fire, mechanical (heating and cooling), plumbing, energy conservation, and eco-friendly materials and construction.

Construction and maintenance codes are frequently adopted by local governments simply by incorporating model codes into local ordinances, generally with customized local or regional provisions that account for local differences in climate and other factors.

These codes are typically administered and enforced by the local government building official in the building department. This official may have complete review and approval authority over single family residential construction, and may become involved in multiple-family residential, subdivision, commercial, and industrial construction as well, after plans for such work are reviewed by the planning commission and other state or county governmental entities. Due to complexity, building officials generally collaborate with in-house or consulting professionals, such as civil engineers, in the performance of these tasks, especially for construction of improvements other than single family homes.

B.   Subdivision and Condominium Regulations

The development of property into "platted subdivisions" of individually-owned lots has been occurring for decades, and has been the subject of regulation for nearly as long. "Condominium" projects, which permit a greater variety of design and ownership options, have existed in Europe for years, but did not make an appearance on the United States development scene until the 1960s. Since then, they have become increasingly popular.

Subdivision "platting" (where a parcel of land is developed with numbered lots) and condominium developments are predominantly regulated under rules established by state law. Local officials should have some familiarity with these subjects because local governments frequently require review and approval under standards specified in ordinances that supplement state regulation.

Platted subdivisions typically involve the development and sale of lots for single family residences. Condominium projects, as explained further below, can involve apartment-type buildings, attached and detached clusters of homes, and "site" condominiums that resemble platted lots for single family residences. An important distinction between a subdivision plat and a condominium project has to do with the manner in which properties are owned. In a platted subdivision, the developer divides a parcel of land into a number of lots, and in many cases includes common areas for entrance amenities, open space, and recreation. Each of the lots is sold to a buyer who will take complete ownership and possession of the lot. The developer also customarily creates a set of covenants and restrictions (commonly known as deed restrictions) which establish a homeowner association. These covenants and restrictions limit the use and design of individual lots, and place the day-to-day governance of the subdivision into the hands of an elected subdivision association consisting of lot owners.

In the case of residential condominium projects, there is a variety of alternatives that govern precisely what it is that an individual buyer purchases. Each ownership arrangement revolves around its unique definition of the term "unit." In all cases, the "unit" will include the residential living space, but from there, there are significant choices, generally determined by the developer based on market demand:

- *Apartment style condo.* This common form of condominium project presents itself like an ordinary apartment building (or grouping of buildings). In this setting, the "unit" will most likely be the interior living space which is the counterpart of what is normally leased by a tenant. Except, in a condominium development, rather than leasing the living space, each resident takes exclusive ownership. Along with the exclusive living space, the purchaser also acquires an interest in "common areas," which support the units and are shared with other unit owners, both within the building and on the grounds. Typical common areas include hallways, lobby, elevators, landscaping, drives, and other amenities. The purchaser may also acquire one or more parking spaces for exclusive use.
- *Pod (cluster) condos.* Another common form consists of a series of "pods" or "clusters" of *attached or detached units*. The total number of units in a pod, and in the entire project, is very flexible, subject to applicable zoning. For this configuration, "the unit" can be limited to merely the interior living space (like in the apartment style) or a unit may include all or a portion of the exterior of the structure as well. The unit may also include or share special ownership rights in a garage, perhaps a yard area, and a driveway adjacent to the unit. The purchaser of such a unit may also acquire a common interest, with the other unit owners, in various streets, parks, open space, landscaping, and other amenities within the development.
- *Site condominiums.* A third condominium arrangement, very comparable to a platted subdivision, is commonly known as a "site condominium."

In this form, the "unit" is the functional equivalent of a subdivision lot. A unit's purchaser has exclusive possession of the entire "lot," and will likely own the entire residence constructed on the lot. Ownership rights, however, are governed by condominium law rather than subdivision platting law. There may be common ownership of streets, parks, open space, landscaping, and other amenities.

In condominium developments, a set of bylaws, rules, and regulations contain the counterparts to the deed restrictions established for platted subdivisions. The precise components and contents of these documents are determined by a combination of state law and developer discretion – and possibly local ordinance if permitted by the state. The existence of bylaws reveals an important characteristic of condominiums, namely that these developments are typically governed by *majority rule of the unit owners* to a greater degree than platted subdivisions.

Before leaving the subject of condominiums, local officials should be aware that this form of ownership is not limited to residential projects. Indeed, development authorization in the condominium law of some states includes the right to create mixed-use developments, industrial developments, office campuses, and even boat docks ("dockominiums").

C. Environmental Regulation

Historically, when persons and entities would cause harm to the land, air, water, and other natural resources, the best form of remedy was a court action under *nuisance law*, as discussed in Chapter 9. A neighboring property owner might file an action claiming that the environmental harm amounts to a private nuisance. Or a number of neighbors, a local government, or both might seek a remedy in court to stop a public nuisance.

As populations concentrated at the beginning of the 1900s, science and industry facilitated land uses which became more complex and impactful. Issues raised by those concerned about environmental preservation and prevention of contamination grew ever more complicated and exacting, to the point that modern standards sometimes measure pollution in *parts per billion*. Potential new harms might last *thousands of years*, and an extensive number of aggrieved parties might be engaged in the effort to stop or otherwise control an activity. Traditional nuisance law proved to be fundamentally inadequate to the tasks newly at hand.

A significant new body of legislated environmental law tackles these scientific issues and complexities on a systematic basis, rather than relying on individual nuisance claims. There are definitions of various parties responsible for causing environment harm, and detailed explanations of thresholds for when various types of substances cross the line into the realm of pollution or contamination. Of course, many of these substances were historically either not understood or nonexistent, but have since been identified as the cause of contamination, pollution, impairment or destruction of natural resources or the public trust therein. Most of this new regime has been developed within the spheres of federal and state law and regulation. As compared to traditional "nuisance" law, the legislative and regulatory system provides greater advanced notice with regard to what is permissible and not permissible, and establishes methods for meaningful adjudication of complex disputes between parties. These laws and regulations are enforced by federal and state administrative officials, and local governments are generally *not* on the front lines of responsibility for these purposes. This is not to suggest, however, that local governments must defer to federal and state administration in *all* areas of natural resource protection.

Particularly in locations in which land and water resources have been exposed to serious degradation, or are prominent in defining local character, local governments have engaged in protection of natural resources. Local regulation, where permissible by state and federal law, has extended to such subjects as managing storm water, protecting wetlands, and preserving woodlands and other sensitive resources. Authority for wetland protection arises under federal and state law, and is not uniformly delegated to local governments. Woodland preservation is likewise not uniformly undertaken by local governments, and in those states where it is, it takes widely varying directions and forms. Local regulations designed to preserve natural resources are invariably subjects of controversy between so-called property rights advocates and environmental protection advocates. Volumes have been written on this rivalry of interests.

In contrast, the need and authority for local *storm water* management is pervasive. Because of its widespread need and application, most local officials will be exposed to storm water management issues. Accordingly, storm water is the local environmental preservation issue that will be addressed here.

Storm water itself is not inherently harmful. Indeed, it is a resource needed to recharge groundwater basins and watersheds. However, where storm water is not flowing in a smooth "sheet" over a natural, vegetated surface, its character can change from an amiable Dr Jekyll to a destructive Mr Hyde;[1] that is, from helpful to potentially catastrophic. In the natural setting, storm water flows relatively slowly over the vegetated ground, and substantial infiltration occurs through abundant permeable surface areas. But where growth and development have occurred, other dynamics come into play. First, there are more impermeable surfaces (rooftops, driveways, streets, and other surfaces used to transport and focus the outlet of storm water) resulting in less infiltration, and causing water to flow at faster, more erosive rates. This is coupled with the intentional channelling of water into "point" discharge outlets. The most problematic scenario, all too common, is where the storm water from an entire property is funnelled into a single outlet pipe, which concentrates the entire discharge impact onto a narrow receiving zone.

The result of such changes occasioned by development can be a severe erosion of surfaces, with sediment and potentially harmful materials (such as petroleum products on streets and fertilizers and pesticides from lawns) carried in suspension all the way to ground and surface water basins, including lakes and wetland areas. The net results of poorly managed storm water can include surface damage, water quality degradation, flooding, and reduction or destruction of habitat.

Local storm water policies aim primarily at reducing the erosive potential of runoff (especially point discharges from drainage outlets) and preventing moving water from encountering and transporting loose sediments and pollutants to groundwater and surface basins. In many cases, local storm water controls require settling ponds or other facilities that slow down the water movement and permit suspended sediments and pollutants to settle out of the storm water before being discharged into groundwater storage or surface water bodies.

A good illustration of a major storm water issue is found in a dispute that was litigated to the Supreme Court: *Tahoe-Sierra Preservation Council, Inc. v. Tahoe Regional Planning Agency.*[2] Here, readers may observe both the cause and consequences of a storm water issue, and the legal issues that might arise in providing solutions. Lake Tahoe is situated within a 500 square mile basin straddling the California-Nevada state line. All parties, noted the court, agreed that Lake Tahoe is "uniquely beautiful." Mark Twain, in his book entitled *Roughing It,* had aptly described the clarity of its waters as "not merely transparent, but dazzlingly, brilliantly so." Unfortunately, the lake's pristine state had deteriorated rapidly over the 40 years preceding the case. As the Lake

Tahoe basin saw increased settlement and development, the vast sloping areas around the lake brought it storm water of a character it had never received before. Development on the sloped areas included impervious artificial surfaces such as roofs, driveways, and streets that carried water at a greater velocity, and picked up sediment and pollutants en route to the lake. Ultimately, it was these sediments and pollutants that were threatening the "noble sheet of blue water" beloved by Twain and countless others.

As a consequence, the States of California and Nevada, five counties, several municipalities, and the Forest Service of the Federal Government initiated a study that temporarily halted development rights on some 2,400 properties over a period of some two and a half years. Not shockingly, this large-scale interference with private property rights motivated the lawsuit that ultimately reached the Supreme Court. While this case obviously portrays an extreme circumstance, it also illustrates how local governments can become engaged in environmental regulation. The plaintiffs in the case argued that the mere stoppage of development rights resulted in an unconstitutional "taking" of private property, and that the government owed them compensation. The case established the significant precedent that merely halting development for a reasonable temporary period of time in order to study how to resolve a legitimate government issue does *not* "categorically" result in a "taking" of private property for which compensation would be required.

D. Regulation of Signs and Billboards

For a variety of reasons, nearly all local governments regulate the use of signage. It is likely, however, that not all officials will agree on the reasons for sign regulation. Some think immediately of promoting vehicle and pedestrian safety, while the thoughts of others focus on signage controls to establish and maintain community character and aesthetic quality. Persons and entities displaying signs will advocate for regulation that permits freer use of signage for effective visibility and business attraction purposes. Of course, local governments generally consider all of these points when regulating.

Here are several considerations that influence communities as they formulate and amend their sign ordinances, either as part of their zoning ordinances or as separate sign codes:

■ *Vehicle and pedestrian safety.* Sign regulations are critically important to maintaining safety on roads and sidewalks. Communities attempt to prescribe an appropriate number, size, location, illumination, and construction of signs. To most, safety is at least one of the indispensable considerations for regulation. Too many signs, and placement in inappropriate locations, makes it difficult for a driver to find driveways, businesses, and other destinations. Signs that are overly large, banners and blow-up objects, have moving parts or images that change suddenly, and other street graphics intended to draw attention can all distract from safe driving. Temporary signs, and signs that are not properly attached to the ground or to buildings, can be blown into roadways during storms, creating traffic safety hazards. Signs in ill-conceived locations can block vision between drivers and pedestrians.

■ *Aesthetics and community appearance.* Because signs often appear immediately adjacent to streets and highways, they can represent an important face of the commercial community. Over time, sign regulations placing an emphasis on aesthetics can have an uplifting effect on a community. Consistently applied standards for size, height, design, lighting, and maintenance can have a significant effect on setting and maintaining the character of a community.

■ *Preservation of scenic views.* In locations where there are scenic areas, such as significant elevation changes or natural surroundings, sign placement and design can have an important and direct impact on scenic views, and also impact indirectly on the economic integrity of a community. Sign regulations, including standards for sign placement, size, and height, can focus on preserving scenic views.

■ *Economic development.* Signs may also be important to the economic health of a community. A well-placed sign with a legible message can attract business. Insufficient or unenforced regulation can have the opposite effect by sending a message that the community it is not fully engaged. Business owners do not want their own signs blocked by neighboring business signs, nor do they want to expend precious resources to compete with their neighbors over sign visibility. Good sign regulation can do a lot to enhance the physical aspects of signs, promote a level playing field, and foster an attractive community for all businesses.

■ *Prevention of blight and reduction of clutter.* Because of their exposure to the elements and construction with materials that are often less permanent than those of the principal building, deteriorating signs can present a negative appearance in a business area. Without sufficient regulation requiring proper construction and maintenance, signs can contribute to blight. In addition, signs can be places where blowing refuse and other materials accumulate, and regulations requiring attention to this situation are reasonable and relevant.

Technological innovations over the past half-century have led to increased use of digital outdoor advertising to convey commercial and other messages. Some digital innovations have generated intense opposition based on concerns for traffic safety due to the distraction of drivers and in the interest of preserving aesthetic integrity. We know that technology will not subside, which means that accommodations, adaptations, and perhaps compromises will be necessary.

Of the various types of signs, few cause as much controversy as "billboards." These signs, practically speaking, are off-premises advertising signs. "Off-premises" means that the message contained on the sign does not relate to an activity or use occurring on the same parcel of property where the sign is located. Unlike on-premises signs, which may identify a business or residence on the same parcel with the sign, billboards are typically utilized to advertise a service or product available elsewhere. To some who view them, billboards are helpful for obtaining information, while for others they are mere visual clutter and blight, impeding scenic natural views. Regardless, they are a ubiquitous feature of the roadside environment in a good part of the United States. There are several hundred thousand billboards nationwide, perhaps because they are an undeniably profitable medium to reach tens of millions of drivers each day, while also providing public service announcements, such as missing person and criminal suspect alerts, and advertising government programs and services.

Recent decisions of the Supreme Court require that local government, in addition to sorting through the issues and goals presented above, also remain mindful that signage regulation must conform with the First Amendment "free speech" protection in the United States Constitution.[3] The First Amendment is easily implicated when regulations impact the "content" of the expressions presented on signs. Content-based regulation must be scrupulously avoided to maintain the constitutional integrity of a sign ordinance – which is to say, to prevent lawsuits and invalidation. The local government attorney is a necessary party to consult when preparing a sign ordinance or amendment.

E. Historic Preservation Regulation

Historic preservation is the twofold process of identifying historic resources and then acting to protect them. Local laws enter the scene as one means of achieving protection.

The United States has seen three distinct "preservation" movements, each with a particular focus: archaeological and tribal resources; natural landscapes (environmental conservation); and buildings, structures or historic sites that were constructed and developed uniquely at specific times.[4] It is in connection with the third category, involving the preservation of historic buildings and structures, that local government has had the most involvement – beginning with a 1930s attempt to regulate demolition and alteration within historic districts[5] In 1978, the Supreme Court confirmed that historic preservation ordinances are, like zoning, supported by the police power authority,[6] placing historic preservation solidly within the sphere of legitimate state and local law.

Presently, in states that have provided enabling authority, numerous local governments have enacted preservation ordinances to maintain historic buildings on private properties. Regulation is not uniform throughout the country, with the primary common theme being restrictions on the *demolition* of private historic properties, either affirmatively or by neglect. Historic preservation ordinances may also restrict or prohibit historic properties from being *altered* in any way that would undermine their historic qualities, particularly relating to visible features. These ordinances are often administered by historic preservation commissions.

F. Overview of Other Non-Zoning Regulations

Local officials will encounter a myriad of other types of land use control regulations not examined in this chapter. These include regulations already on the books when an official takes office, as well as those that will be newly proposed from time-to-time while an official is in office. Some are fairly common across the country; for example, *public land use* regulations, such as traffic, parking and parade controls, and authorization for utilities to occupy space within road rights-of-way.

Other regulations address matters of local concern on *private property*. There are non-zoning ordinances designed to regulate adult entertainment and other amusements. Local governments with *coastlines* on the oceans or great lakes, or *shorelines* on inland lakes, adopt regulations seeking to organize dock and water usage, and to protect and preserve natural resources. Some local governments find it necessary or appropriate to regulate the use of *rental housing* by adopting inspection requirements, regulations for short-term rentals and bed-and-breakfast operations, and (in rare cases) rent controls. Specialized *urban redevelopment* ordinances have been adopted in some cities.

It is a virtual certainty that, over time, officials will interact with citizens who advocate for land use controls touching on new matters of local concern. Some may have long-term implications. Others are shorter term in their relevance, though not always predictably so, such as the intense demand several years ago for specialty regulation of electronic amusement centers (gaming arcades) – which were soon replaced by the gaming capability of home computer systems. When citizen demand arises for a new type of regulation, it is generally appropriate to communicate with state *municipal associations*, which will have other cities, villages, townships or counties as members. A subject matter thought to be unique in one community has often become a concern elsewhere as well. Thinking such matters through on a more regional or statewide basis can often be helpful, regardless of the specific approach ultimately decided on locally.

G.   Last Words

While zoning may be the most powerful land use control tool, this should not be viewed as detracting from the importance of the several *non-zoning* land use control regulations. While zoning has a material and broad impact on the health, safety, and general welfare of the entire community, construction codes similarly impact the health and safety of all individuals throughout the community by promoting the physical integrity of buildings. A very large share of homes in the country are situated either in platted subdivisions or condominium subdivisions. The regulations applicable to subdivision developments have for decades ensured that they are designed to provide organized living arrangements ideal for residential, that provide neighborhood enclaves, free of commercial and industrial impacts, throughout metropolitan areas of the United States. Environmental regulations and sign and billboard regulations seek both to protect human safety and to provide aesthetic protections that enhance quality of life. Historic preservation regulations attempt to retain for future posterity the architectural and other thoughts and life ways of the past. Taken together, all of the non-zoning regulations discussed in this chapter subtly, but significantly, work together to make our local communities better places to live.

H. Now on to the Local Story

If this chapter has invigorated your appetite for practical legal guidance, you can continue the story by exploring the law applicable to your own particular form of local government, and the law of your particular state. Suggested storytellers include both your local government attorney and your state's local government association, which offers training for community officials. Your local story might begin with responses to these questions:

1. How are construction and maintenance codes enforced in our community? Are these codes uniform among communities throughout the state?
2. What types of condominium are permissible in our state? (such as apartment style, pod or cluster style, site condominiums)
3. Do local governments in our state have uniform regulations for storm water protection?
4. Has our community needed to amend its regulation of advertising signs in light of the Supreme Court's 2015 decision in *Reed v. Town of Gilbert, Ariz?*

Notes

1. This reference is to the novel entitled, the *Strange Case of Dr Jekyll and Mr Hyde*, written by Robert Louis Stevenson, and first published in 1886.
2. 535 U.S. 302, 122 S. Ct. 1465, 152 L. Ed. 2d 517 (2002).
3. *Reed v. Town of Gilbert, Ariz.*, 135 S. Ct. 2218 (2015), *City of Ladue v. Gilleo*, 512 U.S. 43 (1994), *Metromedia, Inc. v. City of San Diego*, 453 U.S. 490 (1981).
4. Brown and Rowberry, Historic Preservation Law (in a nutshell), Chap. 1, 2014, West Academic Publishing.
5. *Id.*
6. *Penn Central Transportation Co. v. City of New York*, 438 U.S. 104 (1978).

Chapter 11

Interlocal Agreements

The overwhelming majority of states permit two or more local governments to join forces for the purpose of providing services or engaging in a cooperative venture. These arrangements may involve a transfer of authority from one local government to another, such as a township authorizing a city to provide one or more services. Or it may involve the creation of a new entity, such as a water authority to operate a system serving customers in all participating local governments. By and large, these joint arrangements transfer only discrete authority, with each community retaining its legislative and other broad authorities. In other words, the general practice is to create an interlocal arrangement to perform a narrow function (such as provide public water service) rather than make a wholesale transfer of responsibility for most or all functions to another entity.

For an historical perspective, prior to World War II, the provision of services to accommodate growth and development occurred very simply. In that earlier time, when growth in urban cities reached the limits of city boundaries, and there was a continued demand for growth, there was no need to consider entering into an interlocal arrangement. Instead, those interested in new development were accommodated by the city extending its borders into the adjacent territory. That is, it was common for older urban cities to merely *expand their boundaries* to encompass the area to be newly developed. This process is referred to as *annexation*. The older urban city simply *annexed* relevant parts of an adjacent, typically more rural, town to accommodate new development, and for all purposes the annexed land became a part of the city. The newly expanded city would then extend its existing utility and transportation systems, and its police, fire, and library services, into the annexed areas. The net effect was that, rather than two local governments combining for the provision of services, the city merely expanded its boundaries, and the area in which services were newly provided became part of a single enlarged city, rather than ending up with an older city and newly developing local governments.

After World War II, annexation began to be used less frequently. Rather, the rural towns adjacent to cities have accommodated new development by themselves becoming more urbanized suburban cities, villages, and townships. Nonetheless, there has often been a need to call on the older city to provide services outside the city border in the newly developing suburbs. In other words, the same facilities and services that would have been extended to serve new development *within a city expanded by annexation* are now often *extended by joint venture* to serve new development *outside* the city, in newly formed or expanded "suburban" communities.

Various names are given to these modern cooperative arrangements, such as "intergovernmental cooperation agreements" or, for purposes of this chapter, *"interlocal agreements."*

A.   Parties to Interlocal Agreements

State constitutions and laws have various approaches to interlocal agreements. A state might have several statutes that authorize interlocal agreements for assorted purposes, from enabling their use to provide a single type of service to permitting agreements to jointly provide any activity or service that the participating local governments are authorized to provide on their own. Looking around the country, these agreements are used for a wide variety of practical purposes. In some cases, interlocal agreements take advantage of the *financial strength of all participating communities*, facilitating the establishment of services and facilities that none of the members could have provided individually. Considering the cost of infrastructure and personnel, these joint arrangements facilitate fire and police protection, emergency service, public water, and sanitary sewer service, solid waste disposal, flood protection, and public transportation.

Even where economic feasibility would not prevent a single local government from providing a service or resource, the motivation for acting jointly may simply be to achieve *efficiency*. This rationale might apply to such services as building code administration, road maintenance, parks and recreation, zoning and planning services, purchasing, and tax assessing. As stated by the supreme court of one state, "Generally, 'Interlocal Agreements,' also referred to as 'Interlocal Cooperation Agreements,' are formal vehicles through which municipalities or political subdivisions may eliminate barriers imposed by jurisdictional lines in order to offer public services more efficiently."[1]

Interlocal arrangements may also arise from consumer demand disbursed over two or more communities, where there is an insufficient demand in any one of them. The point here is that a sufficient need for services and resources on the part of citizens and property owners may not exist within the political boundaries of one community, but may reach the required critical level of need within two or more local governments. The arrangement of these local governments becomes organized by an interlocal agreement.

A combining of local government forces for services and facilities arose after World War II as suburban development surrounding older urban communities formed "metropolitan" areas, with the older cities as hubs. Individual developing communities may have made a solo attempt to provide services for police, fire, library, and emergency response, only to later recognize that these services might be more feasible to continue – and certainly more efficient to operate – through a joint cooperation arrangement with other newly developing suburbs. In such cases, one alternative was for two or more developing suburbs to form an *entirely new system* to supply their service needs under an interlocal agreement.

If suburban communities were unable to provide service by combining with each other, they turned in a couple of alternative directions. One option was to look to *county* government to become the intergovernmental service provider for the region. This was achieved through interlocal agreements between the county and the developing suburban governments. As will be discussed below, this arrangement was extremely popular in both Los Angeles County and St. Louis County.

A second option was for newly developing suburban governments to look to the established systems in older urban cities. Throughout the country, there was a scenario of "urban centers" surrounded by newly developing communities, opening the door for urban cities with established service systems to go into the business of selling needed services to those in the newly developing towns. Such service arrangements typically involved an interlocal agreement under which the users in the surrounding towns became new *rate-paying customers*, served by the existing urban systems, which became regional enterprises. A variation on this theme was for suburban communities to *acquire or lease existing assets and operations* from the older city, to be used by a newly created entity which could then serve both the newly developing communities and some or all of the existing customers in the city.

A combination of these approaches developed over a period of some 150 years in Southeast Michigan, where Detroit at the peak of automotive industry expansion became a highly successful service hub for numerous developing suburbs and rural areas in what became the Detroit-metropolitan area. It all began in the mid-1800s, when Detroit established a public water system, soon followed by a sewage disposal service. Over the years, the city's water and sewer systems were repeatedly extended to serve developing local communities in surrounding areas, with the Detroit Water and Sewerage Department growing into one of the largest water and sewer utilities in the United States. Fairly recently, in 2014–2016, a new interlocal entity by the name of the Great Lakes Water Authority (GLWA) was formed to assume management of the Detroit metropolitan utility system, which by this time had expanded service to include 126 municipalities in seven counties.[2] GLWA leases its infrastructure from the city and is operated by an interlocal board consisting of representatives from the City of Detroit, the Counties of Oakland, Macomb, and Wayne, and the State of Michigan.

B. Involving the State as a Party to the Agreement

The use of interlocal cooperation has in some instances been enhanced by involving a state agency as a party to the agreement. For example, with legislative approval, a state agency may take responsibility for facilitating new development, such as constructing freeways or acquiring land to make a recreational project work. Similarly, for economic development purposes, it may be feasible for the state, participating in an interlocal arrangement, to commit in advance to provide funding for a project according to specific terms and conditions. For example, the state may provide funding for certain elements of infrastructure, such as parking, streets, or landscaping, as needed to achieve economic feasibility for a mixed-use development project with low and moderate income housing.

Taking an even wider view of the possible array of parties who may join forces, the State of New York has enacted state law authorizing local governments in the state to enter into interlocal agreements with governmental units from *other states*.[3] This authorization seems to really throw open the door, looking to broadly explore "mutual advantage, and thereby to provide services and facilities in a manner that will accord best with geographic, economic, population, and other factors influencing the needs and development of local communities."[4]

C. The Powers Given to Interlocal Entities

There are two very distinct power limitations that state legislatures have given to interlocal entities. Most commonly, an interlocal entity has only those powers that are *common to all member communities*. The interlocal entity is authorized to "cooperate together to do anything jointly that [member communities] could do individually."[5] A less frequently encountered approach used in some states is that the interlocal entity may exercise any authority *possessed by at least one member*, even if other member communities have no such authority individually. To determine which approach applies in a given state, it is important to be advised of the language contained in the specific state statute enabling the particular type of interlocal agreement.

D. Important Information Available in an Interlocal Agreement

A public official should not hesitate to read an interlocal agreement, either to figure out what is being proposed in a new arrangement or to learn more about an existing one. It is often helpful to understand what specifically to look for, so here is a list of some of the more important items:

- Who are the participating government *parties*?
- What are the stated *purposes*, such as the particular services to be provided and assets to be acquired and constructed?
- How will the interlocal entity be *financed*?

■ What *contributions* of money will be required from each local government, and when are the contributions due?

■ What are the ongoing *responsibilities* of each local government?

■ Who are the *customers* to be served, and are they all treated on equal terms?

■ How are *fees and charges* for customer services determined?

■ What is the maximum *duration* of the agreement, including any extensions?

■ When the agreement *terminates*, how will the assets of the interlocal entity be divided, and will each local government have an opportunity to make arrangements for alternative services?[6]

■ Is each local government able to adequately *represent and protect* its voters on the interlocal board, or are local governments bound to follow a simple majority determination that may not be in the best interest of some communities?

■ Are local governments – and their officials – adequately *insured* by policies that cover actions taken on behalf of the interlocal entity, in the event of claims made for contract liability, or for damage and injury due to negligence? Does the coverage include payment for *attorney fees* for the local governments and their officials if they are named as parties to a case?

E. Two Issues that Public Officials Should Not Overlook

The general orientation of this chapter has emphasized the advantages and versatility provided by interlocal agreements. These joint venture arrangements create opportunities and efficiencies that may not otherwise be feasible – from complicated enterprises such as utility systems to more routine functions such as procurement of vehicles and office supplies at volume pricing. Along with these positive characteristics of interlocal agreements, serious observations have been made revealing that there are issues on the other side of the ledger.[7] In terms of issues that may provide lessons for local government officials, two concerns relating to interlocal agreements will be discussed.

One concern arises from the self-evident point that interlocal arrangements typically expand the constituency and geography of the people and properties service. In other words, if two equally-sized local governments enter into an arrangement, the constituency and geography served will be twice the size. This threatens one of the key advantages of local government policy-making, namely that *those shaping local policy are closer to the people bound by it*. By adding constituency and geography, interlocal agreements tend to move control *farther away from the people*.

A second concern for local officials to consider is the potential for interlocal agreements to impair the political *accountability* of elected officials to their local government voters. In some cases, important decisions may be made by interlocal entities that conflict with the interests of one or more constituent local governments.

1. Regulation Close to the People

There is certainly a legitimate concern that interlocal agreements have the potential of diluting an essential advantage of "local" government by moving control *farther away from the people*.

The focus of Chapter 1 was on the legal character and structure of a "local government," and its relationship with state and federal governments. That discussion quoted a well-respected treatise on *Municipal Corporations*:

> The American people have always acted upon the deep-seated conviction that local matters can be better regulated by the people of the locality than by the state or central authority . . . the fundamental maxim in the American system of government that the *nearer the officers are to the people* they represent, the more easily and readily are reached the evils that result from political corruption and the more speedy and certain the cure. Local self-government is, thus, a guaranty of individual liberty.[8]

The long-standing principle has been that, to the extent possible, *there should be local control over matters of local concern*. In this chapter on interlocal agreements, it is worth briefly circling back to that important point. Local self-government, undertaken with *regulators close to the people*, supports *individual liberty*. The question now at hand is whether this critical characteristic of local government authority might be undermined by the use of interlocal agreements.

In considering this question, we need to remain mindful that interlocal agreements are generally limited in their scope and subject matter. That is, the object in nearly all interlocal arrangements is to accomplish the provision of one, or a very few, services. Rarely do these arrangements involve the whole-sale turnover of authority to another community in a joint venture, or to an interlocal entity. Interlocal agreements are not intended to serve as broad sub-stitutes for the representative government provided in each of the respective constituent entities.[9] Also of significance is the point that intergovernmen-tal entities are limited in the *type of authority* they may exercise. Specifically, unless enabled by the state legislature, they may only exercise *administrative* authority on behalf of the constituent entities, and not *legislative* authority. So, for example, while an intergovernmental transit entity might have authority to establish bus routes within the entire intergovernmental service area, it would not have authority to rezone a neighborhood in a member community in order to allow a new bus station. Overall, the concern that the typical use of interlocal agreements will materially impair the purpose of local government may not have an especially alarming practical impact in actual application. Nonetheless, the concern of a potential erosion of local control contains a ker-nel of truth. When considering the pros and cons of adopting a new interlocal agreement, public officials might add to their check-list of issues the question of whether the proposed arrangement will have sufficient benefit to offset any loss of local control.

2. Political Accountability to Voters

Governance of an interlocal entity is important. This may become most obvi-ous in terms of whether there is an efficient and effective means of operating the intergovernmental service or facility. More subtle, but every bit as import-ant, is whether governance of the interlocal entity has been structured so as to fulfill the *legislative* responsibilities *each local government owes to its voting constituency*.

Successful administrative skills may allow the venture to operate in a finan-cially responsible way, while delivering services consistent with the vision of the interlocal agreement. But *financial* responsibility is distinct from *political* responsibility to voters, which raises issues more difficult to recognize and measure. Voters in each local community elect representatives to make deci-sions *in the interest of the respective local community and its people*. But at the interlocal level, decisions will be made *in pursuit of the broader interlocal entity's overall best interests*, with the interests of individual local communities likely being secondary. Voters in those individual communities may perceive that some decisions of the interlocal entity, although *favorable to the interlocal venture as a whole*, in fact *conflict* with the interests of their own individual community. For example, optimizing an interlocal transportation system's routing for maximum system-wide efficiency may result in certain individual communities receiving substandard (or downright insufficient) coverage. While such routing might be in the interest of the joint entity considered as a whole, the interlocal entity would be exercising government power in a manner that undermines the voting rights of electors in the low-service areas.[10] In other words, it would arguably be *failing to adequately represent* the interests of each participating local government.

Presumably, the political responsibility conflict has a greater likelihood of occurring where there are numerous local government members in the interlocal arrangement. For example, one report of an Advisory Commission on Intergovernmental Relations (which ceased operating in the 1960s) disclosed the extensive use of interlocal contracts between Los Angeles County, California and local government entities within the county. It indicated that in 1959, there were 887 contracts between cities and the County, covering all manner of services – with one or more cities contracting to have practically all governmental services provided by the County.[11] The same Advisory Commission report indicates that 81 of the 98 municipalities in St. Louis County, Missouri signed a total of 241 contracts for the provision of municipal services by the county, and the City of Cleveland, Ohio had 30 contracts with 12 of its suburbs.[12] With such large numbers of local governments, with some – perhaps due to size and financial contribution to the venture – having greater leverage in decision-making, it is a fair bet that, over time, the interests of some individual local governments – perhaps those making smaller financial contributions and having less leverage – will not align with the interests of the interlocal entity as a whole.

The takeaway here this is that, during the negotiations creating an interlocal entity, *care must be taken to ensure that interlocal decisions will not materially undermine the accountability of participating local governments to their voters.* A conscious effort should be made, to the extent feasible, to confirm that the agreement makes every effort to require the interlocal authority to give due consideration to the unique interests of each member local government. Ideally, there should be an identifiable *method* or *mechanism* to prevent action by the interlocal entity which is actually in material conflict with the interests of certain member local governments.

3. Weighing the Advantages and Potential Disadvantages

The potential downsides discussed above must be weighed against the prospective advantages likely to be achieved through the use of interlocal agreements. When negotiating terms, beneficial efforts can be made to minimize encroachment on local control, and to avoid governance structures that might problematically dilute the accountability of interlocal officials to local government electors.

Officials might ask whether there are any realistic action to take if it appears that an interlocal entity is making decisions that conflict with the important interests of their local government and its voters. The first question is whether the local government is entitled to withdraw from the interlocal agreement at the point when such a problem is discovered. Assuming there is an opt-out provision, the next question is whether it is actually feasible to find or create an alternative interlocal arrangement after withdrawing from one that resulted in conflict. If there are no other *existing* interlocal agreements that would be receptive to new participants, it is likely that officials would have a "long and winding road" to navigate in order to *create* an alternative interlocal entity after escaping from one that is well-established in the region. Yet, it is not out of the question. For example, even in the Southeast Michigan region, where a single interlocal entity operates a regional utility system with more than 100 municipalities as customers, a relatively small group of local governments formed a new interlocal entity to provide themselves with alternative utility service.[13]

F. Last Words

In the final analysis, interlocal agreements have the potential to provide services, facilities, and efficiencies that might otherwise be difficult or impossible to achieve by one local government acting alone. These agreements bring to the table individuals with a broader range of knowledge and experience, and also introduce the prospect of a greater and more cost-effective financing capacity. When local governments are willing and able to combine forces with the state, additional financing and other advantages become possible. On balance, the cooperative approach to services and facilities provided by interlocal agreements can be evaluated as a net positive, which presumably explains their popularity. Yet this chapter has also presented cautions about theoretical downsides to the use of interlocal arrangements. The cautions are not intended to discourage the use of this powerful tool, but they should inspire vigilance and creativity when considering and negotiating new interlocal agreements.

G. Now on to the Local Story

If this chapter has invigorated your appetite for practical legal guidance, you can continue the story by exploring the law applicable to your own particular form of local government, and the law of your particular state. Suggested storytellers include both your local government attorney and your state's local government association, which offers training for community officials. Your Local Story might begin with responses to these questions:

1. Does our state permit interlocal agreements? If so:

   a. Are they authorized under the state constitution, state statute, or both?
   b. Are they authorized only for specified purposes, or is it a broad authorization? (A "broad" authorization might, for example, allow local governments to enter into interlocal agreements to provide any service or facility that each party to the agreement could provide on its own.)
   c. By state statute or court decision, can an interlocal agreement make provision for any service or facility that at least one member could provide independently, or is the agreement limited to services and facilities that all members have independent authority to provide?

2. Is our community currently a party to any interlocal agreements? If so, with regard to each one:

   a. Who are the other local government parties?
   b. What is the service or facility provided under the agreement?
   c. What is the reason our community is a party to the agreement? For example, is it because it would not be economically feasible to provide the service or facility on our own, or perhaps because it achieves efficiency?
   d. How is our community represented in the agreement? For example, is our community a member of the governing board of the interlocal entity? Does the arrangement give us enough authority to require that we are receiving fair treatment?

e. Does our community pay for a service provided under the agreement? If so, how is the fee or other payment determined?
f. Does the agreement have an expiration date? If so, what choices would our community have to obtain the service upon expiration of the agreement?

Notes

1. *City of Carmel v. Steele*, 865 N.E.2d 612, 620 (Indiana) (2007).
2. See https://detroitmi.gov/departments/water-and-sewerage-department/resources (accessed in 2020).
3. See 25 New York Jurisprudence, Second Edition, § 317. Interlocal agreements with governmental units of other states (accessed in 2020).
4. *Id.*
5. *Goreham v. Des Moines Metropolitan Area Solid Waste Agency*, 179 N.W.2d 449 (Iowa, 1970).
6. *City of Grandview Heights v. City of Columbus*, 174 Ohio St. 473, 23 Ohio Op. 2d 117, 190 N.E.2d 453 (1963).
7. Baker, Gillette, & Schleicher, *Local Government Law Cases and Materials*, 5th ed., Foundation Press, pp. 829, and following pages (2015); Reynolds, O.B., *Local Government Law*, 5th ed., West Academic, p. 45 (2019); Mandelker, and others, *State and Local Government in a Federal System*, LexisNexis, 7th ed., p. 265 (2010); Frug, Ford & Barron, *Local Government Law Cases and Materials*, 5th Ed, West, pp. 538–40 (2010).
8. McQuillin's Municipal Corporations, § 1:40 (3rd ed.) (accessed in 2020).
9. There are interlocal arrangements with Los Angeles County in the so-called Lakewood plan in which practically all services are transferred to the county. See *Report of the Advisory Commission on Intergovernmental Relations, Metropolitan America: Challenge to Federalism*, printed in Frug, Ford & Barron, *Local Government Law Cases and Materials*, 5th ed, West, pp. 539 (2010).
10. *Education/Instruccion, Inc. v. Moore*, 503 F.2d 1187 (2nd Cir. 1974).
11. See note 9, above.
12. *Id.*
13. Within the southeast Michigan area served by the Great Lakes Water Authority, an interlocal agreement was entered into by the Ypsilanti Community Utilities Authority (YCUA), which provides water and wastewater services to the City of Ypsilanti, Charter Township of Ypsilanti, Pittsfield Township, Augusta Township, Sumpter Township and Superior Township. Moreover, YCUA contracts with an additional separate authority known as the Western Townships Utilities Authority (WTUA) to provide wastewater treatment services for the Townships of Canton, Northville, and Plymouth. See http://www.ycua.org/about.htm (accessed in 2020).

Chapter 12

Eminent Domain and Regulatory Takings

"Eminent domain" and "regulatory takings" are two closely related subjects that are not widely understood by the general public. Even though this material is somewhat technical in nature, it has been included in the book for two important reasons. First, the goal is to provide insights into these two doctrines which can easily arise and have potential for substantial economic implications. Second, local officials without a basic understanding of these doctrines run the risk of being ensnared in unsuspected controversy.

In nearly all scenarios leading to eminent domain and regulatory taking cases, officials exercise their authority in the public interest, with no expectation of adverse response. However, with these doctrines, the possibility of controversy can never be ruled out.

A.   Introductory Overviews

Eminent domain is a power that government *intentionally* exercises to acquire private property from an owner who has not been willing to sell on the terms offered by the government. While this power is almost always exercised for worthwhile purposes, it occasionally leads to heated debate.

A *regulatory taking* case typically arises after the government establishes a regulation on the use of private property to accomplish a legitimate purpose.

The government then learns that it has *unintentionally* caused one or more private properties to be significantly burdened.

Both subjects are "joined at the hip" by what is known as the "Takings Clause" of the Fifth Amendment to the U.S. Constitution, which states that "private property [shall not] be taken for public use, without just compensation."

1. Summary of Eminent Domain

Eminent domain is the power of a sovereign government to acquire private property for public use. Historically, the "sovereign" was the king or queen. All land was ultimately owned by the "crown," and could be repurposed as the king or queen saw fit. One of the remarkable innovations in the United States Constitution was the establishment of a government without a monarch or other all-powerful head of state. Yet the concept of the government as a "sovereign" has survived. The federal government, and each of the state governments, is considered to be a sovereign, each with the implicit power to requisition property for public use, subject to the federal and respective state constitutions. Indeed, a significant characteristic of the power of "eminent domain" is that it can be exercised *even where a private owner is not willing* to voluntarily part with the property, and thus the potential for controversy.

Contrary to federal and state governments, local governments are not considered to be "sovereigns." So, a local exercise of eminent domain requires the state to delegate the authority to exercise this power for specified purposes.

The manner in which the power of eminent domain is exercised is straightforward. After unsuccessfully attempting to secure a voluntary sale of the property, the *government commences a case against the owner* of the property being taken. In the papers filed with the court by the government, various types of relief may be requested, but the two most fundamental requests for relief are these: first, the government asks the court to grant a judgment transferring to the government ownership of the property needed for public use; and second, the government asks the court – typically through a jury – to determine and award to the property owner an amount of money that will *fairly compensate* the owner for the forced transfer of the property.

As explained in greater detail in Chapter 5, the first 10 amendments to the U.S. Constitution (the Bill of Rights) were intended to expressly enumerate protections of the people against actions of the *federal* government. The fifth of these amendments (the Fifth Amendment), includes the basic protection that "private property [shall not] be taken for public use, without just compensation." This provision is known as the "Takings Clause." As indicated in the language of the Fifth Amendment itself, the Takings Clause protects the people in two ways. First, private property may be taken *only* for *public* use. Second, when property is taken by the government, *just compensation* must be paid to the owner. These two components of the Takings Clause will be discussed in greater detail below.

As interpreted by the Supreme Court over the years, the Fourteenth Amendment, which was ratified nearly a century after the Bill of Rights, has the effect of extending the "public use" and "just compensation" requirements of the Fifth Amendment's Takings Clause to protect the people from actions and regulations of the *states*, including local governments. In all 50 states, primarily by *state constitution*, and in one state by statute,[1] states have adopted their own counterparts to the Takings Clause to expressly provide protection parallel to, but not precisely the same as, the Fifth Amendment.

While most may view the topic of eminent domain as being low on the hierarchy of excitement, the 2005 United States Supreme Court decision in *Kelo v. City of New London, Connecticut,*[2] involving a significant exercise of eminent domain, created a national stir. The Supreme Court's decision in the case, interpreting the federal "public use" requirement, turned out to be broadly unpopular with the public. In its wake, constitutions and laws in a large number of states were amended to restrict the exercise of eminent domain in the manner permitted by the Court in *Kelo* (which also will be discussed at length below).

Although the eminent domain power does not directly touch the lives of most people, the reality is that this subject is of major importance to both the government and to those private owners whose property is taken. *For the government*, there are many crucial projects, such as the construction of highways, which simply could not be accomplished in most cases without the ability to acquire specific properties where owners refuse to voluntarily sell. Indeed, the attempt to build a relatively straight highway could be entirely scuttled by one or a few private owners. The importance of eminent domain, and the Fifth Amendment, *for private owners* is that this power gives government the right to force an owner to give up private property, and the Takings Clause serves as a constitutional shield from a government extraction of property for purposes other than public use, or without sufficient compensation to the owner.

2. Summary of Regulatory Takings

The subject of "regulatory takings" is likewise anything but dull. Indeed, a considerable number of lawsuits *against local governments* are filed under this legal doctrine every year. Particular attention should be focused on the point that a regulatory takings case is *filed by property owners against the government*, which is the reverse of eminent domain cases. For this reason, while eminent domain cases are often referred to as "condemnation" cases, regulatory takings cases have been referred to as "inverse condemnation" cases because the property owner sues the government under the authority of the Takings Clause.

Suits by property owners in regulatory takings cases do not focus on a *government-intended* acquisition of private property. Rarely is a claim made that the government had the objective of taking possession of the property in the case. Rather, these suits arise when *the government regulates the use* of property, often by the adoption of a zoning regulation imposing a restriction. The dispute underlying a regulatory takings lawsuit is based on the allegation by a property owner that the *regulation goes too far* in limiting the use of the property. So, the owner sues the government claiming that the overly burdensome regulation is *invalid* because the government has *effectively taken possession of the property*, as if by eminent domain, *but has failed to pay just compensation*.

B. Eminent Domain

The Merriam-Webster dictionary defines eminent domain as the "right of a government to take private property for public use by virtue of the superior dominion of the sovereign power over all lands within its jurisdiction." State governments, as "sovereigns," have the power to make broad use of eminent domain as needed for purposes of public use. Local governments, not themselves sovereigns, may only use this power for the limited purposes delegated to them by the state.

1. The Purposes of Eminent Domain

As a practical matter, when a local government needs private property for a project, such as a street improvement, the government will normally proceed in the first instance like a typical buyer and approach the owner with an offer, seeking a voluntarily sale. It is interesting to compare two types of *unsuccessful negotiations* with a prospective seller: on the one hand where the negotiation is between *two private parties*, and then where the *government* is negotiating to buy. If an owner ultimately refuses to sell to a *private* buyer, that is typically the end of the story. The buyer will need to consider other properties. But this is not the case with a local government if it has been authorized to utilize the power of eminent domain for the particular acquisition. The power of eminent domain *permits the local government to acquire private property for a public use in spite of the owner's rejection of all offers the government is willing to make.* This is a huge authorization. Upon rejection of its offer to purchase, the government can activate this power to compel the owner to relinquish possession of the property. This is referred to as the government's right to "take" private property for public use, and results in an adversarial court proceeding between the government and the property owner.

One of the most common purposes served by the exercise of eminent domain is the construction or expansion of streets and highways. In most cases, this type of construction will require the government to acquire interests in numerous separate properties along the course of the highway, which typically compels the government to deal with an equal number of property owners. Even if we assume that a large number of these owners will be willing to voluntarily part with their property on mutually agreeable terms, government offers to purchase are routinely rejected by at least a handful of owners. There are some who simply do not wish to give up their property. Others may hold out for an amount of money slightly in excess of the fair value of the property. And then there are those rare owners who may recognize that their property is inescapably needed for a project, and hope to leverage this fact for a sale well in excess of market value. In the latter cases, in the absence of the power of eminent domain, the government would be at the mercy of the opportunistic holdouts. It would need to make the choice of either abandoning or redesigning its project or making a purchase at a grossly inflated price. Of course, when the government pays an inflated price, the unfairness is passed on to its taxpayers. This is where eminent domain intervenes. It protects taxpayers, by enabling the government to proceed with its planned public project, and while objecting property owners are not able to keep their property, it guarantees that they at least receive just compensation for the loss.

Other than streets and highways, common purposes for which the government may exercise the power of eminent domain include the acquisition of property for public parks, water lines, sanitary sewer lines, drainage facilities, and the like. In all of these particular examples, the government acquires the property, improves it for the intended purpose, and continues to own it. If the government were instead to acquire property by eminent domain and then transfer it for *private* use or benefit, the former owner could raise the constitutional issue of "public use" and in some cases prevent the government from using eminent domain for the acquisition. However, there are circumstances in which the government may acquire property by eminent domain, with the view of transferring it for private use or benefit, while still complying with the constitutional requirement of "public use."

It is important to note that *having* the power of eminent domain does not mean that it *must* be exercised when an owner refuses to voluntarily sell. Using this power routinely requires the initiation of a lawsuit against a property owner, which can be expensive and burdensome to all involved. Government officials also need to be aware that members of the public frequently sympathize with the private property owner, who may have a legitimate reason for refusing to sell. The short lesson from this is that there may be *political consequences* to taking property by eminent domain. A brief hypothetical may be helpful here.

Let us assume that a local government desires to establish a park, and its highest priority location has been determined based on the legitimate reason that it will provide the maximum accessibility for use. The government makes an offer to purchase the property, but the private owner refuses to sell because the land has been in the owner's family for many generations, and in fact everyone in the area is well aware of this multi-generational ownership. The local government will need to weigh the favorable qualities of the desired park site against both the harm that may result to the private property owner, and also the *appearance of being overbearing* if a sale is forced by eminent domain. An alternative park site may suddenly rise to the top of the priority list!

2. The Two Key Takings Clause Provisions That Protect People's Rights

The two overarching constitutional issues to examine in eminent domain cases are:

1. the "public use" requirement; and
2. the "just compensation requirement.

So far in this discussion, the exercise of eminent domain appears to be straightforward. But now we will complicate the picture somewhat by taking a closer look at the two key constitutional provisions mentioned above. These two provisions, both from the Fifth Amendment Takings Clause, are the "public use" protection and the "just compensation" protection. There are subtle complexities infused into the public use and just compensation protections that make this subject more interesting, but more difficult to grasp.

a.   The "Public Use" Protection

The *public use* protection is not an issue that frequently arises in eminent domain cases. However, when it does become an issue, it has the potential of totally derailing a property acquisition.

Certainly, the concept of "public use" would seem to be straightforward by reading of the words. However, the Supreme Court decided in its wisdom that there is actually more to the story. Indeed, the Court clarified in 1984 that, "this Court long ago rejected any literal requirement that condemned property be put into use for the general public."[3] Alright, if "public use" does not actually mean that the property must be "used by the general public," then just what does it mean?

When a local government files its eminent domain case to seize a property that will be *transferred for private use*, the property's owner may raise the "public use" protection under *federal* or *state* law. Under the *federal* requirement, the meaning of "public use" would be determined based on the Supreme Court's interpretation of the Fifth Amendment, applicable to local governments under the Fourteenth Amendment. Under the respective *state* requirements, the meaning of "public use" would be determined based on the interpretation of *state* constitution and law by the state supreme court. A property owner can challenge under either or both standards, but the claim the property owner is likely to assert will depend on whichever rule, federal or state, provides the most protection to the property owner.

Because there are so many meanings under the laws of the several states, we will focus on the federal rule established by the Supreme Court. Fortunately, this rule provides a fairly straightforward interpretation. Specifically, the federal rule is that the *court will simply defer to the legislative branch of government (congress or a state legislature) to determine whether the purpose for the exercise of eminent domain is for "public use."* If the legislature has delegated to a local government the authority to undertake a particular type of project, and the local government has the authority to use the power of eminent domain to accomplish that project – *even if the property will be transferred to a private interest for use* – the Court has concluded that this satisfies the "public use" requirement of the Fifth Amendment. This is the present rule, followed for over a half-century. However, stay tuned! Considering the separate opinions written by some of the justices on the Court, it will not be surprising if the Supreme Court takes the opportunity in a future case to reconsider the meaning of "public use."

The undemanding rule applied by the Supreme Court during the last half-century has not prevented states from applying their own *state law* rules for the public use protection. And indeed, there are widely divergent rules among the states on the meaning of the term "public use." To be clear, a state is not authorized to countermand the Supreme Court on the meaning of public use when the government's action is challenged under the Fifth and Fourteenth Amendments to the U.S. Constitution. However, each state is free to provide a *stricter* definition of public use to be applied when a party asserts a public use challenge under *state* law and constitution. This state autonomy on the meaning of "public use" became particularly clear following the U.S. Supreme Court opinion in *Kelo*, a 2005 case that captivated the nation.[4]

Kelo involved the taking of several homes from long-time owners who refused the government's offer to purchase. They simply did not wish to part with their homes. Motivating the government's need for these residential properties was a major economic development project in New London, Connecticut, where the government had been able to secure most of the property needed for the project by voluntary sale. The acquisitions at issue in the case were those requiring the use of eminent domain. Following acquisition, these properties would be turned over for *private* development and use – which raised the "public use" question. As the eminent domain case progressed, the sympathy of the nation became more firmly supportive of the residential property owners who refused to sell their homes. They were seen as being subordinated to the business interests that would benefit from the economic development project.

In their challenge of the local government's use of eminent domain, the holdout homeowners relied on the *federal* public use protection. The Supreme Court's decision simply followed the long-established rule, concluding that, since the economic development objectives of the project, including the use of eminent domain, had been permitted under state law, the federal meaning of "public use" was satisfied. Consequently, in the face of overwhelming opposition of the media and the national public, the Court deferred to the legislature and allowed the use of eminent domain to take the properties at issue.

The national sentiment was so strongly opposed to the Court's decision that *more than half the states in the country* amended their state constitutions or laws in order to make it clear that the federal rule of total legislative deference on the meaning of public use would not apply in their states.[5] The real sticking point was the use of eminent domain to take property for conveyance to a private person in order to advance *economic development* objectives. Between protecting individuals in their private ownership rights, and allowing a state or local government to pursue economic development goals, the states have resoundingly chosen to protect private property interests, at least in the eminent domain context.

In the final analysis for local governments, when public officials are informed that property to be taken by eminent domain is proposed to be transferred to a private entity, the officials should confirm that the local government attorney has concluded that there would be compliance under both federal and state rules governing the public use protection.

b. The "Just Compensation" Protection

While "public use" is not an issue that frequently arises in eminent domain cases, the *just compensation* issue is present in virtually every case. In the first papers filed with the court in an eminent domain case, the government makes two requests: first, the government asks the court to transfer ownership; and second, the government seeks a determination of just compensation – the amount to be paid to the property owner in exchange for the property.

Every exercise of eminent domain must include the payment of just compensation to the owner of the property being taken. Specifically, the property owner is entitled to be paid *fair market value* for the property. The customary thought is that the only important aspect of "just" compensation is that the property owner must be paid *at least* an amount equal to fair market value. Rarely do we consider that "fair" might also have a "maximum" component for the government. But in an eminent domain case, it is the *public* (taxpayers) who will pay the price determined by the jury. It is important that the compensation paid is in a *just amount*, not merely *to the individual* whose property is taken, but also to those taxpayers.[6] So, the just compensation calculation attempts to follow the "goldilocks" rule: the award to the property owner should be an amount which is not too low, and not too high, but "just" right.

The property owner must be paid "fair market value" for the property taken.

Fair market value is measured based on the property's "highest and best use."

The "fair market value" awarded in a just compensation case is measured based upon the property's "highest and best use." Both of these phrases carry heavily technical legal meanings, to the extent that conveying a detailed understanding would require diving headlong into definitions, and using hair-splitting legalese. However, a practical way of approaching "fair market value" and "highest and best use" is for the reader to conceptually step into the shoes of a seller and buyer in a real world private sale and purchase transaction, and consider the types of things that would influence the ultimate agreement on a mutually fair price.

Determining fair market value for real estate on the open market customarily involves an investigation of *recent sale prices of comparable properties.* Of course, no two properties are perfectly "comparable," so once a list of reasonably similar property sales has been produced, it is necessary to make *adjustments* to account for the differences between each comparable property and the property to be purchased. For example, adjustments might be made based on a more or less favorable location, zoning, size, services (such as available public transportation), amenities (such as water features and parks) and whatever other factors a buyer might consider relevant.

The "highest and best use" factor requires the government to pay fair market value for *the most valuable use* of the property that is *lawful* and *reasonably feasible.* For example, if a property is being used for farming, but could be used either for a shopping center or for farming, we can assume that the shopping center use would be more valuable on a per-acre basis. So, if a property being used for farming is zoned to permit a shopping center, a knowledgeable real-world buyer and seller would likely agree to a higher price than could be charged for an identical property zoned purely for farming purposes. (This presumes that reasonable demand for a shopping center can be anticipated in the foreseeable future.) Similarly, even where a property is zoned *and* being used for farming, if there is a *reasonable possibility* that the property could be rezoned and feasibly used for a shopping center, this too could boost the open market price agreed to by a knowledgeable buyer and seller.

Of course, these are only the major "just compensation" concepts. There are many other rules and approaches that a court might apply in determining the amount of just compensation due for a particular property, and the rules themselves vary from state-to-state. In addition, a special set of rules apply where the government is merely seeking to acquire a *part* of a property, leaving the remainder of the property to the owner. Various other circumstances likewise warrant special rules, such as the payment of additional compensation for "moving expenses" to an owner who is operating a business concern on the property that will have to be reopened at a new location. States appear uniformly to reject "sentimental value" as a basis for claiming that additional compensation is due, owing to the difficulty of reliably measuring the worth of an individual's sentiment.

Clearly, the calculation of "fair market value" has a subjective character. Consequently, when an eminent domain case goes to trial, the government and the property owner are likely to have very different expectations on the question of fair market value (each backed by the opinion of an expert appraiser). If the parties are unable to reach a settlement prior to trial, the decision on value is typically left for a jury to decide, based on legal guidelines provided by the court.

3. Securing Possession of a Property in Order to Meet a Project Deadline

If an offer to purchase is rejected by the property owner, the local government must decide whether to initiate its eminent domain case. And there's the "rub." Pursuing a lawsuit to completion may take more than a year. The worst case scenario might be a highway project where the government is acquiring land just ahead of active construction, and contracts have already been signed for the portion of the project that will require the use of the property which is yet to be acquired. If the lawsuit is just getting started, this could entirely stop a project in its tracks. Now what?

If a property owner understands that the government is in a weak position due to the urgent need to acquire the property, negotiations on just compensation could tilt decidedly in favor of the property owner's position. Acquiring the property in time to stay on schedule may require the government to pay a premium price – to the detriment of taxpayers. Fortunately, state legislatures around the country have recognized that paying "windfall" prices to such property owners can't be squared with the overall interests of the public. The remedy devised for resolving this problem is a levelling of the playing field by allowing the government to secure possession of the property *before* the trial. Thus, the need to complete a trial in order to determine just compensation will have no bearing on whether the government's project is able to proceed on schedule. The laws that enable this arrangement have been referred to as "quick-take" statutes.

The "quick-take" arrangement is accomplished through a wide variety of legislative schemes among the several states. Generally, as a condition to gaining early possession, the government must pay money to the property owner at the time the right to possession is given to the government. The amount of such payment is based on a specified formula provided by state law. For example, the government may be required to make advance payment of the price determined to be fair by the government's own expert appraiser. If an additional amount is ultimately awarded by the jury, this excess amount must then be paid at the end of the trial. In some states, the government must post a bond to ensure full payment.

Overall, the quick-take statutes seem to balance the interests of all parties.

C. Regulatory Takings

There are many *regulatory taking* cases filed each year against local governments throughout the country.

So, gaining a better understanding of this doctrine would make a great deal of sense.

It appears to be universally acknowledged that the guarantee of just compensation in the Fifth Amendment Takings Clause was written to apply only to instances in which the government *intentionally takes* private property through the power of eminent domain. Yet in 1922 (about 131 years after the Fifth Amendment was ratified) the famous U.S. Supreme Court Justice, Oliver Wendell Holmes, expanded the meaning.

In the 1922 case, Justice Holmes wrote that when a *regulation* "goes too far" in *adversely impacting the use and value* of private property, it can amount *to a government "taking"* of the property.[7] This novel interpretation of the Takings Clause has applied ever since, and is referred to as the "regulatory takings" doctrine. It is important for public officials to understand its fundamentals, as cases filed based on this doctrine represent a meaningful portion of the total number of lawsuits filed against local governments each year – and, considering that the local government had no intent of "taking" the property when it merely enacted its regulation, the property owner's assertion of a taking claim can come as a big surprise to some officials.

The first step is to clearly distinguish regulatory takings from eminent domain. Recall that an eminent domain taking is commenced by the government *intentionally* setting out to take private property from an owner. The *government initiates a lawsuit* seeking a transfer of the property from the private owner to the government, and asking for a determination of the just compensation to be paid to the property owner as required under federal and state Takings Clauses.

In contrast, a regulatory taking scenario might surface without the local government having known that its regulation would "go too far" in impacting a particular property owner's rights. The government will have set out to achieve a legitimate objective, such as protecting a residential neighborhood from the impacts of intense commercial or heavy industrial uses. But lo, and behold! A *private property owner might file a regulatory takings lawsuit* against the government, asserting that the *particular regulation* that the government enacted to achieve its legitimate objective had the *effect* of imposing such a substantial burden on the owner's use of property that it was equivalent to the government filing an eminent domain case.

It is important to note at this juncture that nowhere in the Constitution is there a prohibition on the government *taking* private property. Indeed, it is the presumed understanding that the federal and state governments inherently have the power to take property for public use. But the Fifth Amendment directs that, if private property is going to be taken, the government must pay *just compensation. When a local government enacts a regulation, it has no intention of paying just compensation.* So when the claim is made that the *effect* of the regulation is the *equivalent* of an exercise of eminent domain, the regulatory takings doctrine empowers the *property owner to start a lawsuit* claiming that the application of the regulation causes a taking of the owner's private property, and that the government has failed to pay the required just compensation. Again, there is no constitutional prohibition against the federal or state governments taking private property – the prohibition is only against taking private property *without paying just compensation.* So, the lawsuit filed by the property owner asserts that because the effect of the regulation is essentially *equivalent* to an exercise of eminent domain, its application to the owner's private property is an *unconstitutional taking because the government has not made the required payment of just compensation.*

As a teaching hypothetical, we can consider a variation on a famous 1978 taking case in New York City.[8] Let us assume that a person buys a two-story building formerly used as a bank. The building is located at the main downtown intersection of a major city, and was designed and constructed in the early 1900s with architectural characteristics which are now considered to be exemplars of important historical resources.[9] Let us also assume that the current owner acquired the building with the view of expanding its function and value by *adding eight additional stories over the existing two.* At the time of purchase, a ten-story building was permitted under the ordinances of the city, and there are other ten-story buildings at or near the same intersection. But as plans for the new construction were being prepared, the city enacted an *historic preservation ordinance,* declaring that a specified number of buildings in the city, including the former bank building, happen to be significant historic structures. The ordinance prohibits alteration of buildings within this classification unless a permit is granted by the city's historic commission. The new historic preservation ordinance authorizes a permit only if a proposed alteration would "preserve the essence of the historic resources." Note carefully that the ordinance does not make any provision for the payment of just compensation to an owner who is denied a permit, regardless of impact.

In this hypothetical, the owner of the building applied for but was denied a permit, with the commission commenting that the historic resources of the building are so important that such a dramatic change in the building could not be tolerated. The owner also sought, and was denied, every form of administrative relief available in the city, pertaining to the commission's denial. As a result, the owner was left with the two-story bank building as purchased. Although likely to be a profitable investment, it would produce nowhere near the return that would have been certain had the proposed addition been constructed as planned. In sum, the city's newly enacted historic preservation ordinance had the effect of reducing the owner's development rights to an equivalent extent as if the city had used its power of eminent domain to *take* all of the formerly developable space above the existing building – a space worth millions of dollars.

The Supreme Court has established a three-factor "balancing test" to review most regulatory taking claims. The test involves an analysis under each of three separate factors. The three factors are independently evaluated to determine whether, on balance, they signal that the regulation results in an unconstitutional taking.

The three factors are:

(1) whether the *character of the government's regulation* represents a good faith effort to achieve a legitimate objective, and whether the regulation permits a physical intrusion on the property (analogous to eminent domain);

(2) how severe is the *economic impact of the regulation* on the property; and

(3) to what extent does the regulation interfere with *reasonable investment-backed expectations*.

So, the owner initiates a *regulatory takings* case against the city. How will the court review this case? For most regulatory takings claims, the Supreme Court has established a "balancing test," which identifies three considerations to analyze. The results from the analysis of each of the three considerations are placed on a two-sided scale, with one side representing a "taking" and the other side "no taking." After weighing all three factors together, the balancing test will signal a violation of the Takings Clause only if the scale is heavily weighted-down on the "taking" side.

The three factors of the test present the following issues:

■ First, does the *character of the government's regulation* suggest a good faith effort to achieve a legitimate objective, and does the regulation permit a physical intrusion on the property?

■ Second, how severe is the *economic impact of the regulation* on the property – in other words, what is value of the property *with* and *without* the regulation applied?

■ Third, to what extent does the regulation interfere with *reasonable investment-backed expectations* – that is, would denying the payment of just compensation signal to the local real-estate market that making investments in this community would be so demoralizing that no future investments would be made?[10]

Based on the track record in decided cases around the country, these three factors, and particularly the last two, have left lawyers and judges "dancing on the head of a pin" in attempting to anticipate a conclusion in a regulatory takings scenario.

In our historic preservation hypothetical, applying the three-factor balancing test presents the usual, somewhat ambiguous challenge. Under the first factor, the character of this particular regulation should be deemed to signal "no taking." There was a good faith motive for the regulation, and it does not permit a physical intrusion on the private property at issue. Under the second factor, we find that the owner has been deprived of substantial property value. Yet the Supreme Court has not specified any objective standard that would allow a prediction on how severe a property value reduction must be in order to send a clear "taking" signal on the scale. Although the owner will certainly not profit *as much* as expected, there is no indication that the regulation leaves the owner worse off than before the purchase. So the second factor appears to be a "toss-up" in terms of a "taking" conclusion. The third factor is equally difficult to navigate to an undisputable conclusion. Certainly, the owner and others similarly situated would feel a degree of demoralization at having plans that were viable prior to the regulation crushed by the enactment of the city's regulation. But the Court has provided very little in the way of guidance on how much "demoralization" is "too much." Would it be reasonable for the owner and others to say they would make no other investments in the city as a result? The city would argue that the owner is still likely to make at least some profit in the use of the building – and the owner has not tried proposing a less dramatic change, which might be permissible under the new ordinance. Both sides have viable arguments, and the third factor may also be a "toss-up" in terms of a "taking" conclusion.

Overall, the owner's regulatory takings case against the government appears likely to be an uphill fight – but the city will unfortunately not be able to rest easy until it is safely concluded. There is simply too much subjective flexibility within the three-part balancing test for any outcome in a typical regulatory takings case to be a sure bet.

D. Last Words

From the perspective of a local government going about its daily business, *eminent domain* and *regulatory takings* are very different legal doctrines. Eminent domain will arise only when the government acts *intentionally* to take property needed for a project, while a regulatory takings claim may pop up at almost any time after the government has enacted a regulation impacting the use of property to accomplish a legitimate purpose. Yet these two doctrines are joined at the hip. Both present issues involving the taking of private property, and both involve court confrontations governed by the Takings Clause of the Fifth Amendment to the United States Constitution (as well as corresponding clauses of state constitutions). Both doctrines exist to bar the government from "forcing some people alone to bear public burdens which, in all fairness and justice, should be borne by the public as a whole."[11]

Court decisions on both doctrines reveal the extensive degree to which courts have struggled in their interpretation of the Takings Clause to find just the "right" level of protection for private property rights – particularly in the case of regulatory takings. It took some 131 years after the ratification of the Fifth Amendment for the Supreme Court to make its first holding that a regulatory taking could occur, and the Court has reminded us that the Takings Clause was originally intended to apply only to actions filed under the power of eminent domain – not to regulations enacted by the government.[12] There are many who would nonetheless argue that the Supreme Court is allowing the government to exceed its authority by acquiring property under eminent domain which it intends to transfer for private use, and also that the Court does not often enough hold that a government regulation amounts to a regulatory taking. On the other hand, all things are relative, and considering the lack of protections given to private property ownership by governments throughout the world, it must be conceded that the interpretation of the Fifth Amendment and the Bill of Rights generally provides exceptional property owner protection.

E. Now on to the Local Story

If this chapter has invigorated your appetite for practical legal guidance, you can continue the story by exploring the law applicable to your own particular form of local government, and the law of your particular state. Suggested storytellers include both your local government attorney and your state's local government association, which offers training for community officials. Your local story might begin with responses to these questions:

1. Does our state constitution have a "public use" requirement? If so, how does our state define "public use" in this context? Under what

circumstances would an exercise of eminent domain *fail* to meet this requirement?

2. Under state law, what steps would our community be required to take before commencing a lawsuit to take private property under the power of eminent domain (for example, obtaining an appraisal of the property, making an offer to purchase, and the like)?

3. Some states have "quick-take" authorizations that permit the government to secure early possession of private property – before the trial is held to determine the amount of "just compensation" required to be paid for the property to be taken? "Quick-take" very helpfully avoids situations where the public needs the property sooner than a trial would be likely to conclude. Does our state have this type of authorization?

Notes

1. This protection is provided by state constitution in 49 states, and in the 50th state, North Carolina, protection is provided by state statute.
2. *Kelo v. City of New London*, 545 U.S. 469, 125 S. Ct. 2655; 162 L. Ed. 2d (2005).
3. *Hawaii Housing Authority v. Mitkiff*, 467 U.S. 229 (1984).
4. *Kelo v. City of New London*, above.
5. *Id.*
6. *Searl v. School Dist. No. 2, of Lake County*, 133 U.S. 553, 562 (1890), referring to *Garrison v. City of New York*, 88 U.S. 196, 21 Wall. 196 (1874) (emphasis not in original case text).
7. *Pennsylvania Coal Co. v. Mahon*, 260 U.S. 393 (1922).
8. *Penn Central Transportation Co. v. City of New York*, 438 U.S. 104 (1978).
9. One expert description of such historic resources included "intangible" aspects of cultural heritage—including the architect's designs, or relevant historic styles and building cultures—as well as the "tangible" historic building fabric." Sense of Place, Design Guidelines for New Construction in Historic Districts, A Publication of the Preservation Alliance for Greater Philadelphia (2007), at the following web address: http://www.preservationalliance.com/publications/SenseofPlace_final.pdf (accessed in 2020).
10. A rigorous discussion of "investment-backed expectations" can be found in Michelman, *Property, Utility, and Fairness: Comments on the Ethical Foundations of "Just Compensation" Law*, 80 Harv. L. Rev. 1165, 1233 (1967), a law review that was cited by the Supreme Court in the *Penn Central* opinion, 438 U.S. at 128.
11. *Lingle v. Chevron*, 544 U.S. 528, 537, 125 S. Ct. 2074, 161 L.Ed.2d 876 (2005).
12. *Id.*

Chapter 13

Meet the Court System and Local Attorney

If a guidebook for local officials is going to provide a basic picture of the "law," it certainly must include some discussion of two fundamental institutions: the court system, and the office of the local government attorney. These institutions are important connections between local government and the laws it creates and operates under.

Nearly all local officials are influenced to a degree by the workings of the court system. Legislative body members frequently act in anticipation of how the court might react to their decisions. A consideration for "what the court might do" applies as well to the decision making of many administrative officials, from the CEO to the clerk and treasurer, the assessor, and those enforcing local ordinances.

Similarly, the local government attorney (referenced in this chapter as "the attorney") has a pervasive impact on matters throughout the local government. The attorney has regular interaction with the CEO, the legislative body, the clerk, the local police, and in some communities the officials involved with planning and zoning. At various times, the attorney will communicate with many or most offices in the local government while fulfilling basic legal duties. This chapter offers local officials a look at some of the other professional activities of the attorney, which are not always observable.

A. The Court System

1. The Nature of a Lawsuit

The court system in the United States was established to operate on an *adversary* basis, which means that parties with disagreements come together to advocate their respective positions to neutral finders of law and fact. These "neutrals" are the traditional *judges and juries*. Once the process of advocacy has been completed, such as at the conclusion of a trial, the neutrals are empowered to resolve the disagreement in favor of the party which has presented the most compelling evidence and arguments under the prevailing rules of law. Knowing what happens in court and why can inform the actions of local officials in many respects.

When a case goes to court, the local government can be a *plaintiff* – the party that initiates the case and who seeks relief from one or more other parties. Or the local government can be a *defendant* – the party against whom one or more plaintiffs are pursuing a claim.

Explaining the different types of relief which may be sought in court by the plaintiff requires a bit of history. After the Colonies became states, the American system did not attempt to totally "reinvent" entirely new rules to govern the outcome of disputes. Of course, the federal and state constitutions provided important new rights and guidelines. But aside from these, the states – Louisiana aside[1] – generally adopted a large part of the "common law" of England. In essence then, United States courts would rely on the principles of pre-revolution English law as a basis for deciding many disputes. Of course, American law has undergone substantial change since those early days, based on decisions made by American courts and legislatures. But one of the broad concepts that has had a lasting impact is the division into two separate court systems: courts of "law" and courts of "equity."

2. Separate Courts of "Law" and "Equity"

In early days, plaintiffs would ask *courts of law* for a judgment requiring defendants to pay them money (money damages). These cases involved plaintiffs claiming that a defendant breached a contract, or that the defendant was negligent, resulting in an injury to the plaintiff. In courts of law, *judges* makes decisions on the law applicable to the case, and the parties are entitled to have *juries* determine which party's factual allegations are more likely true, as well as the amount of money to be awarded if the plaintiff is successful.

For the better part of America's history, separate *courts of equity* could also be found. In courts of equity, there are no juries, only judges, and the predominant form of remedy is the "injunction," which is an order compelling a party to stop taking certain action (or in some cases compelling a party to take certain action). In equity, judges make decisions on the law, the facts, and also on precisely what remedy should be granted to provide the appropriate relief to a prevailing plaintiff.

These two courts – law and equity – continued separately until the mid-1900s, when the two courts were formally "merged" into the single court system we know today. While our courts now operate as a single tribunal, there remains a meaningful legal distinction between "claims at law" and "claims in equity." In claims at *law*, just as in the old courts of law, parties are entitled to *juries* to determine the facts and remedy, while in *equity* cases, just as in the old courts of equity, a judge alone determines the law, facts, and remedy. Interestingly, in some cases, a modern plaintiff will seek both a money damage remedy at law and an injunction in equity, and in such cases the vestiges of the old system remain: a jury will be made available to decide the money damage issue, while the judge alone will decide the injunction issue.

3. There are "Civil" Cases and "Criminal" Cases

Cases in the court system are also separated into two distinct categories based on another historical characteristic of some consequence. One category consists of "civil" cases, where parties seeking relief must prove their cases "by a preponderance of the evidence," meaning they have demonstrated that their position is at least more likely true than not true. Civil plaintiffs bring claims on their own behalf, seeking money damages or various types of equitable relief (such as injunctions or declarations of property ownership rights). The other category consists of "criminal" cases, where the party bringing the claim is the prosecutor (or district attorney, attorney general or state's attorney) acting on behalf of "the people" against a defendant. Criminal charges must be proved "beyond a reasonable doubt," a far more demanding standard. The "remedy" in a criminal case may involve *probation* or confinement in *jail or prison* if a defendant is found "guilty."

At the local government level, the attorney may take on the role of public prosecutor on behalf of the community, charging defendants with *misdemeanors* (minor crimes carrying a relatively small maximum fine or brief confinement as penalty) in order to *enforce* local ordinances and codes. These cases may include traffic offenses where the charging police officer has written a traffic ticket under local ordinance rather than state law. Many states also make provision for the local government to charge local ordinance violations, including traffic offenses, as "civil" wrongdoing, rather than "criminal" cases.

In all civil and criminal cases (with the exception of pure equity cases and civil enforcement of ordinance violations) the parties are permitted to demand a jury to make findings of fact, and in some cases to determine the severity of the outcome, based on instructions on the law provided by the court. It is worth noting, however, that in a limited number of cases, as a matter of strategy, the attorneys and parties may *waive* the right to a jury and allow the judge alone to make all findings and determine all outcomes.

4. Important Components of a Civil Case: Before Trial

Summary of a Civil Lawsuit

■ Case is filed.

■ Parties conduct "discovery."

■ Parties typically discuss settlement.

■ Parties file "motions" with the court for relief before a trial is held.

■ Case is mediated or facilitated with goal of settlement.

■ If no settlement is reached the case will be resolved at a formal "trial."

■ Based on the trial, a judgment will be entered for the prevailing party.

■ The party losing at trial will generally have the right to ask an appeals court to review the trial court proceedings.

In civil cases, important "pre-trial" steps are built into the court process, between the date a case is filed and the date it is ready for trial. One of these pre-trial steps is known as "discovery." Each of the parties is entitled to obtain documents from the opposing party, as well as ask written and verbal questions, in the attempt to "discover" the full picture of facts surrounding both the claims brought by the plaintiff and the defenses to those claims asserted by the defendant. Discovery allows the parties to narrow the issues that are actually in dispute, avoid surprises in the courtroom, and gain a relatively good insight on what specific questions the judge or jury will face at the end of the case. In other words, discovery attempts to avoid a "trial by ambush." In light of advances in technology, such as electronic record keeping, the process of discovery (including "e-discovery") has become more complex, sometimes requiring the assistance of technical experts.

Aside from trial preparation, the information "discovered" may be used by attorneys in communications with their clients, to more meaningfully evaluate the strengths and weaknesses of their respective cases. The parties can better understand the likely consequences of committing to the great time, expense, and risks associated with a trial, and thus take more measured and realistic positions during settlement negotiations.

Another pre-trial step involves the right of the parties to formally ask the court to *dismiss* all or some part of the claims filed by the plaintiff, or to dismiss one or more of the defenses asserted by the defendant. This procedural path takes into consideration that the purpose for having a trial in the first place is to resolve *disputed issues of fact and law*. What if the case filed by plaintiff has not asserted a valid claim under the law (even if everything stated is true) or if the defendant has not asserted a legitimate defense to the plaintiff's legitimate claims? What if the parties learned during "discovery" that there *are* no disputed facts that need to be resolved in the case? Court rules make provision for each of these possibilities by allowing either of the parties to file a "motion" (a request for a formal response from the court) seeking a ruling on specific questions *prior to trial*, such as whether the plaintiff or defendant should immediately prevail, in whole or in part.

A further pre-trial step is a relatively new addition to the litigation process. Known as "mediation," or "facilitation," it is based on the philosophy that parties should be given opportunity, and assistance, to settle their differences before resorting to the all-or-nothing war known as a trial. Mediation and facilitation can take many forms, but the common thread is to improve the prospects of settling a dispute by allowing a knowledgeable and neutral *arbiter* to assist the parties in evaluating their respective cases and arriving at a settlement. Mediators and facilitators provide a pair of fresh, neutral eyes to examine what a trial might look like, and what the finders of law and fact are likely to conclude. This experience can provide significant assistance to parties in evaluating their settlement positions. However, these proceedings produce only *recommendations* on settlement, not a binding outcome – unless the parties agree otherwise. In some cases, the parties may go a step further in pursuing a resolution of their case without a full trial. Specifically, they may voluntarily agree to a *binding* arbitration that brings their dispute to a final resolution outside the regular court process (although a court may be called upon to enforce an award given in arbitration).

After "discovery," motions to dismiss, and mediation, but before trial begins, the judge in a case will often call the parties to the courthouse for one or more "pre-trial conferences." The agenda for a pre-trial conference is variable, depending on the particular judge. The process is likely to reveal what each party expects to do at trial, how long the trial is expected to last, and perhaps the nature of any technical issues expected to arise during the trial. The court may also take a last opportunity to assist the parties in settling the case rather than proceeding to trial.

An illustrative (though extreme) story of such "assistance" from a judge involves a case where the claim for money damages was expected to require a very lengthy trial, which the court was not looking forward to. The court called the parties in for a pre-trial conference in the late afternoon of a well-known national holiday, having learned during pre-trial that the hold-up on settlement was that the president of the defendant corporation was refusing to authorize a money payment that the attorneys from both sides had agreed would be a fair settlement. The judge, formulating his strategy of "assistance," ordered the attorney for the defendant to call the company president, whose office was in another city, and advise him that his presence would be required at the pre-trial. The president, were he to comply, would be forced to spend the evening of this national holiday apart from his family. One brief phone call later, the defendant's attorney announced that payment had been authorized! The case was settled. Trial courts have considerable discretion in managing cases.

If all efforts to achieve a settlement prove unsuccessful, the case will be formally presented at a trial. Depending on the subject matter and desires of the parties, there might be a jury trial or non-jury trial. At the conclusion of the trial, either the jury or the court (if there is no jury) will determine all disputed issues of fact, and a judgment will be rendered for the party that has presented the most persuasive case on the facts and law.

5. Cases May be Filed in Federal or State Court

There are separate federal and state court systems. Most cases involving local governments are filed in state court. This is the natural outgrowth of the fact that most regulations creating and governing local governments are state laws. Nonetheless, officials will occasionally encounter cases initiated in federal court. A reasonable question is: what influences whether a case belongs in one court or the other?

Federal courts hear disputes involving the federal constitution and laws, and cases involving certain disputes between parties from different states. There are various types of federal laws and constitutional provisions that may involve a local government. For example, there are federal civil rights laws, interstate business regulations, and many other laws regulating interests protected under the federal constitution. Another example of a "federal issue" is a plaintiff who asserts that, in the design and construction of a building or sidewalk, a local government has violated the federal law requiring accessibility for disabled persons, namely, the Americans with Disabilities Act.[2] More broadly, based on the ratification of the Fourteenth Amendment, many of the protections enumerated in the Bill of Rights apply directly to the states (including local governments). These include the protections of free speech, religious rights, due process, equal protection, and restrictions on the government "taking" property from private owners. Cases filed to seek protection or implementation of these laws and constitutional provisions may be initiated in federal court.

There are 94 federal trial-court districts throughout the country, divided among 12 regional "circuits." Each federal circuit, along with a 13th circuit applicable to the District of Columbia (the "DC Circuit") has a circuit court of appeals.

On the other hand, cases predominantly involving state laws, or the provisions in state constitutions, are within the purview of state courts. Local governments are created and conduct business primarily under state law and constitution. Indeed, one of the most important reasons for the existence of local governments is to promote and protect the interests of citizens and property under the "police power," which is a state's power to promote and protect the public health, safety, and general welfare. This power is used, for example, to enact zoning regulations, license businesses, prevent nuisances, adopt traffic regulations, and the like. The police power is reserved to the states under the Tenth Amendment to the U.S. Constitution. So, unless there is also a federal law or constitutional provision at issue (which might be joined in the same case with a police power dispute), cases pursuing or challenging exercises of the police power will typically be filed in state court.

To avoid surprises, it is important to clarify that where a lawsuit is filed claiming a violation of federal law or constitution, the state courts will often have "concurrent jurisdiction" with the federal court to consider and adjudicate the claims.[3] For example, a plaintiff may file certain federal civil rights claims either in the federal court or the state court.

In short, when a plaintiff asserts that a local government or its officials are violating state law or the state constitution, the case will generally be filed in state court. But when the plaintiff contends that the local government or its officials are violating a federal law or constitutional provision, the case may, but often need not, be filed in federal court.

6. *Appealing a Trial Court's Decision*

When the final decision has been entered by a trial court in a state or federal case, the party (or parties) aggrieved by the decision generally has a *right to appeal* the decision to a higher court. Our adversarial system acknowledges that no courts or proceedings are perfect and so allows a "reviewing court" to take another look at any suggested errors that occurred during the trial proceedings. This does not involve an entirely new trial. Rather, a *transcript* is prepared of the trial and related proceedings. This transcript, along with any exhibits and tangible evidence presented to the trial court, serves as a "record" of the trial, and the decision on appeal is based on this record.

In all or nearly all states, as well as in the federal court system, there are *two levels* of appeal, the first of which is an *intermediate* appellate court – between the trial court and the supreme court. In most instances, a party has a *right* to have an intermediate appellate court review the trial proceedings and decision. But the highest court in each state, and in the federal system, usually called the *supreme court*,[4] accepts cases only on a discretionary basis. Cases will generally only be accepted by a supreme court when the decision hinges on a broad issue with the potential to affect many future disputes, not merely the individual parties in the case at hand. In some cases, the supreme court will consider whether to establish a new rule of law or determine whether to change the precedent from earlier cases.

7. *Judicial Philosophy*

For those who may be interested, there is a subject not discussed extensively outside professional legal circles that offers important insight into many court decisions. A controversy about judicial philosophy, raging for decades, involves two fundamentally opposing views on how the Constitution should be interpreted over time. There is the "original meaning" doctrine, and there is the "living constitution" doctrine. The debate can reach a fevered pitch when the subject under review involves the Constitution and original Bill of Rights.

There are many nuances and disagreements on both sides of the argument, which the reader will be gratified to hear will be left for other books and informative material. Here, the discussion will be limited to a brief summary of the two competing positions. Recognize that this summary is not presented as an authoritative statement on this subject. It is intended to present only the crux of the dispute, while attempting to present the position of both sides in an even-handed manner. With luck, it will inspire further study on the subject.

a. Original Meaning Doctrine

On one side of the debate are the "Originalists," who take the position that the Constitution (and its amendments) should be interpreted on the basis of what those ratifying the Constitution (or a later amendment) understood its meaning to be *at that time*. If the particular language used requires interpretation, it is necessary to ascertain the original meaning from historical sources, rather than applying the current meanings of words. Originalists advocate that each provision in the Constitution has one meaning, fixed in time, unchanging. To the extent that the original meaning is no longer fitting and beneficial for society, the correct course of action is to use the *majoritarian* mechanism embedded in the Constitution to address such a situation: namely, the Constitution should be amended.

The primary *critique* of the Originalist approach is that the *majoritarian process* for amending the Constitution can be lengthy and arduous. Because the amendment process can take years and requires overwhelming public support, it cannot keep pace with the current needs of society. Holding to a single, unchanging meaning for each constitutional provision leaves society unable to effectively adapt to a changing world over time.

b. Living Constitution Doctrine

On the other side of the debate is the "Living Constitution" camp. Supporters of this doctrine see no obligation to allow the past alone to rule the present,[5] and argue that changed circumstances in society should factor into the Court's interpretation of constitutional provisions. This makes the Constitution a *living* document that should be interpreted based on present-day circumstances, without the necessity of amending the actual words. The Court described this methodology in one of its latest applications: "Courts must exercise reasoned judgment in identifying interests of the person so fundamental that the State must accord them its respect. History and tradition guide and discipline the inquiry but do not set its outer boundaries."[6]

The chief *critique* of the Living Constitution approach is that the *judicial process* of re-interpretation is *too far removed from the people*. When five unelected justices have the authority to re-interpret the meaning of a constitutional provision, they are effectively *ratifying a new constitutional amendment* without the people ever voting on it.

The hope is that these summaries will lend greater meaning to reports on Court decisions interpreting constitutional provisions, and aid in understanding the arguments on this subject that will inevitably arise.

B. The Local Government Attorney

Allow me to introduce you to the local government attorney, who from here on will be known as "the attorney."

1. Part of the Face of the Community

To members of the public, the attorney is part of the face of the community – a face presented at various proceedings and negotiations that arise between the local government and its citizens and property owners. The attorney is perhaps most visible while making regular appearances at public meetings of the local legislative body and other boards and commissions. In broad and idealistic terms, the attorney's mission during these appearances is to provide technical and practical advice, enabling the local government, the people of the community, and the law to work together for the public good.

2. The Attorney's Regular Duties

Duties of the Local Government Attorney

- Provide advice to officials and bodies, either verbally or by written opinion.
- Attend meetings of the legislative body and administrative bodies (such as the planning commission or zoning board of appeals).

■ Perform "transactional" work, such as legal research, and preparation of documents such as legal opinions, ordinances, and contracts, and assist in negotiations.
■ Represent the local government in court.

The attorney provides legal advice and counsel to the local government CEO and legislative body, while routinely communicating with officers, department heads, and often the employees of the local government. Legal counselling may take the form of verbal advice, formal legal opinions, or the preparation of documents such as contracts, resolutions, and ordinances. In working with a local government, there are very few areas of law the attorney does not encounter. Key subjects on which the attorney must be well-versed include property and zoning law, federal, and state constitutional law, civil rights law, criminal law, contract law, negligence law, labor and employment law, property taxation law, administrative law, ethics law, construction law, election law, and environmental law. All of these subjects are "business as usual" for local governments, and so likewise for the attorney. If a need arises, the attorney may bring in "outside counsel" to consult on one or more of these subjects, such as labor and employment law.

The attorney plays a major role in the overall achievement of the government's duties and responsibilities. Considering that most policy decisions have legal ramifications, the attorney is frequently consulted during the course of deliberations, and in many instances is called upon to either directly formalize decisions or indirectly provide guidance. The attorney's experience and expertise regularly reveals alternative ways of saying, describing or doing things that will enhance results and minimize liability or other adverse outcomes.

In our litigious society, the attorney will typically spend time working with the CEO and other officials to improve outcomes in lawsuits filed, or to be filed, in defense of the local government or in pursuit of its policies. Meanwhile, the attorney must also represent the local government in the enforcement of traffic regulations and local ordinances.

3. *The Attorney at Public Meetings*

At public meetings, the attorney may on occasion play a prominent role in presenting a particular agenda item. For example, the attorney may brief the public on the current state of negotiations with a large developer, or in a major lawsuit. For the most part, however, the attorney may have the *appearance* of playing a relatively minor role at public meetings. This appearance is illusory.

While officials deliberate policy, the attorney must keep vigilant watch, ensuring proper adherence to numerous procedural requirements, which can be less than straightforward. Constraints on acceptable behavior by public officials derive from such diverse sources as the Open Meetings Sunshine Law (see Chapter 2), Roberts Rules of Order (see Chapter 3), and the Due Process Clause (see Chapter 5) if administrative decisions are on the docket. The attorney must also ensure that "public hearings" are scheduled when required by law as a condition to taking final action on matters. At the same time, while focusing on the several *procedural* issues, the attorney must closely follow the *substance* of the public body's discussion, in order to provide specific legal advice on any *policy* questions that may arise.

Members of the public may occasionally insist at meetings that the attorney represents each individual citizen and taxpayer. However, for various ethical and practical reasons, the attorney's only *true* client is the local government itself, unless state law or local charter dictates otherwise.

4. Transactional Work

Aside from meeting appearances and attending to court matters, perhaps the bulk of the attorney's work consists of "transactional" services. These will include consultation, legal research, and preparation of documents such as legal opinions, ordinances, and ordinance amendments, as directed by the legislative body, chief executive officer, planning commission, planning department, and ordinance enforcement officials. There are also various types of contracts that must be negotiated and written.

Another hat worn by the attorney relates to a special type of contract that may periodically require considerable time to negotiate and administer. Namely, there are labor agreements with employees, as well as related labor and employment legal issues that the attorney must attend to.

During the course of elections, the attorney may be called upon to provide advice on such things as the legality of certain election signs, petitions seeking to place propositions on the ballot, or the valid residency of a candidate.

The attorney is also expected to stay abreast of new developments in applicable law. Whenever adjustments to local ordinance or procedure may be required in light of the changes in the law that regularly occur, the attorney must call it to the attention of the CEO, legislative body, and other relevant officials.

5. Court Appearances

There are several assignments that will take the attorney to court. Perhaps the most obvious and consequential is a general civil case, where the attorney will (1) represent the local government as a plaintiff seeking relief from another party; or (2) represent the local government when it is named as a defendant. In some instances, officials of the local government are named as individual defendants, and the attorney may also represent them.[7] If a money damage claim is asserted against the local government or its officials, an attorney assigned by the government's insurance carrier may appear with, or in lieu of, the attorney to defend the case.

Local ordinance enforcement might be pursued in the general civil court, primarily when the local government is attempting to "enjoin," that is stop, a party from continuing to violate a local regulation or state law.

Alternatively, analogous to the enforcement of traffic regulations, ordinances may be enforced in the court having authority over cases commenced by the issuance of a citation or ticket. The relief sought in this type of case is typically a fine in an amount sufficient to deter future violations. The penalty for a violation might be a criminal misdemeanor (lower crime), or in some states ordinance enforcement can involve a "civil" ticket and payment of a fine.

The attorney will also defend the local government in a specialized tribunal that hears challenges to the annual property tax assessment.

6. The Attorney Might Be an Employee or a Consultant

The local government's arrangement with the attorney can take a variety of forms.

a. In-house

One common arrangement is for the attorney to be "in-house," which means the attorney is an *employee* of the local government, and there may be a department of the government, often referred to as the "law department," headed by the attorney. In relatively small communities, the department may consist exclusively of the attorney, and in larger communities there may be the attorney and one or more assistant attorneys, who are all employees of the local government.

b.   Retained Law Firm

Another common arrangement, frequently in small or medium-sized communities, consists of the community retaining an attorney as *consultant* to the local government, often from a law firm that specializes in local government law. A retained attorney is treated in similar fashion to an in-house attorney, and other members of the firm may serve as assistant attorneys to handle special areas of law, such as labor and employment law and ordinance enforcement.

c.   Special Counsel

In most arrangements, the local government may retain one or more attorneys to serve as "special counsel," to assist the principal local government attorney, who would be known as the "general counsel for the local government." Special counsel may, for example, assist the local government on the issuance of municipal bonds to finance a project, or negotiate and provide advice on labor agreements.

7.   *Anatomy of a Legal Opinion*

Routinely, the legislative body, CEO, and clerk of the local government need legal opinions from the attorney as part of the performance of their normal functions. Occasionally, so might the treasurer, department heads, FOIA administrator, and other employees of the local government. Some opinions can be provided on a relatively informal basis, and need not be recorded. However, official government business regularly requires a formal written opinion, in which the attorney must exercise carefully considered judgment to interpret the law and explain how it applies to a unique set of facts.

How does the attorney go about preparing such an opinion? The process requires a series of measured steps designed to maximize the *reliability* of the ultimate conclusions presented to the local government. Here are three of the essential steps:

a.   Ascertaining the Provable Facts

When a legal opinion is challenged, experience shows, opposing parties will not always agree on the facts. Consequently, the first step in the process of preparing an opinion is to ascertain the relevant facts that have given rise to the *need* for an opinion. This step is frequently not merely a matter of gathering objective details that are readily available. In addition to examining the relevant objective facts, it is often necessary to rely on details from potential witnesses.

b.   Interpreting the Law That Will Govern the Opinion

Having in hand the most reliable set of facts available, the attorney must then isolate the law that will govern the opinion. This often begins with identifying the statutory law – created by the legislature – that speaks to the legal issue to be addressed in the opinion. With statutes as a starting point, the attorney must then determine how past court decisions have *interpreted* the legislative enactments in similar circumstances. It is unlikely that any past case on the subject will have had identical facts. (In the rare event that such a case exists, the case is said to be "controlling," and allows the attorney to give a very confident opinion.) Most frequently, research will produce a series of cases that merely *relate to* the specific question at hand, providing clues about what the courts are *likely* to conclude with regard to the specific facts involved. Courts themselves must attempt to determine what the legislature had in mind as they attempt to follow the cardinal rule in interpreting case law on a particular statute: ascertaining and giving effect to the *intent* of the legislature when it created the statute. This typically leaves considerable room for weighing and balancing various factors – which leads into the next level of analysis. Namely, the attorney must anticipate the precise principles of law, and sometimes personal philosophy, that the court will choose to rely on in reaching its ultimate conclusion.

c.   Predicting Philosophies and Inclinations of Likely Trial and Appellate Judges

To the extent the information is available, it is prudent for the attorney to consider the inclinations and past decisions of the actual sitting judges likely to rule on the particular issues at hand if a court challenge arises. Indeed, for an opinion on local policy of great significance, the attorney might consider the legal philosophies not only of the *trial* judges, but also of the *appellate* judges who may ultimately be called upon.

In sum, the hallmark of a legal opinion is that it is full of moving parts. Many are very subjective, requiring a multi-layered exercise of discretion. For that reason, it will be a rare occasion indeed for a public official to receive any opinion from the attorney expressing an unequivocal "yes" or "no."

8. *Short Questions and Answers*

A few other brief points that should assist in painting a picture of the attorney will be addressed here in a question-and-answer format:

a. Who Should Consult the Attorney?

Should every local government official be individually permitted (or encouraged) to seek clarification on the law directly from the attorney?

For a variety of reasons, it would be appropriate for the local government's legislative body to establish a *policy* on whether individual officials should be permitted or encouraged to seek guidance directly from the attorney. In formulating such a policy, it is necessary to consider the additional expense to the community, the availability of the attorney for these purposes, and whether the community's needs might best be served by funneling all such contact through the CEO, for efficiency and uniformity purposes.

b. Should the Attorney Participate in Politics?

Even in states where local officials are elected on a ballot without party affiliations, local government is a world of politics and public policy debates. Won't the attorney, working in this world, inevitably choose sides when giving advice?

This is an extremely relevant question for all local government attorneys. Officials often assume that the decisions of the attorney are driven by political motives. While the attorney may well stay abreast of political conditions, the wiser course is to maintain uniform respect over time by impartially following the facts and law as a consistent compass. The attorney represents the local government as a whole, not one or a few officials, and in the best of worlds will see many officials come and go over the course of a career. So when there is a debate, and the attorney must provide an opinion that will promote a resolution, the opinion will generally be governed by the facts and law, not angled to favor one side or the other in the debate.

c. What if I Disagree with the Attorney?

When the attorney provides advice, do officials have the authority to disagree with or choose to disregard such advice?

The best course of action is to discuss a disagreement with the attorney, or with the CEO (depending on the local policy), rather than disregard it. A review of the discussion above on the "Anatomy of a legal opinion" will clarify that there are sure to be weighty legal considerations behind virtually every opinion rendered. In many instances, the attorney begins from a basic legal principle and extrapolates to reach the conclusion initially offered as advice. While the basic principle itself is likely to be immovable, it is often possible to explore an alternate means of expressing or executing it that will resolve the disagreement. On the other hand, simply brushing aside legal advice runs a significant risk of creating liability.

d. Why Must the Attorney's Opinion be Confidential?

Communications from the attorney's office are marked "confidential and privileged." Shouldn't government be more transparent?

Confidentiality between attorney and client is a long tradition in both public and private sectors, and for good reason. It promotes frank and honest discussion that would often be impossible if there were an expectation of disclosure. To ethically perform the function of legal counsel, it is necessary to provide unvarnished advice and opinions to clients, including public officials and bodies of officials, explaining their rights, obligations, and liabilities. The fact that the attorney's client is a "public body" does not lessen the need for frankness and honesty, and thus for confidentiality. It is frequently in the public interest to keep legal advice confidential. Indeed, it is a good policy to ask for and receive straightforward advice from the attorney. In order to avoid accidental disclosure of information that could ultimately be harmful to the community, the attorney regularly designates communications as "confidential and privileged."

e. Should the Attorney Be Making Policy Decisions?

At what point should a public official defer to the attorney in making policy decisions for the local government?

The short answer is that policy decisions are the province of public officials, not of the attorney. The attorney should be relied on for *advice* as to whether a proposed policy decision is permitted or not permitted under the law. In sensitive cases, the attorney may assist by identifying *limits* on actions or in the wording of new policy. But officials should not allow substitution of the attorney's judgment for their own.

C. Last Words

A character in a Shakespeare play famously declares, "The first thing we do, let's kill all the lawyers."[8] That character is Dick the Butcher, who backs a rebel seeking to overthrow the government. Dick may be a deeper thinker than you first expect. If your goal is to take control of the government, a promising strategy is to undermine law and order. In that sense, Shakespeare is actually paying a compliment to attorneys and judges for the stability they bring to society.[9]

The point of this chapter is that officials gain an advantage by understanding the court system and local government attorney. The courts, as an institution, have developed over centuries, and continue even today as a work in progress. At the center of this institution remains the notion that truth can best be discovered when opposed parties present their cases before a neutral court. Facing an ever-larger volume of cases filed each year, courts have added the new dimension of *mediation* or *facilitation* to the overall process, utilizing a neutral *arbiter* to assist the parties in identifying a satisfactory voluntary *settlement*, rather than face the risks of a win-lose trial. But a majority of the steps leading to final resolution of a case remain the same, whether achieved by trial or by mediation. The parties must file their claims and defenses with the court, undergo "discovery" to fully reveal the facts and circumstances underlying the dispute, and participate in "motion" filing to focus the issues and perhaps achieve an early end to the case.

Central to the functioning of courts, and an indispensable resource for guidance on the law, is the local government attorney. While the attorney of course represents the local government in various types of court proceedings, a larger share of the attorney's time is spent researching, formulating, and providing advice designed to help the local government stay *out* of the courthouse. The attorney also drafts opinions and all manner of other binding documents on behalf of the local government. Cultivating a basic understanding of both the court and the local government attorney can remove a needless cloud of ambiguity on both institutions, and open the door to smoother relations and greater collaboration.

D. Now on to the Local Story

If this chapter has invigorated your appetite for practical legal guidance, you can continue the story by exploring the law applicable to your own particular form of local government, and the law of your particular state. Suggested storytellers include both your local government attorney and your state's local government association, which offers training for community officials. Your local story might begin with responses to these questions:

1. Does our community enforce its ordinances by issuing "civil" (no jail possibility) citations, or criminal citations (which carry the prospect of a short jail sentence) to alleged violators? In some cases, rather than issuing a citation, does the community start a civil action seeking an "injunction" ordering a party to stop the violation?
2. Is the attorney for our community hired on an "in-house" or "consultant" basis?
3. Does our community have a formal policy on whether individual officials should be permitted or encouraged to seek guidance directly from the attorney?
4. Similarly, if an official disagrees with the attorney, is there a formal procedure for resolving the dispute (other than a confrontation at a public meeting)?

Notes

1. In Louisiana, prior to statehood, the "Napoleonic Code" was adopted, incorporating a predominantly French influence.
2. 42 U.S.C. 12101 *et seq.*
3. Examples of the types of cases frequently filed under a federal law in state court are those charging that a local government or its officials have violated the civil rights of person in the land use or law enforcement context under 42 U.S.C 1983.
4. The highest court is not referred to as the "supreme court" in all states. For example, in New York, there is a supreme court, but the highest court is the "court of appeals."
5. *Obergefell v. Hodges*, 135 S. Ct. 2584, 2598, 192 L.Ed.2d 609 (2015).
6. *Id.*
7. There are certain situations in which the local government and one or more officials have conflicting positions in a case. This may require the attorney to represent the local government while another attorney, or attorneys represent the official(s).
8. Henry VI, Part 2, Act IV, Scene 2.
9. The underlying meaning of Shakespeare's line is of course impossible to know with certainty. This chapter's commentary is consistent with an article appearing in the *New York Times* (June 17, 1990) Section LI, p. 12 of the National edition, by Debbie Vogel, with the headline: "Kill the Lawyers, A Line Misinterpreted."

Chapter 14

Avoiding Personal Liability

We live in a society with diverse views. In and of itself, this is a positive. However, we also inhabit a litigation-charged society that is often inclined to go to court when unfavorable outcomes and events occur. This is particularly important for local officials who may face a claim for personal liability when a private party alleges that a decision or action violates certain rights protected under federal law. Or a person may claim to have been harmed by the negligent wrongdoing of an official under state law and seek personal liability for money damages. When such claims arise, local officials generally want to know whether "governmental immunity" will provide a shield from personal financial exposure.

> There are doctrines of governmental immunity under both federal and state law that may provide complete insulation of an official from personal liability depending on the facts of the particular case.

Both federal and state law include doctrines of governmental immunity that may provide insulation. Depending on the facts of the particular case, a public official may be completely immune from personal liability. For claims arising under federal law, the essence of the immunity rules apply throughout the country. Immunity from claims arising under state law will vary from state to state.

In many cases, local governments provide policies of liability insurance that may provide coverage for some or all of a claim made against an official. Of course, having coverage is not a certainty, and the mere *probability* of coverage (especially partial coverage) typically will not provide adequate comfort for an official who has been served with a new lawsuit. Regardless, securing a fundamental understanding of the subject of immunity will permit local officials to work with the local government attorney in a more meaningful way, and perhaps to sleep a little easier at night.

The goal here is to provide local officials with some of the basic deciding factors that will allow or deny use of the governmental immunity "shield" from federal and state liability in a given case. It is important to keep in mind that the *facts and circumstances* underlying each individual claim will ultimately dictate whether government immunity will apply. It would not be practical to attempt an explanation of each of the separate rules the several states have developed on this subject. However, there is a sufficient common conceptual core of these rules to allow this analysis to be instructive.

The idea of government immunity harkens back to the old common law rule that "the king can do no wrong." Of course, in our system of government, the federal and state governments take the place of kings and queens (with slightly less authority over our lives!). Under the old English common law doctrine, immunity transferred from the royals to all levels of government and government officials. This same full-blanket coverage was recognized for some time in the United States, but in recent times it has begun to unravel.

For local government officials, *federal* liability issues most frequently arise under the post-civil war federal civil rights laws enacted in 1871, and particularly 42 U.S.C. § 1983. As a civil-rights law, § 1983 makes local officials *personally liable* for action by the local government that *deprives rights, privileges or immunities secured by federal constitution and law*.[1] This needs some unpacking. Here, "action by local government" means official implementation or execution of a policy, ordinance, regulation, or decision. And most importantly for the sanity of modern officials, the *deprivations* of rights referred to are only those deprivations that are *unconstitutional* or *unlawful* at the federal level. § 1983 was created to force unwilling state and local governments to obey the new federal recognition of full civil rights for all persons, including the recently freed slaves.

As set out below, § 1983 allows a party to seek money damage relief where rights are deprived under "color of law," meaning any situation where a party asserts that the deprivation of rights has occurred under a law, local ordinance or custom. It reads, in part:

> Every person who, under color of any statute, ordinance, regulation, custom, or usage, of any State or Territory or the District of Columbia, subjects, or causes to be subjected, any citizen of the United States or other person within the jurisdiction thereof to the deprivation of any rights, privileges, or immunities secured by the Constitution and laws, shall be liable to the party injured in an action at law, suit in equity, or other proper proceeding for redress

Again, the only wrongdoing that creates liability under § 1983 is deprivation of a right or a claim of entitlement that is protected by the Constitution or federal law. Moreover, the liability is purely individual – a public official supervising others is not liable under § 1983 for the actions of those being supervised.

While the focus of this chapter is on immunity from liability for the *individual* public official, a related subject is the liability of the government body itself. In cases arising under § 1983, neither Congress nor the Supreme Court has seen fit to provide local governments themselves with any immunity – even where harm is caused only incidentally by officials acting in good faith.[2] This means that where this chapter discusses immunity under § 1983, it is purely a question of protecting *individual* officials from being personally liable. Where a deprivation occurs under § 1983, the local government body may still be on the hook to pay damages.

For *state law* purposes, an early erosion of the immunity shield appeared under state law when it was decided that immunity should *not* apply in cases in which a local government is acting based on a *profit-making* motive. Instead, state immunity would provide protection from liability only for harm caused in connection with the performance of a "governmental function." More recently, courts and legislatures also began to reject the assumption that government should always be free of tort liability – even during performance of governmental functions. Modernly, nearly all states have carved out their own unique, enumerated list of non-immune activities, such as the negligent operation of motor vehicles (where insurance is likely to be available). State constitution and law spell out the full scope and circumstances in which immunity for local governments and their public officials will apply.

The examination below will start with a more detailed analysis of immunity under federal law, and then turn to state law. The rules at both the federal and state levels have sought to "strike a proper balance between protecting decisions made by government agencies as well as elected and appointed government officials and providing redress for injuries caused by those decisions."[3]

A. Federal Law: Absolute and Qualified Immunity

Absolute Immunity under Federal Law

Liability of local officials that may be subject to immunity arises under federal law chiefly in context of civil rights lawsuits such as those filed under 42 U.S.C. § 1983. There are rules which, depending on the facts of the particular case, may provide either "absolute" or "qualified" immunity.

Absolute immunity under § 1983 has been granted to *legislators, judges, and prosecutors.*

Absolute "legislator" immunity applies to local legislators acting within the legitimate sphere of legislative activity. For example, *enacting an ordinance* is a legislative act for these purposes.

The absolute immunity granted to "judges" applies when a person has *acted within the judicial scope of authority.* Agencies can be "functionally equivalent" to judges, depending on the *function performed.* For example, a county construction board of appeals has been found to meet this test after confirming the adversary nature of the process used in their proceedings.

For local officials, liability (and potential immunity) under federal law is an issue that arises chiefly in context of civil rights lawsuits, such as those filed under 42 U.S.C., § 1983, although there are other federal statutes which are relevant. There are rules which, depending on the facts of the particular case, may provide either "absolute" or "qualified" immunity.

1. Absolute Immunity for Officials

Absolute immunity under § 1983 has been granted to *judges, legislators, and prosecutors*. When absolute immunity applies, there will be no personal liability on the part of the official.

Absolute "legislative" immunity applies to local legislators acting within the legitimate "sphere" of legislative activity. Whether a local official is acting within that legislative sphere is not determined based on the motive or intent of the action, or on the name or predominant function of the person or body taking the action, but only on the legislative nature of the act itself. For example, *enacting an ordinance* is a legislative act, so legislative immunity should apply.[4] But *applying* or *administering* an ordinance is outside the legislative sphere and so not protected by legislative immunity – even if done by a government body with a title that sounds very "legislative" or that performs some legislative functions.

For a specific example, consider a final site plan approval, which is an *administrative* act, not a *legislative* one. If an ordinance delegates the administrative act of final site plan approval to the community's legislative body, the body is acting within the administrative sphere when approving or denying the site plan – it is the act that matters, not the legislative title of the body. Because the officials on the legislative body are acting outside the legislative sphere while approving or denying the site plan, they are unprotected by legislative immunity while taking that action.[5] (As discussed below, federal qualified immunity might apply depending on the facts and circumstances).[6] By the same reasoning, a regional planning commission, which is a non-legislative body, may have certain limited powers of a legislative nature. Individuals serving on the commission may benefit from absolute legislative immunity while exercising those limited legislative powers.[7]

The absolute immunity granted to *judges* applies when they have acted within the judicial scope of authority. Such immunity has also been extended to officials and agencies who act in a "quasi-judicial" capacity – that is, while conducting hearings similar to court proceedings. The Supreme Court has observed that adjudication by agencies can be "functionally equivalent" to adjudication by judges.[8] Again, the ultimate analysis would explore the *function performed*, rather than the title of the position held. A reviewing court would want to know whether decisions are made in a process similar to a court proceeding, where two adversaries are involved, witnesses are questioned, and the official or body then determines which side should prevail. For example, a New Jersey federal district court followed this line of reasoning to find the members of a county construction board of appeals absolutely immune from personal liability due to the adversarial nature of their review process.[9]

What about the zoning boards of appeals, which states frequently recognize as quasi-judicial bodies? While the Supreme Court appears not to have weighed in on this precise issue, judicial immunity for ZBA members would presumably depend on such things as whether similar bodies had sovereign immunity under traditional common law in the 19th century, when § 1983 was enacted, and whether the nature of the decision-making process could be characterized as being adversarial, like the proceedings held in court. The more the process moves away from being purely "administrative" and instead resembles an adversarial court proceeding, the stronger the argument for judicial immunity.

2. Qualified Immunity for Officials

Qualified Immunity under Federal Law

The Supreme Court has observed that: "The doctrine of qualified immunity protects government officials from liability for civil damages insofar as their conduct does not violate clearly established statutory or constitutional rights of which a reasonable person would have known . . . "

Qualified immunity balances two important interests – the need to hold public officials accountable when they exercise power irresponsibly and the need to shield officials from harassment, distraction, and liability when they perform their duties reasonably.

When public officials are sued *personally* under § 1983 (for example, as Janet Smith, rather than as City Mayor) they may be in a position to assert *qualified immunity*. (As always, the availability of immunity will depend on the underlying facts and circumstances). If successfully asserted, qualified immunity will prevent personal liability for monetary damages.

In 2009, Justice Alito wrote an opinion for a *unanimous* Supreme Court, stating the rule of qualified immunity for officials:

> The doctrine of qualified immunity protects government officials "from liability for civil damages insofar as their conduct does not violate clearly established statutory or constitutional rights of which a reasonable person would have known." Harlow v. Fitzgerald, 457 U.S. 800, 818, 102 S. Ct. 2727, 73 L.Ed.2d 396 (1982). Qualified immunity balances two important interests—the need to hold public officials accountable when they exercise power irresponsibly and the need to shield officials from harassment, distraction,, and liability when they perform their duties reasonably.[10]

When an official acts in a way that *violates a rule that has been clearly established*, qualified immunity probably will *not* apply. This includes any rule that the official *actually* knew about or that a reasonable person *should* have known about. Where qualified immunity *can* be available is in situations where there *was no clear rule* against the official's behavior, or where there was *no reasonable way for the official to know* that the action taken was against the rules. In legal terms, qualified immunity operates to ensure that, before they may be subjected to suit for their conduct, officials must be *on notice* that the conduct would be unlawful.[11]

The Court offered this further clarification in 2017:

> Qualified immunity attaches when an official's conduct "does not violate clearly established statutory or constitutional rights of which a reasonable person would have known. . . . for a right to be clearly established, [the rule on] the statutory or constitutional question [must be] beyond debate."[12]

In summary, when a § 1983 case is filed against a public official who raises qualified immunity as a shield against personal money damages, the plaintiff bringing the case must demonstrate two things in order to avoid qualified immunity. *First*, the plaintiff must show that there has been a violation of rights protected under federal constitution or by federal law. *Second*, the plaintiff must show that the official clearly knew (or clearly should have known) at the time the action was taken that it would be a violation of those rights.

B. State Law: Liability Allowed under Exceptions to Governmental Immunity

State Government Immunity

State constitutions and law often broadly establish the general rule that officials are immune from liability, but then specify particular circumstances in which officials may be liable, that is, state law will establish specific *exceptions to immunity* are created.

Three common circumstances in which negligence cases are permitted are: (1) where public buildings (or other specified public places) have been neglected to the point of becoming unsafe; (2) where government personnel have operated motor vehicles negligently during the course of employment; and (3) where neglect has caused a street, highway or sidewalk to fall into an unsafe or defective condition.

Under state law, governmental immunity for public officials varies from state to state, based on the treatment provided in the state's constitution and law. As noted above, while old common law rules dictated that "the king can do no wrong," the modern rule in most states no longer springs directly from tradition. Rather, nearly all states begin by broadly proclaiming governmental immunity as a general principle, but then specify various *exceptions* to immunity. Under the specific circumstances named in each exception established by a state, governmental immunity is *waived*, meaning that liability is permitted based on harm caused by a public official's negligent actions.

Three circumstances (among many others) in which negligence cases are commonly permitted are: (1) where public buildings (or other specified public places) have been neglected to the point of becoming unsafe; (2) where government personnel have operated motor vehicles negligently during the course of employment; and (3) where neglect has caused a street, highway or sidewalk to fall into an unsafe or defective condition.

Consider this example. In the State of Wyoming, the legislature has provided that "a governmental entity and its public employees while acting within the scope of duties are granted immunity from liability for any tort except as provided by W.S. § 1–39–105 through § 1–39–112."[13] This means that, in general, Wyoming public officials have the benefit of governmental immunity. But under the specific circumstances named in §§ 105 through 112, immunity is *waived*, and there may be liability for torts. Unless a claim falls within one of these exceptions stated in W.S. § 1–39–105 through § 1–39–112, the claim is blocked by immunity and may not be asserted in court.

Examining the first exception, stated in § 105, Wyoming has provided that "A governmental entity is liable for damages resulting from bodily injury, wrongful death or property damage caused by the negligence of public employees while acting within the scope of their duties in the operation of any motor vehicle, aircraft or watercraft."[14] This first exception waives immunity for harm caused by officials while negligently operating vehicles. A close reading reveals that this particular waiver makes the *governmental entity* itself responsible, while the individual official who commits the negligent act remains immune from any *personal* liability.

From the standpoint of the party who suffers personal injury or property damage due to the negligence of a public official, government immunity is a *denial of recovery* that would have been available had the official instead been employed by a private company. On the other hand, unlike private employees, the theory is that public officials are *servants of the public*, and the public at large has a strong interest in protecting the freedom of public officials to confidently engage in their duties:

> The doctrine [of governmental immunity] represents a balance between the need of public officers to perform their functions freely and an aggrieved party's right to seek redress. Government decision makers exercising discretionary functions are immune from suit because the courts should not chill legislative discretion in policy formation by imposing tort liability, nor should government employees be stripped of their independence of action or intimidated by the fear of personal liability and vexatious suits. Thus, immunity serves two policies: It shields those governmental acts and decisions impacting on large numbers of people in a myriad of unforeseen ways from individual and class actions, the continual threat of which would make public administration all but impossible, and it preserves the autonomy of coordinate branches of government.[15]

When a case is filed as a result of harm or injury caused by the negligence of a public official, with important exceptions (including the three noted above), states have provided immunity for ordinary negligence. However, to the extent that wrongdoing extends beyond negligence, and can be characterized as being within the realm of an *intentional tort*, most states permit the victim to recover. Similarly, if the public official has acted with *gross* negligence, immunity will rarely, if ever, apply. "Gross" negligence is extreme behavior involving a knowing violation. Some states exclude from immunity action taken with "reckless disregard" for the legality or potential consequences – sometimes called "wilful and wanton" conduct.[16]

The theme unifying most state law exceptions from immunity is this "crossing of the line" from sloppy mistake (negligence) over to something more sinister. It would be difficult to argue, for example, that a balancing of public interests favors sheltering an official from personal liability for an assault and battery simply because the perpetrator was a government employee.

C. Last Words

In the formation of this country, a monumental decision was made to omit "the Royals" from involvement in the government structure. Nonetheless, the benefit of total immunity for government and its officials – which had historically been enjoyed by the Royals – was transferred to the new system, where it endured for some time. Today, we operate with two separate arrangements, one federal and one state. Immunity in the federal system applies to civil rights claims made against officials under federal constitution or law. In the state system, each of the respective states has maintained broad immunity for officials while carving out specific types of claims for which liability may apply – predominantly based on the negligence of officials, and especially in those instances where insurance coverage might be available. It is no secret that members of our society seem ever more willing to rely on courts to sort out their differences. So, those offering their time as public officials have good reason to be interested in identifying those circumstances in which they could be held personally liable for actions taken and decisions made while performing their official duties.

While it would be a false comfort to assure officials that they will be totally insulated from liability in all cases, it can be extremely beneficial simply to gain a working knowledge of those circumstances in which there may be liability. To that end, this chapter has attempted to plant a fundamental understanding of the nature of governmental immunity in the United States, and the types of circumstances in which its protection may apply.

D. Now on to the Local Story

If this chapter has invigorated your appetite for practical legal guidance, you can continue the story by exploring the law applicable to your own particular form of local government, and the law of your particular state. Suggested storytellers include both your local government attorney and your state's local government association, which offers training for community officials. Your local story might begin with responses to these questions:

1. Does our local government carry liability coverage for the acts and negligence of officials in the performance of their duties? If so:

   a. Under what circumstances will coverage be provided or denied?
   b. What is the amount of coverage?
   c. Would an official be required to pay a deductible, or pay for legal representation?

2. Has the state legislature provided by law for broad governmental immunity for the ordinary negligence of local government officials, subject to stated exceptions? If so, what are the specific exceptions where personal liability might apply? If not, under what circumstances would local officials enjoy governmental immunity for ordinary negligence?

3. Has the legislature permitted liability on the part of local officials for:

   a. Wrongful intentional torts?
   b. Actions taken with gross negligence?
   c. Actions taken with reckless disregard?

Notes

1. *Monell v. New York City Department of Social Services*, 436 U.S. 658 (1978). Liability may also arise if an official did not affirmatively act in a way that violated rights, but acted with "deliberate indifference" so as to violate rights.
2. *Owen v. City of Independence*, 445 U.S. 622 (1980).

3. D.L. Mandelker, et al., State and Local Government in a Federal System, 7th ed., p 658, LexisNexis (2010).
4. *Bogan v. Scott-Harris*, 523 U.S. 44 (1998).
5. *Scott v. Greenville County*, 716 F.2d 1409, 1422 (4th Cir, 1983).
6. *Haskell v. Washington Township*, 864 F2d 1266 (6th Cir, 1988).
7. *Lake County Estates, Inc v. Tahoe Regional Planning Agency*, 440 U.S. 391 (1979).
8. *Butz v. Economou*, 438 U.S. 478, 513 (1978). (federal hearing examiner or administrative law judge).
9. *Akins v. Deptford Township*, 813 F. Supp. 1098, 1102 (1993).
10. *Pearson v. Callahan*, 555 U.S. 223, 231 (2009).
11. *Id.* at 244.
12. *White v. Pauly*, 137 S. Ct. 548, 551–552, 196 L.Ed.2d 463 (2017). The cases also note that, even if the law was clearly established, the public official may attempt to prove that qualified immunity should nonetheless apply: "Usually, if the law was clearly established at the time of the relevant events, the qualified immunity defense will fail. *Harlow v. Fitzgerald*, 457 U.S. 800, 818–19, 102 S. Ct. 2727, 73 L.Ed.2d 396 (1982). "Nevertheless, if the official pleading the defense claims extraordinary circumstances and can prove that he neither knew nor should have known of the relevant legal standard, the defense should be sustained." *Id.* at 819, 102 S. Ct. 2727. Exceptional circumstances which may render an official's conduct objectively reasonable and therefore justify qualified immunity include reliance on a state statute or regulation, Roska, 328 F.3d at 1248, 1251, and reliance on the advice of legal counsel, V–1 Oil Co. v. Wyo. Dep't of Envtl. Quality, 902 F.2d 1482, 1488 (10th Cir.1990). It is the defendant's burden to claim such extraordinary circumstances and prove that his conduct was objectively reasonable." *Mimics, Inc. v. Village of Angel Fire*, 394 F.3d 836, 842 (10th Cir. 2005). However, a very recent case decided by the Supreme Court provides an insight on when an official "should know" that actions violate constitutional rights even in the absence of a clear law or court decision. In *Taylor v. Riojas*, 592 U.S. ___, Case No. 19-1261, decided November 2, 2020, a set of extreme facts relating to the conditions a prisoner was subjected to led to the conclusion that, even in the absence of "clearly established" law, qualified immunity did not apply.
13. W.S. §1–39–104.
14. W.S. § 1–39–105.
15. 57 Am. Jur. 2d Municipal, etc., Tort Liability § 2, Public Policy (accessed in 2020).
16. *City of Jackson v. Gardner*, 108 So. 3d 927 (Miss. 2013).

Index

For Product Safety Concerns and Information please contact our EU
representative GPSR@taylorandfrancis.com
Taylor & Francis Verlag GmbH, Kaufingerstraße 24, 80331 München, Germany

www.ingramcontent.com/pod-product-compliance
Lightning Source LLC
Chambersburg PA
CBHW050346270326
41926CB00016B/3618